Betty Crocker

One-Dish Meals

Casseroles,

Skillet Meals,

Stir-Fries and

More for Easy,

Everyday Dinners

WILEY

Wiley Publishing, Inc.

For general information on our other products and services or to obtain technical support please contact our Customer Care Department within the U.S. at 800-762-2974, outside the U.S. at 317-572-3993 or fax 317-572-4002.

Wiley also publishes its books in a variety of electronic formats. Some content that appears in print may not be available in electronic books. For more information about Wiley products, visit our web site at www.wiley.com.

Library of Congress Cataloging-in-Publication Data:

Crocker, Betty.
   Betty Crocker one-dish meals : casseroles, skillet meals, stir-fries, and more for easy, everyday dinners.—1st ed.
      p. cm.
   Includes index.
   ISBN 0-7645-4419-5 (pbk. : alk. paper)
1. Casserole cookery. I. Title: One-dish meals.

   TX693 .B54 2005
   641.8/2 22   2004011940

Manufactured in the United States of America

10 9 8 7 6 5 4 3 2 1

Cover photo: Garlic Shepherd's Pie (page 125)

General Mills, Inc.

Betty Crocker Kitchens

Director, Book and Online Publishing: Kim Walter
Manager, Book Publishing: Lois L. Tlusty
Editor: Heidi Losleben
Recipe Development and Testing: Betty Crocker Kitchens
Food Stylists: Betty Crocker Kitchens
Photography: General Mills Photo Studios

Wiley Publishing, Inc.

Publisher: Natalie Chapman
Executive Editor: Anne Ficklen
Senior Production Editors: Jennifer Mazurkie, Michael Olivo
Cover Design: Jeffrey Faust
Book Design: Richard Oriolo
Interior Layout: Holly Wittenberg
Manufacturing Manager: Kevin Watt

The Betty Crocker Kitchens seal guarantees success in your kitchen. Every recipe has been tested in America's Most Trusted Kitchens™ to meet our high standards of reliability, easy preparation and great taste.

FIND MORE GREAT IDEAS AND SHOP FOR NAME-BRAND HOUSEWARES AT

BettyCrocker.com

Dear Friends,

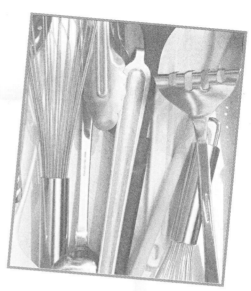

Are you a fan of one-stop shopping? Are you ready to go head-to-head with the daily question of "What's for Dinner?" Then you'll really enjoy *Betty Crocker One-Dish Meals*. Make dinner easy and inviting with this fresh look at what can go into just one dish—and come out a meal.

Inside, you'll find more than 300 recipes that give you dinner all in one dish. They are quick to fix and range from tried-and-true classics like Chicken Pot Pie with Herb Crust and Hearty Tomato Soup, to updated flavors such as Lamb and Lentil Casserole and Mexican Steak Stir-Fry. These super convenient recipes include soups; stews and chilies; skillet dishes; casseroles, gratins and pizzas; as well as slow cooker suppers, salads and grilled meals. Who could ask for more?

All the recipes use everyday, on-hand ingredients and provide big-easy taste in one dish. There's something to please just about everyone. Cleanup is a snap too. It's minimum fuss and maximum results for time-crunched home cooks.

There are also helpful sections, including Tools of the Trade, which offers tips on choosing cookware; stocking your pantry; freezing and microwaving meals; and potluck pointers. Flavor Boosters suggests ways to enhance your meal with add-ins and toppings and Lighten Up shows you how to trim fat and calories from your diet. There's a one-dish meal for (almost) every occasion such as potlucks, brunches and casual at-home gatherings.

Betty Crocker One-Dish Meals is your ticket to an easy fabulous family meal.

Warmly,

Betty Crocker

Contents

Tools of the Trade

To whip up great-tasting one-dish meals, it's important to have the right utensils on hand. Whether you're adding to an already extensive collection of pots and pans, or you're just starting to stock your kitchen cabinets, it's wise to buy good-quality cookware. You—and your family—will reap the benefits for years to come.

One-Dish Cookware Basics

Most recipes in this book call for one of the standard-size utensils specified on the following page. If you're unsure of the capacity of a dish, look for measurements on the bottom or under the handles. Or, use a measuring cup to see how many cups of water it takes to fill the dish to the brim.

DISH IT UP

	DESCRIPTION	SIZES	APPROXIMATE VOLUME	GOOD FOR
Baking Dish	A square or rectangular shallow dish that is ovenproof	8 × 8 × 2-inch 11 × 7 × 1 1/2-inch 13 × 9 × 2-inch	8 cups 6 cups 15 cups	Casseroles, lasagna
Casserole	A covered or uncovered ovenproof utensil, often round or oval in shape, in which food can be baked and served	1 1/2-quart 2-quart 3-quart	1 1/2 cups 8 cups 12 cups	Casseroles, stews, cassoulets
Dutch Oven/ Stockpot	A cast-iron pot or kettle with a close-fitting cover; some Dutch ovens have handles	4- to 14-quart	16–56 cups	Soups, stews, chilies
Saucepan	A covered or uncovered round and generally deep pan	1- to 4-quart	4–16 cups	Soups
Skillet/frying pan	A covered or uncovered shallow pan with flared or straight sides and one long handle	8-inch 10-inch 12-inch		Stir-fries, skillet dinners
Slow Cooker	An electric "casserole" with a ceramic liner; heating coils in the outer metal shell heat the liner	1- to 6-quart	4–24 cups	Soups, stews, chilies, less tender cuts of meat
Wok	A round-bottomed cooking utensil with two handles, typically made of rolled steel	Varies		Stir-fries

Don't Have It?

To get the best results, it's a good idea to stick with the cooking utensil specified in the recipe. In a pinch, use the following substitutions:

- For a 1- to 1 1/2-quart casserole, use a square baking dish, 8 × 8 × 2 inches.

- For a 2-quart casserole, use a rectangular baking dish, 11 × 7 × 1 1/2 inches.

- For a 3-quart casserole, use a rectangular baking dish, 13 × 9 × 2 inches.

Skillet Smarts

- Use a flat-bottomed pan of medium weight for even, quick heat and uniform cooking.

- If you're cooking with gas, adjust the flame to the pan size; on an electric stove, fit the heating unit to the size of the pan.

- Use the lowest setting possible to achieve the desired cooking method. Turning the heat up and down can create hot spots and cause sticking.

- Always use the skillet size called for in a recipe. Not only does it affect the cooking time, it also affects the evaporation of liquids.

- Different skillet materials have different heating properties. See the chart that follows for more information.

Common Materials of One-Dish Utensils

Although you may be tempted to buy an entire set of pots and pans at once, keep in mind that no one metal is ideal for all purposes. Look for utensils and materials that suit your personal style and the kinds of food you commonly cook. Remember, there's no rule about having all your pots and pans match!

POTS AND PANS 101

	PROS	CONS
Aluminum	Conducts heat well Moderately priced Lightweight and sturdy	Can react with acidic ingredients Finish can scratch
Anodized Aluminum	Extremely hard metal surface Low-stick Available in chip-, stain- and scratch- resistant finishes Good for freezer Can go from stovetop to oven	Finish can spot and fade in dishwasher
Cast Iron (regular)	Retains heat well Fairly inexpensive Has a nonstick finish after seasoning Doesn't react with or absorb food flavors (after seasoning)	Doesn't conduct heat well Often lends a metallic taste to foods Tends to rust
Ceramic/ Stoneware	Retains heat well Available in many styles and motifs Most can go from freezer to microwave or oven to dishwasher	May discolor over time
Copper	Conducts heat well Heavy duty Lined with tin or stainless steel to keep it from interacting with certain foods	Very expensive Not nonstick Requires polishing Needs to be relined about every 10 years
Earthen Ware	Retains heat well Hard and durable Can be washed in dishwasher	Doesn't conduct heat well Must cool slowly and completely before washing to prevent cracking

Enamelware (cast iron or stainless steel)	Durable
	Flameproof and ovenproof
	Good for freezer
	Can go from stovetop to oven
	Enameled *cast iron* conducts heat well
	Easy to clean
	Doesn't react with acids
		Enamel can chip
		Enameled *stainless steel* does not
		   conduct heat well
		Light-colored enamelware may not
		   brown foods as easily as dark-colored
		   and may discolor
		May crack if overheated

Glass	Retains heat well Economical and practical Coordinates well with other tableware Microwave and dishwasher safe Nonreactive to acids Easy to clean	Doesn't conduct heat well Can break easily with sudden temperature changes
Stainless Steel	Doesn't react with acidic or alkaline foods Corrosion resistant Extremely durable Easy to clean Doesn't easily scratch or dent	Doesn't conduct heat well Can burn food in spots

Flavor Boosters

One-dish meals are flavorful in and of themselves, but if you'd like to add more zip or zest to casseroles, skillets, soups or salads, try the following add-ins and toppings:

- Add plain or flavored feta cheese to a salad.

- Sprinkle shredded Swiss cheese over individual servings of soup.

- Intensify the flavor of vegetables by seasoning them with balsamic vinegar or soy sauce.

- Use a flavored pasta sauce instead of plain.

- Sprinkle canned French-fried onions over the top of casseroles.

- Add a dash of soy sauce to skillet and stir-fry dishes.

- Stir a tablespoon or two of pesto into a pot of soup.

- Substitute flavored mayo for plain in pasta salads.

Lighten Up

In addition to being convenient, flavorful and easy to clean up, one-dish meals can also be good for you. To trim the fat and calories from your diet:

- Grease baking dishes and skillets with cooking spray. In addition to the cans you can buy at stores, you can also buy refillable spray canisters at kitchenware shops and fill with your own olive or canola oil.

- Use fat-free or reduced-fat dairy products such as milk, buttermilk, yogurt, cottage cheese and other cheeses.

- Use egg whites or fat-free egg product (made of egg whites and flavoring) instead of whole eggs.

- Reduce the amount of meat in a recipe but keep the portion size the same by upping the amount of beans, rice, vegetables, etc.

- Reduce the amount of cheese and nuts in recipes. Try sprinkling them on top of a dish rather than mixing them in.

- Trim excess fat from meat and poultry.

- Use fat-free or reduced-sodium broths.

Freezer-Friendly Foods

One benefit of one-dish meals is that they can be made ahead and stored in the freezer. To get the best results when freezing, keep the following in mind:

- A one-dish meal that has been frozen needs to be baked slightly longer than one that is baked immediately after being made. Most need about 10 to 15 minutes longer, but it's a good idea to check the dish during baking time and adjust the time accordingly.

- Casseroles may be frozen before or after they are baked.

- Recipes with a low-fat sauce or condensed-soup base usually freeze well.

- If a recipe calls for sour cream, wait to add the sour cream after thawing and reheating the dish.

- Crisp toppings, such as nuts, crushed chips or bacon bits, should be added after the dish is thawed.

- Fresh potatoes do not freeze well. Some dairy products such as sour cream (see above), half-and-half and ricotta and cottage cheese are also not recommended for freezing.

- To make sure meats, vegetables, pastas and grains don't overcook when reheated, cook them just until tender the first time around.

- Cool foods before placing them in the freezer.

- Store foods at 0°F or colder.

- Freeze foods in sizes that are suitable for your family. Individual sizes are a good idea, as is enough for one family meal.

- Use airtight containers that are microwavable or can be go directly from the freezer to the oven.

- For best quality, use frozen casseroles within three months.

Zap It! Reheating Foods in the Microwave

A microwave makes quick work of reheating one-dish foods. For food-safety reasons, it's recommended to bring the internal temperature to 140°F. An instant-read thermometer is helpful to determine whether the food is hot enough at its center. Do not leave a thermometer in the food while microwaving; use it to check the temperature only after reheating.

- Moist foods reheat best, and covering foods adds speed and even heating. Pizzas and other crisp or crunchy foods reheat best when heated on a browning dish or a microwave rack, so the bottom doesn't get soggy.

- Tightly cover casseroles with microwavable plastic food wrap to speed reheating. Fold back a corner or cut a few slits in the plastic wrap to vent the steam. Stir or rotate the casserole once or twice during reheating. Casseroles that can't be stirred, such as lasagna, benefit from a standing time to allow the heat to equalize throughout the food.

- Smaller, individual servings heat more quickly than full recipes because the microwaves are able to penetrate the food more deeply and heat the center more quickly.

- To avoid overcooking, casseroles containing eggs, cheese or large chunks of meat should be heated at a lower power setting.

One-Dish Meals for (Almost) Every Occasion

No doubt about it: one-dish meals are varied and versatile. From easy, cheesy casseroles and slow-simmering slow cooker dishes to quick stir-fries and toss-together salads, there's a flavor and a cooking method to please just about everyone.

Kid-Friendly

The following yummy recipes feature familiar flavors kids love, from noodles and cheese to taco chips and tater nuggets.

Best for Brunch

Served with a cup of hot coffee, a glass of fresh OJ and a sprinkling of fresh fruit, these one-dish meals make for a virtually fuss-free brunch.

Good for Casual At-Home Gatherings

Hey, hey, the gang's all here so—instead of being stuck in the kitchen—why not enjoy their company with one of these easy-to-prepare, yet impressive, meals?

Beef Stroganoff,* page 68
Beer and Cheese Soup, page 35
Cheddar Burgers and Veggies, page 298
Easy Philly Cheesesteak Pizza, page 241
Easy Turkey Lasagna, page 157
Four-Cheese Pesto Pizza, page 260
French Onion Soup, page 233
Greek Pita Pizzas, page 258
Italian Bean Soup, page 29
Meatball Sandwich Casserole, page 132
Mediterranean Chicken Packets,* page 306
Mediterranean Pot Roast, page 191
New England Clam Chowder, page 52

Paella on the Grill,* page 303
Pesto Ravioli with Chicken, page 76
Skewered Steak Dinner, page 299
Skillet Lasagna, page 64
Southwestern Chicken BLT Salad, page 269
Steak and Potato Soup, page 19
Steak Caesar Salad, page 263
Super-Easy Chicken Manicotti,* page 139
Taco Pizza, page 238
Thai Chicken Pizzas, page 242
Turkey Chili, page 57
Tuscan Panzanella Salad,* page 294

Great Make-and-Take Dishes

Your schedule is packed; how are you going to find the time to make a potluck dish for the PTA meeting at 7:00? Let these make-ahead and slow cooker dishes do the work.

Dill-Turkey Chowder, page 210
Easy Bean and Kielbasa Soup, page 229
Easy Pork Chili, page 224
Greek Chicken Salad, page 270
Hearty Beef Chili, page 186
Italian Beef Stew, page 187
Potato and Ham Chowder, page 215

Ratatouille Bean Stew, page 234
Ravioli with Sausage and Peppers, page 218
Smoky Ham and Navy Bean Stew, page 216
Southwestern Pork Stew, page 222
Turkey Chili Verde, page 208
Turkey Tabbouleh Salad, page 274
Zesty Italian Beef Tips, page 194

* Show-Stopper Recipes—also great for more elegant get-togethers

Helpful Hints for Making and Taking Dishes to Share

Whether you're toting treats to a potluck or a picnic, it's important, for food safety reasons, to keep them at a proper temperature. Insulated coolers and thermoses were invented for that very purpose. Before you transfer any food to a storage container, make sure it's either thoroughly heated or thoroughly chilled. Partially cooked foods should not be packed.

- Preheat or chill thermoses for at least 30 minutes before adding food. To preheat, pour boiling or very hot water in the thermos and replace the top. To cool a thermos, fill it with ice water and replace the top. Cool down insulated coolers by filling them with ice water or ice cubes. Close the lid and allow the cooler to chill for 45 minutes to 1 hour.

- Keep hot and cold foods separated.

- For more insulation, wrap several towels or layers of newspaper around hot food containers.

- Place frozen ice packs or bags of ice around or on top of cold foods.

- Don't peek! To keep hot foods hot and cold foods cold, try not to open thermoses and coolers until you are ready to eat.

Slow Cooker Take-Along Tips

- As mentioned above, wrapping a towel or newspaper around your container will help insulate it. There are also insulated totes designed specifically for slow cookers.

- To make sure your slow cooker stays flat in your car, place it in a box or other container. Keep in mind the floor of your car is a flat surface—the seat of your car is not.

- Attach rubber bands around the handles and lid to secure the lid when traveling.

- Serve the food within an hour, or plug in the slow cooker and set it on the Low heat (or "Keep Warm") setting to stay warm for up to 2 hours.

- Be sure to put your name or an identifiable mark somewhere on your slow cooker. Many slow cookers look alike, so it's easy to grab the wrong one.

Hearty Soups, Stews and Chilies

Cheesy Lasagna Soup

PREP **20 min** COOK **20 min** BROIL **2 min** SERVINGS **6**

1 pound lean ground beef

1 medium onion, sliced

2 large green bell peppers, cut into 1-inch pieces

2 cloves garlic, finely chopped

2 cups water

2 cans (14 1/2 ounces each) diced tomatoes in olive oil, garlic and spices, undrained

1 can (6 ounces) tomato paste

2 cups uncooked mafalda (mini-lasagna noodle) pasta or wide egg noodles (4 ounces)

1 tablespoon packed brown sugar

1 1/2 teaspoons Italian seasoning, crumbled

1/4 teaspoon pepper

1 1/2 cups Italian-style croutons

1 1/2 cups shredded part-skim mozzarella cheese (6 ounces)

1. Cook beef, onion, bell peppers and garlic in 4-quart Dutch oven over medium heat 8 to 10 minutes, stirring occasionally, until beef is brown and onion is tender; drain. Stir water, diced tomatoes and tomato paste into beef mixture.

2. Stir in remaining ingredients except croutons and cheese. Heat to boiling; reduce heat to low. Cover and simmer about 10 minutes, stirring occasionally, until pasta is tender.

3. Set oven control to broil. Pour hot soup into 6 oven-proof soup bowls or casseroles (do not use glass). Top each with 1/4 cup croutons. Sprinkle with cheese. Broil soup with tops 3 to 4 inches from heat 1 to 2 minutes or until cheese is melted.

1 SERVING Calories 430 (Calories from Fat 160) | Fat 18g (Saturated 8g) | Cholesterol 70mg | Sodium 910mg | Carbohydrate 40g (Dietary Fiber 5g) | Protein 27g % DAILY VALUE Vitamin A 28% | Vitamin C 64% | Calcium 28% | Iron 20% EXCHANGES 2 Starch, 2 Vegetable, 2 1/2 Medium-Fat Meat, 1 Fat CARBOHYDRATE CHOICES 2 1/2

BETTY'S TIP
Instead of using your broiler to melt the cheese, why not let the hot soup melt the cheese on its own? It cuts down on prep time, and kids will love the ooey-gooey strings of cheese that form as a result.

Steak and Potato Soup

1. Cut beef into 1/4-inch strips; cut strips into 1-inch pieces. Heat oil in 8-quart stockpot or Dutch oven over medium-high heat. Cook and stir beef in oil 4 to 5 minutes or until brown; add onion and garlic. Cook and stir 2 minutes.

2. Stir in remaining ingredients. Heat to boiling; reduce heat to low. Cover and simmer 12 to 15 minutes, stirring occasionally, until vegetables are tender.

1 SERVING Calories 330 (Calories from Fat 90) | Fat 10g (Saturated 3g) | Cholesterol 80mg | Sodium 960mg | Carbohydrate 28g (Dietary Fiber 4g) | Protein 33g   % DAILY VALUE Vitamin A 100% | Vitamin C 20% | Calcium 6% | Iron 30%   EXCHANGES 1 1/2 Starch, 1 Vegetable, 4 Very Lean Meat, 1 Fat CARBOHYDRATE CHOICES 2

2-pound boneless beef sirloin steak (1 inch thick)

2 tablespoons vegetable oil

1 1/2 cups coarsely chopped onions

3 cloves garlic, finely chopped

2 pounds small red potatoes, cut into 3/4-inch pieces

3 cups baby-cut carrots, cut lengthwise into fourths

1 bag (1 pound) frozen cut green beans

2 tablespoons chopped fresh or 2 teaspoons dried basil leaves

1/2 teaspoon freshly ground black pepper

6 cans (14 ounces each) beef broth

3 tablespoons steak sauce

BETTY'S TIP

It's a snap to cut the steak into slices of even thickness if you pop it into the freezer for about 20 minutes first.

Homemade Chicken Soup

1 pound boneless, skinless chicken breasts, cut into 1-inch pieces

1/4 cup all-purpose flour

1 tablespoon vegetable oil

1 medium onion, chopped (1/2 cup)

1/4 teaspoon garlic powder

1 can (49 1/2 ounces) chicken broth

1 cup baby-cut carrots

1 tablespoon chopped fresh parsley, if desired

1 teaspoon dried thyme leaves

2 medium stalks celery, sliced

1 cup uncooked farfalle (bow-tie) pasta or wide egg noodles (2 ounces)

1. Toss chicken with flour. Heat oil in 4-quart Dutch oven over medium-high heat. Cook chicken, onion and garlic in oil about 5 minutes, stirring occasionally, until chicken is no longer pink in center.

2. Stir in remaining ingredients except pasta. Heat to boiling. Stir in pasta; reduce heat to low. Simmer uncovered about 15 minutes or until vegetables and pasta are tender.

1 SERVING Calories 335 (Calories from Fat 90) | Fat 10g (Saturated 2g) | Cholesterol 80mg | Sodium 1680mg | Carbohydrate 23g (Dietary Fiber 2g) | Protein 36g   **% DAILY VALUE** Vitamin A 100% | Vitamin C 4% | Calcium 4% | Iron 16%   **EXCHANGES** 1 Starch, 1 Vegetable, 4 Lean Meat   **CARBOHYDRATE CHOICES** 1 1/2

BETTY'S TIP

Short on time? Toss in two 6-ounce packages of refrigerated diced cooked chicken breasts instead of cooking the chicken breasts.

African Peanut–Chicken Soup

PREP **20 min**   COOK **20 min**   SERVINGS **6**

1. Heat oil in 4-quart saucepan or Dutch oven over medium-high heat. Cook and stir chicken, onion and garlic in oil 4 to 5 minutes or until chicken is no longer pink in center.

2. Stir in remaining ingredients except peanut butter. Heat to boiling; reduce heat to low. Cover and simmer 10 to 12 minutes, stirring occasionally, until vegetables are tender.

3. Stir in peanut butter. Cook over low heat, stirring constantly, until peanut butter is blended and soup is hot.

1 SERVING Calories 355 (Calories from Fat 155) | Fat 17g (Saturated 4g) | Cholesterol 50mg | Sodium 980mg | Carbohydrate 22g (Dietary Fiber 4g) | Protein 28g % DAILY VALUE Vitamin A 100% | Vitamin C 34% | Calcium 4% | Iron 10% EXCHANGES 1 1/2 Starch, 3 Lean Meat, 1 1/2 Fat CARBOHYDRATE CHOICES 1 1/2

1 tablespoon vegetable oil

1 1/4 pounds boneless, skinless chicken breasts, cut into 1-inch pieces

1 small onion, cut into thin wedges

1 clove garlic, finely chopped

2 medium dark–orange sweet potatoes, peeled and coarsely chopped

1 medium green bell pepper, chopped (1 cup)

2 cans (14 ounces each) chicken broth

1 can (11 1/2 ounces) tomato juice

1/2 teaspoon ground ginger

1/8 to 1/4 teaspoon ground red pepper (cayenne)

1/2 cup crunchy peanut butter

BETTY'S TIP

For a "soup-er" special presentation, plop a mound of hot cooked rice in the middle of each bowl of soup and sprinkle chopped peanuts, flaked coconut and sliced green onions over the top.

Chicken and Vegetable Bow-Tie Soup

1 teaspoon vegetable oil

1 stalk celery, thinly sliced

3 cans (14 ounces each) chicken broth

2 cups water

1 bag (1 pound) frozen broccoli, carrots and cauliflower (or other combination)

2 cups cubed cooked chicken

1 cup uncooked farfalle (bow-tie) pasta or wide egg noodles (2 ounces)

1/4 teaspoon poultry seasoning

PREP **10** min   COOK **20** min   SERVINGS **6**

1. Heat oil in 4-quart saucepan or Dutch oven over medium-high heat. Cook celery in oil 2 to 3 minutes, stirring frequently, until crisp-tender.

2. Add broth and water; heat to boiling. Add frozen vegetables; heat to boiling.

3. Stir in remaining ingredients; reduce heat to low. Simmer about 15 minutes, stirring occasionally, until pasta and vegetables are tender.

1 SERVING Calories 180 (Calories from Fat 55) | Fat 6g (Saturated 1g) | Cholesterol 40mg | Sodium 990mg | Carbohydrate 11g (Dietary Fiber 3g) | Protein 20g % DAILY VALUE Vitamin A 40% | Vitamin C 20% | Calcium 4% | Iron 8% EXCHANGES 1/2 Starch, 1 Vegetable, 2 1/2 Very Lean Meat, 1/2 Fat CARBOHYDRATE CHOICES 1

BETTY'S TIP

No bow-tie pasta in the pantry? Other medium-size pasta shapes, such as shells, rotini or fusilli, work too. Up the fun factor by mixing several shapes.

Oriental Chicken Noodle Soup

PREP **10 min**   COOK **10 min**   SERVINGS **4**

1.   Heat water to boiling in 3-quart saucepan. Break block of noodles; reserve seasoning packet. Stir noodles, chicken, bok choy and carrot into water. Heat to boiling; reduce heat to low. Simmer uncovered 3 minutes, stirring occasionally.

2.   Stir in contents of seasoning packet and sesame oil.

1 SERVING Calories 205 (Calories from Fat 70) | Fat 8g (Saturated 2g) | Cholesterol 60mg | Sodium 340mg | Carbohydrate 11g (Dietary Fiber 1g) | Protein 22g   % DAILY VALUE Vitamin A 62% | Vitamin C 4% | Calcium 2% | Iron 8%   EXCHANGES 1/2 Starch, 1 Vegetable, 2 1/2 Lean Meat   CARBOHYDRATE CHOICES 1

3 cups water

1 package (3 ounces) chicken-flavor ramen noodle soup mix

2 cups cut-up cooked chicken

2 medium stalks bok choy (with leaves), cut into 1/4-inch slices

1 medium carrot, sliced (1/2 cup)

1 teaspoon sesame oil, if desired

BETTY'S TIP

If you wind up with more bok choy than you need, use the extra to make a simple side salad. Top with a few sliced radishes and a tangy vinaigrette dressing.

Hearty Turkey-Barley Soup

1 pound ground turkey breast

2/3 cup uncooked quick-cooking barley

2 cans (14 ounces each) beef broth

1 can (14 1/2 ounces) diced tomatoes, undrained

1 jar (1 pound 10 ounces) tomato pasta sauce (any variety)

2 cups (from 1-pound bag) frozen sweet peas, potatoes and carrots (or other combination)

PREP **5 min**   COOK **35 min**   SERVINGS **4**

1. Cook turkey in 4-quart Dutch oven over medium heat 8 to 10 minutes, stirring occasionally, until no longer pink; drain.

2. Stir barley, broth, tomatoes and pasta sauce into turkey. Heat to boiling, stirring occasionally; reduce heat to low. Cover and simmer 15 minutes.

3. Stir in frozen vegetables. Cover and simmer about 10 minutes or until barley is tender.

1 SERVING Calories 380 (Calories from Fat 80) | Fat 9g (Saturated 2g) | Cholesterol 50mg | Sodium 1400mg | Carbohydrate 51g (Dietary Fiber 7g) | Protein 24g   % DAILY VALUE Vitamin A 64% | Vitamin C 24% | Calcium 8% | Iron 16%   EXCHANGES 3 Starch, 1 Vegetable, 2 Lean Meat   CARBOHYDRATE CHOICES 3

BETTY'S TIP

Quick-cooking barley is aptly named. It takes only 10 to 12 minutes to cook; regular barley needs 45 to 50 minutes. This hardy grain is also packed with protein—1 cup has the same amount as an 8-ounce glass of milk.

Turkey-Ginger Tortellini Soup

PREP **15 min**   COOK **20 min**   SERVINGS **4**

1. Cook and drain tortellini as directed on package; set aside. Heat water, vinegar, soy sauce, broth and gingerroot to boiling in 3-quart saucepan; reduce heat to low.

2. Stir bok choy stems (reserve leaves), turkey and onions into saucepan. Simmer uncovered 15 minutes. Stir in bok choy leaves, mushrooms and tortellini. Simmer just until leaves are wilted.

1 SERVING Calories 235 (Calories from Fat 80) | Fat 9g (Saturated 3g) | Cholesterol 100mg | Sodium 830mg | Carbohydrate 12g (Dietary Fiber 1g) | Protein 26g   % **DAILY VALUE** Vitamin A 28% | Vitamin C 14% | Calcium 8% | Iron 12%   EXCHANGES 1/2 Starch, 1 Vegetable, 3 Lean Meat   CARBOHYDRATE CHOICES 1

1 package (7 ounces) dried cheese-filled tortellini

2 1/4 cups water

2 tablespoons rice wine or white wine vinegar

2 tablespoons soy sauce

1 can (10 1/2 ounces) condensed chicken broth

1 to 2 tablespoons finely chopped fresh gingerroot or 1 to 2 teaspoons ground ginger

2 cups sliced bok choy (stems and leaves)

2 cups cut-up cooked turkey

2 green onions, sliced

1 cup enoki mushrooms (3 1/2 ounces)

BETTY'S TIP

Finely chopping the fresh ginger takes a bit more time than using ginger from a can, but the extra flavor is worth it. It's hard to believe those gnarled-looking roots you see at the grocery store taste so sweet and delicious.

Rio Grande Turkey Soup

1 can (14 ounces) chicken broth

1 can (28 ounces) whole tomatoes, undrained

1 jar (16 ounces) thick-and-chunky salsa

2 to 3 teaspoons chili powder

1/2 bag (1-pound size) frozen corn, broccoli and red peppers (or other combination)

1 cup uncooked cavatappi or shell pasta (3 ounces)

2 cups cut-up cooked turkey or chicken

1/4 cup chopped fresh parsley

PREP 5 min   COOK 20 min   SERVINGS 6

1. Heat broth, tomatoes, salsa and chili powder to boiling in 4-quart Dutch oven, breaking up tomatoes. Stir frozen vegetables and pasta into soup. Heat to boiling; reduce heat.

2. Simmer uncovered about 12 minutes, stirring occasionally, until pasta and vegetables are tender. Stir in turkey and parsley; cook until soup is hot.

1 SERVING Calories 215 (Calories from Fat 45) | Fat 5g (Saturated 1g) | Cholesterol 40mg | Sodium 890mg | Carbohydrate 27g (Dietary Fiber 4g) | Protein 20g   % DAILY VALUE Vitamin A 48% | Vitamin C 50% | Calcium 8% | Iron 16%   EXCHANGES 1 Starch, 2 Vegetable, 1 1/2 Lean Meat   CARBOHYDRATE CHOICES 2

BETTY'S TIP

The spiciness of this Southwest-inspired soup can vary a great deal depending on the type of salsa you use. Hot or not? It's your call.

Split Pea Soup

PREP **20 min**   COOK **2 hr 10 min**   SERVINGS **8**

1. Heat all ingredients except carrots to boiling in 4-quart Dutch oven, stirring occasionally; reduce heat to low. Cover and simmer 1 hour to 1 hour 30 minutes.

2. Remove ham bone; let stand until cool enough to handle. Remove ham from bone. Remove excess fat from ham; cut ham into 1/2-inch pieces.

3. Stir ham and carrots into soup. Heat to boiling; reduce heat to low. Cover and simmer about 30 minutes or until carrots are tender and soup is desired consistency.

2 1/4 cups dried split peas (1 pound), sorted and rinsed

8 cups water

1/4 teaspoon pepper

1 large onion, chopped (1 cup)

2 medium stalks celery, finely chopped (1 cup)

1 ham bone, 2 pounds ham shanks or 2 pounds smoked pork hocks

3 medium carrots, cut into 1/4-inch slices (1 1/2 cups)

1 SERVING Calories 185 (Calories from Fat 45) | Fat 5g (Saturated 2g) | Cholesterol 15mg | Sodium 210mg | Carbohydrate 31g (Dietary Fiber 12g) | Protein 16g   % DAILY VALUE Vitamin A 18% | Vitamin C 2% | Calcium 2% | Iron 10%   EXCHANGES 2 Starch, 1 Very Lean Meat   CARBOHYDRATE CHOICES 2

BETTY'S TIP

Sorting and rinsing peas is much easier than it sounds. First, you want to toss any grit or discolored peas you come across. Then, put the split peas in a bowl of water and throw away any skins or peas that float to the top. Last, rinse the peas in a colander and start cooking!

Black Bean Soup

1 slice bacon

1 medium onion, chopped (1/2 cup)

1 large clove garlic, finely chopped

1 can (14 ounces) chicken broth

1 medium carrot, coarsely chopped (1/2 cup)

1 medium stalk celery, coarsely chopped (1/2 cup)

2 tablespoons finely chopped fresh parsley

1/2 teaspoon dried oregano leaves

1/2 teaspoon crushed red pepper

1 can (15 ounces) black beans, rinsed and drained

4 lemon wedges

PREP 20 min   COOK 20 min   SERVINGS 4

1. Cut bacon crosswise into 1/2-inch strips. Cook bacon in 3-quart saucepan over medium heat 1 minute, stirring constantly. Do not drain. Add onion and garlic. Cook about 5 minutes, stirring frequently, until onion is tender. Remove from heat.

2. Stir broth, carrot, celery, parsley, oregano and red pepper into saucepan. Heat to boiling; reduce heat to low. Cover and simmer 10 minutes.

3. While soup is cooking, place 1/2 cup of the beans in small bowl; mash with fork. Stir whole beans and mashed beans into soup. Heat about 1 minute or until soup is hot. Serve with lemon wedges.

1 SERVING Calories 170 (Calories from Fat 20) | Fat 2g (Saturated 1g) | Cholesterol 0mg | Sodium 910mg | Carbohydrate 33g (Dietary Fiber 8g) | Protein 13g   % DAILY VALUE Vitamin A 60% | Vitamin C 6% | Calcium 10% | Iron 8%   EXCHANGES 2 Starch, 1/2 Very Lean Meat   CARBOHYDRATE CHOICES 2

Meatless Black Bean Soup Substitute 1 tablespoon vegetable oil for the bacon and use vegetable broth instead of chicken broth.

BETTY'S TIP

Instead of using a chef's knife to chop the parsley, try using kitchen scissors to snip the leafy portion of the parsley into very small pieces.

Italian Bean Soup

PREP **10 min**   COOK **20 min**   SERVINGS **6**

1. Heat oil in 3-quart saucepan over medium-high heat. Cook onion and garlic in oil, stirring frequently, until onion is tender. Stir in remaining ingredients. Heat to boiling; reduce heat to low.

2. Cover and simmer 12 to 15 minutes or until macaroni is tender.

1 SERVING Calories 250 (Calories from Fat 35) | Fat 4g (Saturated 1g) | Cholesterol 25mg | Sodium 770mg | Carbohydrate 38g (Dietary Fiber 6g) | Protein 22g   % DAILY VALUE Vitamin A 4% | Vitamin C 4% | Calcium 8% | Iron 24%   EXCHANGES 2 Starch, 1 Vegetable, 2 Very Lean Meat   CARBOHYDRATE CHOICES 2 1/2

1 teaspoon vegetable oil

1 medium onion, chopped (about 1/2 cup)

1 clove garlic, finely chopped

1 1/2 cups chopped fully cooked smoked reduced-sodium ham (about 3/4 pound)

1 cup uncooked elbow macaroni (about 4 ounces)

1/2 teaspoon Italian seasoning

1/8 teaspoon red pepper sauce

3 roma (plum) tomatoes, seeded and chopped (about 1 cup)

1 medium stalk celery, cut into 1/4-inch diagonal slices (about 1/2 cup)

2 cans (14 ounces each) reduced-sodium chicken broth

1 can (15 to 16 ounces) great northern beans, rinsed and drained

BETTY'S TIP

Go all out Italian by serving this satisfying soup with a Caesar salad and chunks of garlic cheese bread. Top it off with a scoop of yummy spumoni ice cream for dessert.

Italian Sausage and Mostaccioli Soup

1 pound turkey Italian sausage links, cut into 1-inch pieces

2 cups broccoli flowerets

1 cup uncooked mostaccioli or penne pasta (3 ounces)

2 1/2 cups water

1/2 teaspoon dried basil leaves

1/4 teaspoon fennel seed, crushed

1/4 teaspoon pepper

1 medium onion, chopped (1/2 cup)

1 clove garlic, finely chopped

1 can (28 ounces) roma (plum) tomatoes, undrained

1 can (10 1/2 ounces) condensed beef broth

PREP 10 min   COOK 25 min   SERVINGS 6

1. Cook sausage in 4-quart Dutch oven over medium-high heat, stirring occasionally, until brown; drain.

2. Stir in remaining ingredients, breaking up tomatoes. Heat to boiling; reduce heat to medium-low. Cover and cook about 15 minutes, stirring occasionally, until pasta is tender.

1 SERVING Calories 310 (Calories from Fat 90) | Fat 10g (Saturated 3g) | Cholesterol 45mg | Sodium 2080mg | Carbohydrate 26g (Dietary Fiber 3g) | Protein 29g   % DAILY VALUE Vitamin A 16% | Vitamin C 40% | Calcium 8% | Iron 18%   EXCHANGES 1 Starch, 2 Vegetable, 3 Lean Meat   CARBOHYDRATE CHOICES 2

BETTY'S TIP

Out of fennel seed? Throw in a pinch of dried tarragon leaves instead. It will add a light touch of licorice flavor to this hearty soup.

Southwest Cheese Soup

PREP **5 min**   COOK **10 min**   SERVINGS **4**

1 cup milk

1 package (16 ounces) process cheese spread loaf, cut into cubes

1 can (15 1/4 ounces) whole kernel corn, drained

1 can (15 ounces) black beans, rinsed and drained

1 can (10 ounces) diced tomatoes and green chilies, undrained

Chopped fresh cilantro, if desired

1. Mix all ingredients except cilantro in 4-quart Dutch oven.

2. Cook over medium-low heat about 10 minutes, stirring frequently, until cheese is melted and soup is hot. Sprinkle each serving with cilantro.

1 SERVING Calories 575 (Calories from Fat 225) | Fat 25g (Saturated 17g) | Cholesterol 95mg | Sodium 2580mg | Carbohydrate 65g (Dietary Fiber 10g) | Protein 33g % DAILY VALUE Vitamin A 34% | Vitamin C 16% | Calcium 70% | Iron 24% EXCHANGES 4 Starch, 1 Vegetable, 2 Medium-Fat Meat, 2 Fat CARBOHYDRATE CHOICES 4

Southwest Sausage and Cheese Soup Stir in 1/2 pound chorizo sausage, cooked and drained, in step 1.

BETTY'S TIP

Warm corn bread nicely complements this unbelievably easy cheesy soup, and crunchy tortilla chips make delicious dippers.

Rich Cream of Mushroom Soup

1 pound mushrooms

1/4 cup butter or margarine

3 tablespoons all-purpose flour

1/2 teaspoon salt

1 cup whipping (heavy) cream

1 can (14 ounces) chicken broth

1 tablespoon dry sherry, if desired

Freshly ground pepper

PREP **5 min**   COOK **15 min**   SERVINGS **6**

1. Slice enough mushrooms to measure 1 cup; chop remaining mushrooms. Melt butter in 3-quart saucepan over medium heat. Cook sliced and chopped mushrooms in butter about 10 minutes, stirring occasionally, until mushrooms are golden brown.

2. Sprinkle with flour and salt. Cook, stirring constantly, until thickened. Gradually stir in whipping cream and broth; heat until hot. Stir in sherry. Sprinkle with pepper.

1 SERVING Calories 235 (Calories from Fat 190) | Fat 21g (Saturated 9g) | Cholesterol 45mg | Sodium 620mg | Carbohydrate 7g (Dietary Fiber 1g) | Protein 5g   % DAILY VALUE Vitamin A 14% | Vitamin C 12% | Calcium 2% | Iron 4%   EXCHANGES 1 Vegetable, 1/2 High-Fat Meat, 3 1/2 Fat   CARBOHYDRATE CHOICES 1/2

BETTY'S TIP

There is no "right" kind of mushroom for this soup, so don't be afraid to experiment with different varieties to find your favorite. Crimini, portabella and shiitake are all good ones to try.

Home-Style Potato Soup

1 can (14 ounces) chicken broth

1 pound potatoes, peeled and cut into fourths (about 3 medium)

1 1/2 cups milk

1/4 teaspoon salt

1/8 teaspoon pepper

1/8 teaspoon dried thyme leaves

2 medium green onions, sliced (1/4 cup)

1. Heat broth and potatoes to boiling in 3-quart saucepan; reduce heat to low. Cover and simmer about 15 minutes or until potatoes are tender. Do not drain. Break potatoes into smaller pieces with potato masher or large fork. (Mixture should be lumpy.)

2. Stir milk, salt, pepper, thyme and onions into saucepan. Heat over medium heat, stirring occasionally, until hot. Do not let soup boil.

1 SERVING Calories 110 (Calories from Fat 20) | Fat 2g (Saturated 1g) | Cholesterol 5mg | Sodium 530mg | Carbohydrate 17g (Dietary Fiber 1g) | Protein 5g **% DAILY VALUE** Vitamin A 4% | Vitamin C 8% | Calcium 8% | Iron 2% **EXCHANGES** 1 Starch, 1/2 Fat **CARBOHYDRATE CHOICES** 1

Potato-Cheese Soup Make Home-Style Potato Soup as directed. When soup is finished and very hot, gradually stir in 1 1/2 cups shredded Cheddar cheese until it is melted.

BETTY'S TIP

For added flavor and color, sprinkle your favorite baked potato topping over each serving of soup. Bacon bits, shredded Cheddar cheese and additional green onions will all taste great.

Spicy Noodle Soup

3 cans (14 ounces each) vegetable broth

1 jar (16 ounces) salsa

1 can (15 ounces) black beans, rinsed and drained

1 can (11 ounces) vacuum-packed whole kernel corn, drained

1 package (5 ounces) Japanese curly noodles

1/3 cup chopped fresh cilantro or parsley

1 tablespoon lime juice

1 teaspoon chili powder

1/4 teaspoon ground cumin

1/4 teaspoon pepper

2 tablespoons grated Parmesan cheese

1. Heat broth to boiling in 4-quart Dutch oven. Stir in remaining ingredients except cheese; reduce heat to medium.

2. Cook 5 to 6 minutes, stirring occasionally, until noodles are tender. Sprinkle with cheese.

1 SERVING Calories 205 (Calories from Fat 20) | Fat 2g (Saturated 1g) | Cholesterol 0mg | Sodium 1660mg | Carbohydrate 43g (Dietary Fiber 7g) | Protein 11g   % DAILY VALUE Vitamin A 24% | Vitamin C 14% | Calcium 10% | Iron 18%   EXCHANGES 2 1/2 Starch   CARBOHYDRATE CHOICES 3

BETTY'S TIP

Sour cream also makes a tasty topping for this soup. Look for bottles of squeezable sour cream in the dairy section of your supermarket.

Beer and Cheese Soup

1. Melt butter in 2-quart saucepan over medium heat. Cook onion in butter, stirring occasionally, until tender. Stir beer, carrot and celery into butter. Heat to boiling; reduce heat to low. Cover and simmer 10 minutes.

2. Stir in remaining ingredients except sour cream and cheese. Heat to boiling; reduce heat to low. Cover and simmer 30 minutes; remove from heat. Stir in sour cream. Sprinkle with cheese.

1 SERVING Calories 265 (Calories from Fat 200) | Fat 22g (Saturated 13g) | Cholesterol 65mg | Sodium 1090mg | Carbohydrate 9g (Dietary Fiber 1g) | Protein 10g   % DAILY VALUE Vitamin A 58% | Vitamin C 2% | Calcium 18% | Iron 2%   EXCHANGES 1/2 Starch, 1/2 High-Fat Meat, 4 Fat   CARBOHYDRATE CHOICES 1/2

2 tablespoons butter or margarine

1 medium onion, chopped (1/2 cup)

1 can or bottle (12 ounces) beer

1 medium carrot, finely chopped (1/2 cup)

1 medium stalk celery, finely chopped (1/2 cup)

2 cups chicken broth

1 teaspoon salt

1 teaspoon ground cumin

1/4 teaspoon ground nutmeg

Dash of ground cloves

Dash of pepper

1 cup sour cream

4 ounces Cheddar or Monterey Jack cheese, cut into 1/4-inch cubes (1 cup)

BETTY'S TIP

Add a little crunch to this creamy soup by tossing a handful of freshly popped popcorn over each bowl before serving.

Cream of Broccoli Soup

1 1/2 pounds broccoli

2 cups water

1 large stalk celery, chopped (3/4 cup)

1 medium onion, chopped (1/2 cup)

2 tablespoons butter or margarine

2 tablespoons all-purpose flour

2 1/2 cups chicken broth

1/2 teaspoon salt

1/8 teaspoon pepper

Dash of ground nutmeg

1/2 cup whipping (heavy) cream

Shredded cheese, if desired

PREP **35 min**   COOK **20 min**   SERVINGS **8**

1. Remove flowerets from broccoli; set aside. Cut stalks into 1-inch pieces, discarding any leaves.

2. Heat water to boiling in 3-quart saucepan. Add broccoli flowerets and stalk pieces, celery and onion. Cover and heat to boiling; reduce heat to low. Simmer about 10 minutes or until broccoli is tender (do not drain).

3. Carefully place broccoli mixture in blender. Cover and blend on medium speed until smooth.

4. Melt butter in 3-quart saucepan over medium heat. Stir in flour. Cook, stirring constantly, until mixture is smooth and bubbly; remove from heat. Stir in broth. Heat to boiling, stirring constantly. Boil and stir 1 minute.

5. Stir broccoli mixture, salt, pepper and nutmeg into saucepan. Heat just to boiling. Stir in whipping cream. Heat just until hot (do not boil or soup may curdle). Serve with cheese.

1 SERVING Calories 125 (Calories from Fat 70) | Fat 8g (Saturated 5g) | Cholesterol 25mg | Sodium 520mg | Carbohydrate 8g (Dietary Fiber 2g) | Protein 5g   **% DAILY VALUE** Vitamin A 12% | Vitamin C 42% | Calcium 4% | Iron 4%   **EXCHANGES** 2 Vegetable, 1 1/2 Fat   **CARBOHYDRATE CHOICES** 1/2

Cream of Cauliflower Soup Substitute 1 head cauliflower (about 2 pounds), separated into flowerets, for the broccoli. Add 1 tablespoon lemon juice with the onion in step 2.

BETTY'S TIP

Knock a few minutes off your prep time by using 3 packages (10 ounces each) of frozen chopped broccoli instead of fresh broccoli.

Ratatouille Soup

1. Heat oil in 4-quart Dutch oven over medium-high heat. Cook onion and garlic in oil about 3 minutes, stirring occasionally, until onion is tender.

2. Stir in remaining ingredients. Heat to boiling; reduce heat to low. Cover and simmer about 10 minutes or until vegetables are crisp-tender.

1 SERVING Calories 85 (Calories from Fat 25) | Fat 3g (Saturated 1g) | Cholesterol 0mg | Sodium 420mg | Carbohydrate 11g (Dietary Fiber 3g) | Protein 4g   % DAILY VALUE Vitamin A 16% | Vitamin C 22% | Calcium 2% | Iron 4%   EXCHANGES 2 Vegetable, 1/2 Fat   CARBOHYDRATE CHOICES 1

1 tablespoon olive or vegetable oil

1 small onion, chopped (1/4 cup)

1 clove garlic, finely chopped

1 small eggplant (1 pound), cut into 1/2-inch cubes

3 medium tomatoes, coarsely chopped (2 1/4 cups)

1 medium zucchini, cut into 1/2-inch slices (2 cups)

1 small green bell pepper, chopped (1/2 cup)

1 can (10 1/2 ounces) condensed chicken broth

1 broth can water

1/4 teaspoon salt

1/4 teaspoon pepper

BETTY'S TIP

You can throw this hearty dish together in no time when you cut up the veggies the night before.

Minestrone Soup

1 can (28 ounces) whole tomatoes, undrained

1 can (15 to 16 ounces) great northern beans, undrained

1 can (8 ounces) kidney beans, undrained

1 can (about 8 ounces) whole kernel corn, undrained

2 medium stalks celery, thinly sliced (1 cup)

1 small zucchini, sliced (1 cup)

1 medium onion, chopped (1/2 cup)

1 cup shredded cabbage

1/2 cup uncooked elbow macaroni or broken spaghetti

1 1/4 cups water

2 teaspoons vegetable bouillon granules

1 teaspoon Italian seasoning

1 clove garlic, finely chopped

Grated Parmesan cheese

1. Heat all ingredients except cheese to boiling in 4-quart Dutch oven, breaking up tomatoes; reduce heat to low.

2. Cover and simmer about 15 minutes, stirring occasionally, until macaroni is tender. Serve with cheese.

1 SERVING Calories 275 (Calories from Fat 10) | Fat 1g (Saturated 0g) | Cholesterol 0mg | Sodium 810mg | Carbohydrate 51g (Dietary Fiber 9g) | Protein 15g   % DAILY VALUE Vitamin A 12% | Vitamin C 24% | Calcium 14% | Iron 30%   EXCHANGES 3 Starch, 1 Vegetable   CARBOHYDRATE CHOICES 3 1/2

BETTY'S TIP

Parmesan cheese from a can works fine in this veggie-packed soup, but freshly grated Parmesan cheese will give you a richer, sharper and nuttier flavor—and add an extra special touch.

Wild Rice Soup

1. Melt butter in 3-quart saucepan over medium-high heat. Cook celery, carrot, onion and bell pepper in butter about 4 minutes, stirring occasionally, until tender.

2. Stir in flour and pepper. Stir in wild rice, water and broth. Heat to boiling; reduce heat to low. Cover and simmer 15 minutes, stirring occasionally.

3. Stir in half-and-half, almonds and parsley. Heat just until hot (do not boil or soup may curdle).

1 SERVING Calories 215 (Calories from Fat 100) | Fat 11g (Saturated 6g) | Cholesterol 30mg | Sodium 450mg | Carbohydrate 22g (Dietary Fiber 2g) | Protein 7g   **% DAILY VALUE** Vitamin A 60% | Vitamin C 16% | Calcium 8% | Iron 6%   **EXCHANGES** 1 Starch, 1 1/2 Vegetable, 2 Fat   **CARBOHYDRATE CHOICES** 1 1/2

Chicken–Wild Rice Soup Stir in 2 cups cubed cooked chicken or turkey with the half-and-half.

*To toast nuts, bake uncovered in ungreased shallow pan in 350° oven about 10 minutes, stirring occasionally, until golden brown. Or cook in ungreased heavy skillet over medium-low heat 5 to 7 minutes, stirring frequently until browning begins, then stirring constantly until golden brown.

2 tablespoons butter or margarine

2 medium stalks celery, sliced (1 cup)

1 medium carrot, coarsely shredded (1 cup)

1 medium onion, chopped (1/2 cup)

1 small green bell pepper, chopped (1/2 cup)

3 tablespoons all-purpose flour

1/4 teaspoon pepper

1 1/2 cups cooked wild rice

1 cup water

1 can (10 1/2 ounces) condensed chicken broth

1 cup half-and-half

1/3 cup slivered almonds, toasted,* if desired

1/4 cup chopped fresh parsley

BETTY'S TIP

This is a great recipe to keep in mind the next time you make wild rice as a side dish. Just make a little more wild rice than you need, and freeze the extra so you have it on hand to make this soup.

Hearty Tomato Soup

2 tablespoons butter
or margarine

1 medium onion, finely
chopped (1/2 cup)

1 clove garlic, finely
chopped

1/2 teaspoon paprika

1 1/2 teaspoons chopped
fresh or 1/2 teaspoon
dried basil leaves

2 packages (3 ounces each)
cream cheese, softened

1 1/4 cups milk

2 cans (10 3/4 ounces
each) condensed tomato
soup

2 cans (14 1/2 ounces
each) whole tomatoes,
undrained

PREP **15 min**   COOK **10 min**   SERVINGS **8**

1. Melt butter in 3-quart saucepan over medium heat.
    Cook onion and garlic in butter about 2 minutes, stirring
    occasionally, until onion is tender; remove from heat.

2. Stir paprika, basil and cream cheese into onion mix-
    ture. Gradually stir in milk and soup. Beat with hand
    beater or wire whisk until cheese is melted and soup is
    smooth.

3. Stir in tomatoes, breaking up tomatoes. Heat over medium
    heat, stirring frequently, until hot.

1 SERVING Calories 195 (Calories from Fat 110) | Fat 12g (Saturated 7g) |
Cholesterol 35mg | Sodium 710mg | Carbohydrate 19g (Dietary Fiber 2g) |
Protein 5g   % DAILY VALUE Vitamin A 20% | Vitamin C 22% | Calcium 10% |
Iron 8%   EXCHANGES 4 Vegetable, 2 Fat   CARBOHYDRATE CHOICES 1

BETTY'S TIP

This rich tomato soup tastes wonderful by itself, but pair it with a
hot-from-the-griddle grilled cheese sandwich, and it's a classic comfort food combo few will be able to pass up.

Cheesy Vegetable Soup

PREP **5 min**   COOK **10 min**   SERVINGS **4**

1. Heat cheese and milk in 3-quart saucepan over low heat, stirring occasionally, until cheese is melted.

2. Stir in chili powder. Stir in rice and vegetables; cook until hot.

1 SERVING Calories 285 (Calories from Fat 45) | Fat 5g (Saturated 5g) | Cholesterol 0mg | Sodium 600mg | Carbohydrate 43g (Dietary Fiber 4g) | Protein 17g   **% DAILY VALUE** Vitamin A 100% | Vitamin C 18% | Calcium 46% | Iron 6%   **EXCHANGES** 1 1/2 Starch, 1 Vegetable, 1 Milk, 1 Fat   **CARBOHYDRATE CHOICES** 3

4 ounces reduced-fat process cheese spread loaf, cubed

3 1/2 cups fat-free (skim) milk

1/2 teaspoon chili powder

2 cups cooked brown or white rice

1 bag (1 pound) frozen cauliflower, carrots and asparagus (or other combination), thawed and drained

BETTY'S TIP

Get a head start on making this incredibly easy cheesy soup by cooking your favorite rice ahead of time. Rice can be frozen up to six months when you store it in an airtight container or resealable plastic food-storage bag.

Ham 'n Corn Chowder

1 1/2 cups milk

1/2 cup chopped thinly sliced fully cooked ham

1 bag (1 pound) frozen whole kernel corn

1 can (10 3/4 ounces) condensed cream of celery soup

2 medium green onions, sliced (2 tablespoons)

1. Mix milk, ham, corn and soup in 3-quart saucepan. Heat to boiling, stirring occasionally; reduce heat to low.

2. Simmer uncovered 10 minutes, stirring occasionally. Sprinkle with onions.

1 SERVING Calories 245 (Calories from Fat 70) | Fat 8g (Saturated 3g) | Cholesterol 20mg | Sodium 860mg | Carbohydrate 32g (Dietary Fiber 3g) | Protein 11g   % DAILY VALUE Vitamin A 14% | Vitamin C 6% | Calcium 16% | Iron 6%   EXCHANGES 1 1/2 Starch, 1/2 Milk, 2 Fat   CARBOHYDRATE CHOICES 2

BETTY'S TIP

A quick stop at your supermarket deli counter or salad bar will provide you with the ham and green onions called for in this quick-to-fix recipe.

Chunky Vegetable Chowder

PREP **15** min   COOK **15** min   SERVINGS **6**

1. Melt butter in 4-quart Dutch oven over medium heat. Cook bell peppers and onions in butter 3 minutes, stirring occasionally.

2. Stir in water, potatoes, thyme and salt. Heat to boiling; reduce heat to low. Cover and simmer about 10 minutes or until potatoes are tender.

3. Stir in remaining ingredients; cook until hot (do not boil).

1 SERVING Calories 270 (Calories from Fat 70) | Fat 8g (Saturated 4g) | Cholesterol 20mg | Sodium 580mg | Carbohydrate 47g (Dietary Fiber 5g) | Protein 7g   % DAILY VALUE Vitamin A 12% | Vitamin C 48% | Calcium 6% | Iron 14%   EXCHANGES 3 Starch, 1/2 Fat   CARBOHYDRATE CHOICES 3

1 tablespoon butter or margarine

2 medium bell peppers, coarsely chopped (2 cups)

8 medium green onions, sliced (1/2 cup)

3 cups water

3/4 pound new potatoes, cubed (2 1/2 cups)

1 tablespoon chopped fresh or 1 teaspoon dried thyme leaves

1/2 teaspoon salt

1 cup half-and-half

1/8 teaspoon pepper

2 cans (14 3/4 ounces each) cream-style corn

BETTY'S TIP

If bell peppers are in season, use one red and one green pepper to jazz up the color of this chunky chowder.

Beef-Barley-Vegetable Stew

1 tablespoon vegetable oil

1 pound beef stew meat, cut into 1-inch pieces

1 cup dry red wine or water

1 teaspoon chopped fresh or 1/4 teaspoon dried rosemary leaves, crumbled

1/4 teaspoon pepper

1 clove garlic, finely chopped

1 can (10 1/2 ounces) condensed beef broth

1 can (14 1/2 ounces) whole tomatoes, undrained

1/2 cup uncooked barley

1 cup broccoli flowerets

2 medium carrots, sliced (1 cup)

1 medium onion, cut into wedges

4 ounces medium mushrooms, cut in half (1 1/4 cups)

PREP 10 min   COOK 1 hr 55 min   SERVINGS 4

1. Heat oil in 4-quart Dutch oven over medium heat. Cook beef in oil, stirring occasionally, until brown. Stir wine, rosemary, pepper, garlic, broth and tomatoes into beef, breaking up tomatoes. Heat to boiling; reduce heat to low. Cover and simmer 1 hour.

2. Stir in barley. Cover and simmer about 30 minutes or until beef is almost tender. Stir in remaining ingredients. Cover and simmer about 20 minutes or until vegetables are tender.

1 SERVING Calories 420 (Calories from Fat 155) | Fat 17g (Saturated 6g) | Cholesterol 70mg | Sodium 620mg | Carbohydrate 34g (Dietary Fiber 7g) | Protein 30g   % DAILY VALUE Vitamin A 100% | Vitamin C 34% | Calcium 8% | Iron 28%   EXCHANGES 2 Starch, 3 Medium-Fat Meat, 1 Fat   CARBOHYDRATE CHOICES 2

BETTY'S TIP

The hearty, healthful ingredients in this savory stew make it a great choice for chilly winter evenings. Enjoy a bowl with a thick wedge of wheat bread and a glass of red wine.

Quick Beef and Vegetable Stew

1 pound lean beef boneless sirloin

1 bag (1 pound) frozen stew vegetables, thawed and drained

1 can (15 ounces) chunky garlic-and-herb tomato sauce

1 can (14 ounces) beef broth

2 cans (5 1/2 ounces each) spicy eight-vegetable juice

1. Remove fat from beef. Cut beef into 1/2-inch cubes. Spray 10-inch nonstick skillet with cooking spray; heat over medium-high heat. Cook beef in skillet, stirring occasionally, until brown.

2. Stir in remaining ingredients. Heat to boiling; reduce heat to low. Simmer uncovered 5 minutes, stirring occasionally.

1 SERVING Calories 265 (Calories from Fat 55) | Fat 6g (Saturated 2g) | Cholesterol 65mg | Sodium 860mg | Carbohydrate 25g (Dietary Fiber 3g) | Protein 27g   **% DAILY VALUE** Vitamin A 14% | Vitamin C 24% | Calcium 4% | Iron 18%   **EXCHANGES** 1 Starch, 2 Vegetable, 3 Very Lean Meat, 1/2 Fat   **CARBOHYDRATE CHOICES** 1 1/2

BETTY'S TIP

This satisfying stew has many ingredients that can be substituted for others. Instead of frozen stew vegetables, use your favorite frozen veggie mix, or switch the chunky garlic-and-herb tomato sauce for regular tomato sauce. If you're trying to lower the fat in your diet, use low-fat beef broth instead of regular.

Classic Beef Stew

PREP **15 min**   COOK **3 hr 30 min**   SERVINGS **8**

1 pound beef stew meat, cut into 1/2-inch pieces

1 medium onion, cut into eighths

1 package (8 ounces) baby-cut carrots (about 30)

1 can (14 1/2 ounces) diced tomatoes, undrained

1 can (10 1/2 ounces) condensed beef broth

1 can (8 ounces) tomato sauce

1/3 cup all-purpose flour

1 tablespoon Worcestershire sauce

1 teaspoon salt

1 teaspoon sugar

1 teaspoon dried marjoram leaves

1/4 teaspoon pepper

1 1/2 pounds new potatoes, cut into fourths (about 12 potatoes)

2 cups sliced mushrooms (about 5 ounces) or 1 package (3.4 ounces) fresh shiitake mushrooms, sliced

1. Heat oven to 325°.

2. Mix all ingredients except potatoes and mushrooms in ovenproof 4-quart Dutch oven. Cover and bake 2 hours, stirring once.

3. Stir in potatoes and mushrooms. Cover and bake 1 hour to 1 hour 30 minutes or until beef and vegetables are tender.

1 SERVING Calories 245 (Calories from Fat 65) | Fat 7g (Saturated 3g) | Cholesterol 35mg | Sodium 810mg | Carbohydrate 28g (Dietary Fiber 4g) | Protein 17g   % DAILY VALUE Vitamin A 100% | Vitamin C 20% | Calcium 4% | Iron 18%   EXCHANGES 1 Starch, 2 Vegetable, 1 1/2 Medium-Fat Meat CARBOHYDRATE CHOICES 2

BETTY'S TIP

Try to cut the meat and veggies into similar sizes so that all the ingredients in this stick-to-your-ribs stew get done at the same time.

Greek Beef and Onion Stew

PREP **15 min**   COOK **2 hr 15 min**   SERVINGS **6**

1. Heat oil in 4-quart Dutch oven over medium heat. Cook chopped onion and garlic in oil, stirring occasionally, until onion is tender. Remove onion and garlic; set aside. Cook beef in remaining oil in Dutch oven about 25 minutes, stirring occasionally, until all liquid has evaporated and beef is brown; drain.

2. Return onion and garlic to Dutch oven. Stir in remaining ingredients except white onions and cheese. Heat to boiling; reduce heat to low. Cover and simmer 1 hour.

3. Stir in white onions. Cover and simmer about 45 minutes or until beef and white onions are tender. Remove bay leaf and cinnamon. Sprinkle with cheese.

1 SERVING Calories 435 (Calories from Fat 215) | Fat 24g (Saturated 8g) | Cholesterol 95mg | Sodium 520mg | Carbohydrate 15g (Dietary Fiber 3g) | Protein 33g **% DAILY VALUE** Vitamin A 10% | Vitamin C 10% | Calcium 4% | Iron 22% **EXCHANGES** 1 Starch, 4 Medium-Fat Meat, 1 Fat **CARBOHYDRATE CHOICES** 1

3 tablespoons olive or vegetable oil

1 medium onion, chopped (1/2 cup)

2 cloves garlic, finely chopped

2 pounds beef boneless chuck, tip or round, cut into 1-inch cubes

1/2 cup dry red wine or water

2 tablespoons red wine vinegar

1/2 teaspoon salt

1/4 teaspoon coarsely ground pepper

1 dried bay leaf

1 stick cinnamon

1 can (8 ounces) tomato sauce

1 1/2 pounds small white onions, peeled (about 12)

Crumbled feta cheese

BETTY'S TIP

Pita bread triangles are great for dunking into this flavorful stew, and a bowl of Kalamata olives served on the side keeps the Greek theme going.

New England Baked Bean Stew

PREP **10 min**   COOK **20 min**   SERVINGS **4**

1/2 pound boneless, skinless chicken breasts, cut into 1/2-inch pieces

1/2 pound fully cooked Polish sausage, cut into 1/2-inch slices

1 can (15 to 16 ounces) great northern beans, rinsed and drained

1 can (15 to 16 ounces) dark red kidney beans, rinsed and drained

1 can (14 1/2 ounces) diced tomatoes with olive oil, garlic and spices, undrained

1 tablespoon packed brown sugar

4 medium green onions, sliced (1/4 cup)

1. Spray 12-inch nonstick skillet with cooking spray; heat over medium-high heat. Cook chicken in skillet 3 to 5 minutes, stirring occasionally, until brown.

2. Stir in remaining ingredients except onions. Cook uncovered over medium-low heat 8 to 10 minutes, stirring occasionally, until chicken is no longer pink in center.

3. Stir in onions. Cook 3 to 5 minutes, stirring occasionally, until onions are crisp-tender.

1 SERVING Calories 525 (Calories from Fat 170) | Fat 19g (Saturated 6g) | Cholesterol 65mg | Sodium 1150mg | Carbohydrate 64g (Dietary Fiber 15g) | Protein 40g   **% DAILY VALUE** Vitamin A 6% | Vitamin C 12% | Calcium 18% | Iron 48%   **EXCHANGES** 4 Starch, 1 Vegetable, 4 Very Lean Meat, 1 Fat   **CARBOHYDRATE CHOICES** 4

BETTY'S TIP

Pick up a 6-ounce package of cooked chicken breast slices in the meat department of your grocery store, and you can skip the first step altogether.

Chicken Stew with Potatoes

PREP **15 min**   COOK **25 min**   SERVINGS **4**

1. Mix all ingredients in 3-quart saucepan. Heat to boiling, stirring occasionally; reduce heat to low.

2. Cover and simmer 15 to 20 minutes, stirring occasionally, until potatoes are tender and chicken is no longer pink in center.

1 SERVING Calories 330 (Calories from Fat 70) | Fat 8g (Saturated 2g) | Cholesterol 55mg | Sodium 580mg | Carbohydrate 40g (Dietary Fiber 5g) | Protein 25g % DAILY VALUE Vitamin A 24% | Vitamin C 44% | Calcium 6% | Iron 18% EXCHANGES 2 Starch, 2 Vegetable, 2 Lean Meat CARBOHYDRATE CHOICES 2 1/2

2 cups broccoli flowerets

1 cup water

3/4 pound small red potatoes (about 6 potatoes), cut into fourths

3/4 pound boneless, skinless chicken breasts, cut into 1-inch cubes

1 jar (12 ounces) chicken gravy

BETTY'S TIP

If broccoli isn't one of your family's favorite veggies, use 2 cups of cut green beans instead.

Southwestern Pork and Potato Stew

1 pound lean pork
boneless shoulder

1 tablespoon all-purpose
flour

1 medium onion, chopped
(1/2 cup)

3 cloves garlic, finely
chopped

2 1/4 cups fat-free
reduced-sodium chicken
broth

1 teaspoon dried thyme
leaves

1/2 teaspoon ground
cumin

2 tablespoons chopped
fresh or canned jalapeño
chilies

3 cups (from 1-pound bag)
frozen broccoli, corn and
red peppers (or other
combination)

PREP **15 min**   COOK **35 min**   SERVINGS **4**

1. Trim fat from pork. Cut pork into 1-inch cubes. Toss pork with flour. Spray 4-quart Dutch oven with cooking spray; heat over medium-high heat. Cook pork, onion and garlic in Dutch oven, stirring occasionally, until pork is brown.

2. Stir broth, thyme, cumin and chilies into pork. Cook 15 minutes.

3. Stir in vegetable mixture. Heat to boiling; reduce heat to low. Cover and simmer about 10 minutes or until pork is no longer pink in center.

1 SERVING Calories 320 (Calories from Fat 135) | Fat 15g (Saturated 5g) | Cholesterol 70mg | Sodium 380mg | Carbohydrate 18g (Dietary Fiber 3g) | Protein 30g   **% DAILY VALUE** Vitamin A 62% | Vitamin C 78% | Calcium 4% | Iron 10%   **EXCHANGES** 1 Starch, 1 Vegetable, 3 Lean Meat, 1 Fat   **CARBOHYDRATE CHOICES** 1

BETTY'S TIP

In a pinch, 1 tablespoon of ready-to-use minced garlic can be used instead of the garlic cloves. Look for jars of it in the produce department of your supermarket.

Spicy Fish Stew

PREP 5 min   **COOK** 20 min   **SERVINGS** 4

1/2 cup clam juice

4 cloves garlic, finely chopped

3 cups packaged fresh (refrigerated) stir-fry vegetables

1/2 pound cod fillets, cubed

1 1/2 tablespoons chopped fresh or canned jalapeño chilies

2 tablespoons fish sauce or reduced-sodium soy sauce

1 tablespoon packed brown sugar

4 cups hot cooked rice

1. Heat 1/4 cup of the clam juice to boiling in 10-inch nonstick skillet. Cook garlic in clam juice 1 minute.

2. Stir in stir-fry vegetables. Cook about 8 minutes, stirring frequently, until liquid has evaporated.

3. Stir in fish, chilies, fish sauce, brown sugar and remaining clam juice. Heat to boiling; reduce heat to medium. Cook uncovered 10 minutes. Serve with rice.

1 SERVING Calories 305 (Calories from Fat 10) | Fat 1g (Saturated 0g) | Cholesterol 30mg | Sodium 610mg | Carbohydrate 56g (Dietary Fiber 2g) | Protein 18g   **% DAILY VALUE** Vitamin A 18% | Vitamin C 32% | Calcium 6% | Iron 18%   **EXCHANGES** 3 Starch, 2 Vegetable, 1/2 Very Lean Meat   **CARBOHYDRATE CHOICES** 4

BETTY'S TIP

Mix up the flavor of this sweet and spicy stew by experimenting with different kinds of fish. Halibut, orange roughy or haddock will all taste great.

New England
Clam Chowder

1/4 cup cut-up uncooked bacon or lean salt pork

1 medium onion, chopped (1/2 cup)

2 cans (6 1/2 ounces each) minced clams

1 medium potato, finely chopped (1 cup)

1/2 teaspoon salt

Dash of pepper

2 cups milk

1. Cook bacon and onion in 2-quart saucepan over medium heat, stirring frequently, until bacon is crisp and onion is tender. Drain clams, reserving liquid. Add enough water, if necessary, to clam liquid to measure 1 cup. Stir clams, clam liquid, potato, salt and pepper into bacon and onion. Heat to boiling; reduce heat to low.

2. Cover and simmer about 15 minutes or until potato is tender. Stir in milk. Heat, stirring occasionally, just until hot (do not boil).

1 SERVING Calories 235 (Calories from Fat 45) | Fat 5g (Saturated 2g) | Cholesterol 70mg | Sodium 490g | Carbohydrate 19g (Dietary Fiber 1g) | Protein 29g   % DAILY VALUE Vitamin A 14% | Vitamin C 20% | Calcium 24% | Iron 100%   EXCHANGES 1 Starch, 1/2 Milk, 3 Very Lean Meat   CARBOHYDRATE CHOICES 1

BETTY'S TIP

If you have access to fresh clams, go ahead and use them instead of canned clams. Chop up 1 pint of shucked fresh clams and stir them, with their liquid, in with the potato, salt and pepper.

Oyster Stew

1/4 cup butter or margarine

1 pint shucked oysters, undrained

2 cups milk

1/2 cup half-and-half

1/2 teaspoon salt

Dash of pepper

1. Melt butter in 1 1/2-quart saucepan over low heat. Cook oysters in butter, stirring occasionally, just until edges of oysters curl.

2. Heat milk and half-and-half in 2-quart saucepan over medium-low heat until hot. Stir in salt, pepper and oyster mixture; heat until hot.

1 SERVING Calories 285 (Calories from Fat 180) | Fat 20g (Saturated 12g) | Cholesterol 115mg | Sodium 700mg | Carbohydrate 12g (Dietary Fiber 0g) | Protein 14g   % DAILY VALUE Vitamin A 20% | Vitamin C 4% | Calcium 24% | Iron 46%   EXCHANGES 1 Milk, 1 Medium-Fat Meat, 3 Fat   CARBOHYDRATE CHOICES 1

BETTY'S TIP

If fresh oysters are available, by all means use them! When shopping for fresh oysters, look for oysters that are plump, of similar size and smell fresh. The liquid they are packaged in should be clear, not cloudy. Oysters taste best when used within two days.

Shrimp Gumbo

1/4 cup butter or margarine

2 medium onions, sliced

1 medium green bell pepper, cut into thin strips

2 cloves garlic, finely chopped

2 tablespoons all-purpose flour

3 cups beef broth

1/2 teaspoon red pepper sauce

1/4 teaspoon salt

1/4 teaspoon pepper

1 dried bay leaf

1 package (10 ounces) frozen cut okra, thawed and drained

1 can (14 1/2 ounces) whole tomatoes, undrained

1 can (6 ounces) tomato paste

1 pound uncooked peeled deveined medium shrimp, thawed if frozen and tails peeled

3 cups hot cooked rice

1/4 cup chopped fresh parsley

PREP **20 min**   COOK **1 hr**   SERVINGS **6**

1. Melt butter in 4-quart Dutch oven over medium heat. Cook onions, bell pepper and garlic in butter 5 minutes, stirring occasionally. Stir in flour. Cook over medium heat, stirring constantly, until bubbly; remove from heat.

2. Stir in remaining ingredients except shrimp, rice and parsley, breaking up tomatoes. Heat to boiling; reduce heat to low. Simmer uncovered 45 minutes, stirring occasionally.

3. Stir shrimp into gumbo. Cover and simmer about 5 minutes or until shrimp are pink and firm. Remove bay leaf. Serve soup in bowls over rice. Sprinkle with parsley.

1 SERVING Calories 295 (Calories from Fat 80) | Fat 9g (Saturated 5g) | Cholesterol 125mg | Sodium 1,120mg | Carbohydrate 40g (Dietary Fiber 5g) | Protein 19g   **% DAILY VALUE** Vitamin A 34% | Vitamin C 44% | Calcium 12% | Iron 24%   **EXCHANGES** 2 Starch, 2 Vegetable, 1 Lean Meat, 1 Fat   **CARBOHYDRATE CHOICES** 2 1/2

BETTY'S TIP

A shortcut to breaking up the tomatoes in step 2 is to snip them with kitchen scissors.

Classic Chili

PREP **15 min**   COOK **1 hr 25 min**   SERVINGS **4**

1 pound lean ground beef

1 medium onion, chopped (1/2 cup)

1 clove garlic, finely chopped

1 can (14 1/2 ounces) diced tomatoes, undrained

1 can (8 ounces) tomato sauce

1 tablespoon chili powder

3/4 teaspoon ground cumin

1/4 teaspoon salt

1/4 teaspoon pepper

1 can (15 or 16 ounces) kidney or pinto beans, rinsed and drained, if desired

1. Cook beef, onion and garlic in 3-quart saucepan over medium heat 8 to 10 minutes, stirring occasionally, until beef is brown; drain.

2. Stir in remaining ingredients except beans. Heat to boiling; reduce heat to low. Cover and simmer 1 hour, stirring occasionally.

3. Stir in beans. Heat to boiling; reduce heat to low. Simmer uncovered about 10 minutes, stirring occasionally, until desired thickness.

1 SERVING Calories 295 (Calories from Fat 155) | Fat 17g (Saturated 6g) | Cholesterol 65mg | Sodium 740mg | Carbohydrate 12g (Dietary Fiber 3g) | Protein 23g % DAILY VALUE Vitamin A 30% | Vitamin C 22% | Calcium 6% | Iron 18% EXCHANGES 2 Vegetable, 3 Medium-Fat Meat CARBOHYDRATE CHOICES 1

Cincinnati-Style Chili For each serving, spoon about 3/4 cup beef mixture over 1 cup hot cooked spaghetti. Sprinkle each serving with 1/4 cup shredded Cheddar cheese and 2 tablespoons chopped onion. Top with sour cream if desired.

BETTY'S TIP

Want to increase the heat? Increase the chili powder, add 1/2 teaspoon red pepper sauce or add a jalapeño chili, seeded and finely chopped, to the mix.

White Chili

PREP 15 min   COOK 25 min   SERVINGS 6

1 tablespoon vegetable oil

2 medium onions, chopped (1 cup)

2 cloves garlic, finely chopped

3 cups chicken broth

2 tablespoons chopped fresh cilantro or 1/2 teaspoon ground coriander

2 tablespoons lime juice

1 teaspoon ground cumin

1/2 teaspoon dried oregano leaves

1/4 teaspoon red pepper sauce

1/4 teaspoon salt

1 can (11 ounces) white shoepeg or whole kernel corn, drained

1 can (15 to 16 ounces) great northern beans, drained

1 can (15 to 16 ounces) butter beans, drained

2 cups chopped cooked chicken breast

1. Heat oil in 4-quart Dutch oven over medium heat. Cook onions and garlic in oil, stirring occasionally, until onions are tender.

2. Stir in remaining ingredients except chicken. Heat to boiling; reduce heat to low. Simmer uncovered 20 minutes. Stir in chicken; simmer until hot.

1 SERVING Calories 235 (Calories from Fat 55) | Fat 6g (Saturated 1g) | Cholesterol 40mg | Sodium 920mg | Carbohydrate 28g (Dietary Fiber 7g) | Protein 24g   % DAILY VALUE Vitamin A 2% | Vitamin C 6% | Calcium 28% | Iron 16%   EXCHANGES 2 Starch, 2 1/2 Very Lean Meat   CARBOHYDRATE CHOICES 2

BETTY'S TIP

Provide bowls of shredded cheese, crushed tortilla chips, chopped green onions, diced tomatoes, chopped fresh cilantro, sliced avocado and sour cream so everyone can "accessorize" their chili as they see fit.

56   Betty Crocker   One-Dish Meals

Turkey Chili

1. Cook turkey and onions in 6-quart Dutch oven over medium heat about 15 minutes, stirring occasionally, until turkey is no longer pink and onions are tender; drain.

2. Stir in remaining ingredients, breaking up tomatoes. Heat to boiling; reduce heat to low. Simmer uncovered 1 hour 15 minutes.

1 SERVING Calories 320 (Calories from Fat 55) | Fat 6g (Saturated 1g) | Cholesterol 50mg | Sodium 1200mg | Carbohydrate 38g (Dietary Fiber 10g) | Protein 28g   % DAILY VALUE Vitamin A 40% | Vitamin C 34% | Calcium 14% | Iron 32%   EXCHANGES 2 1/2 Starch, 3 Very Lean Meat, 1/2 Fat   CARBOHYDRATE CHOICES 2 1/2

2 pounds ground turkey

2 large onions, chopped (2 cups)

3 cans (28 ounces each) whole tomatoes, undrained

3 cans (15 to 16 ounces each) beans (such as kidney, great northern, black, chili or lima), drained

1 can (15 ounces) tomato sauce

1 can (4.5 ounces) chopped green chiles, undrained

1/4 cup chili powder

1 tablespoon ground cumin

1/2 teaspoon salt

1/2 teaspoon pepper

BETTY'S TIP

Express yourself! Use aerosol cans of process cheese spread to squirt a fun design or special message onto individual servings of chili.

Vegetarian Chili

2 medium potatoes, unpeeled and cut into 1/2-inch cubes (about 10 ounces)

1 medium onion, chopped (1/2 cup)

1 small yellow bell pepper, finely chopped (about 1/2 cup)

1 can (15 to 16 ounces) garbanzo beans, rinsed and drained

1 can (15 to 16 ounces) kidney beans, rinsed and drained

1 can (28 ounces) whole tomatoes, undrained

1 can (8 ounces) tomato sauce

1 tablespoon chili powder

1 teaspoon ground cumin

1 medium zucchini, cut into 1/2-inch slices

1. Place all ingredients except zucchini in 4-quart Dutch oven, breaking up tomatoes. Heat to boiling, stirring occasionally; reduce heat to low. Cover and simmer 10 minutes.

2. Stir in zucchini. Cover and simmer 5 to 7 minutes, stirring occasionally, until potatoes and zucchini and tender.

1 SERVING Calories 400 (Calories from Fat 35) | Fat 4g (Saturated 1g) | Cholesterol 0mg | Sodium 1090mg | Carbohydrate 87g (Dietary Fiber 20g) | Protein 24g   **% DAILY VALUE** Vitamin A 42% | Vitamin C 72% | Calcium 18% | Iron 50%   **EXCHANGES** 5 Starch, 2 Vegetable   **CARBOHYDRATE CHOICES** 6

BETTY'S TIP

Zucchini comes in all sorts of sizes. For this recipe, look for a medium zucchini between 4 and 8 inches long.

BettyCrocker.com

Sizzling Skillet Dishes

Skillet Beef Stew

1 pound lean ground beef

1 jar (18 ounces) seasoned gravy for beef

1/4 cup ketchup

8 unpeeled small red potatoes, cut into fourths

2 cups frozen whole or cut green beans (from 1-pound bag), thawed and drained

1. Spray 12-inch nonstick skillet with cooking spray; heat over medium-high heat. Cook beef in skillet 3 to 5 minutes, stirring frequently, until light brown.

2. Stir gravy, ketchup and potatoes into beef. Heat to boiling; reduce heat to medium-low. Cover and cook 10 minutes.

3. Stir in beans. Cover and cook 10 to 15 minutes, stirring occasionally, until vegetables are tender.

1 SERVING Calories 410 (Calories from Fat 160) | Fat 18g (Saturated 8g) | Cholesterol 65mg | Sodium 980mg | Carbohydrate 34g (Dietary Fiber 4g) | Protein 29g   **%DAILY VALUE** Vitamin A 12% | Vitamin C 12% | Calcium 4% | Iron 24%   **EXCHANGES** 2 Starch, 1 Vegetable, 3 Medium-Fat Meat **CARBOHYDRATE CHOICES** 2

Skillet Turkey Stew Substitute ground turkey for the ground beef and turkey gravy for the beef gravy.

BETTY'S TIP

Leaving the skins on the potatoes not only pumps up the flavor and nutrients of this family-friendly skillet dish, it also cuts down on the prep work.

Beef-Taco-Rice Skillet

PREP **5 min**   COOK **14 min**   STAND **10 min**   SERVINGS **5**

1. Cook beef in 10-inch skillet over medium heat 8 to 10 minutes, stirring occasionally, until brown; drain.

2. Stir seasoning mix, water, salsa and corn into beef. Heat to boiling; stir in rice. Boil 1 minute; remove from heat. Cover and let stand 8 minutes.

3. Fluff rice mixture with fork; sprinkle with cheese. Cover and let stand 1 to 2 minutes or until cheese is melted. Sprinkle lettuce around edge of skillet; sprinkle tomato in circle next to lettuce. Serve with sour cream.

1 SERVING Calories 440 (Calories from Fat 170) | Fat 19g (Saturated 9g) | Cholesterol 70mg | Sodium 670mg | Carbohydrate 44g (Dietary Fiber 3g) | Protein 26g   %DAILY VALUE Vitamin A 30% | Vitamin C 12% | Calcium 14% | Iron 20%   EXCHANGES 3 Starch, 2 High-Fat Meat   CARBOHYDRATE CHOICES 3

1 pound lean ground beef

1 envelope (1 1/4 ounces) taco seasoning mix

1 1/2 cups water

1 cup thick-and-chunky salsa

1 cup frozen whole kernel corn (from 1-pound bag)

1 1/2 cups uncooked instant rice

3/4 cup shredded taco-seasoned cheese (4 ounces)

1 cup shredded lettuce

1 medium tomato, chopped (3/4 cup)

Sour cream, if desired

BETTY'S TIP

On the slim chance you have leftovers, turn them into taco filling or use them in wrap sandwiches for lunch the next day.

Skillet Goulash

1 pound lean ground beef

1 1/2 cups uncooked fine egg noodles (3 ounces)

1/2 cup water

1 medium onion, chopped (1/2 cup)

1 medium stalk celery, chopped (1/2 cup)

1 can (15 ounces) Italian-style tomato sauce

PREP **10 min**   COOK **32 min**   SERVINGS **4**

1. Cook beef in 10-inch skillet over medium heat 8 to 10 minutes, stirring occasionally, until brown; drain.

2. Stir in remaining ingredients. Heat to boiling; reduce heat to low. Cover and simmer 15 to 20 minutes, stirring occasionally, until noodles are tender. (Add a small amount of water if necessary.)

1 SERVING Calories 440 (Calories from Fat 190) | Fat 21g (Saturated 7g) | Cholesterol 80mg | Sodium 640mg | Carbohydrate 38g (Dietary Fiber 3g) | Protein 25g **%DAILY VALUE** Vitamin A 18% | Vitamin C 16% | Calcium 4% | Iron 20% **EXCHANGES** 2 1/2 Starch, 2 1/2 Medium-Fat Meat, 1 Fat **CARBOHYDRATE CHOICES** 2 1/2

BETTY'S TIP

These days, grocery store shelves are practically bursting with tomato sauce varieties. Don't be afraid to experiment by trying different flavors with this dish. Garlic and onion, extra-thick and zesty are some tasty examples to try.

Easy Taco Dinner

1. Cook beef and onion in 10-inch skillet over medium heat 8 to 10 minutes, stirring occasionally, until beef is brown; drain.

2. Stir in seasoning mix and water. Heat to boiling; reduce heat to low. Simmer uncovered, stirring occasionally, 10 minutes. Spoon beef mixture onto chips. Top with remaining ingredients.

1 SERVING Calories 615 (Calories from Fat 340) | Fat 38g (Saturated 13g) | Cholesterol 80mg | Sodium 850mg | Carbohydrate 47g (Dietary Fiber 6g) | Protein 25g   %DAILY VALUE Vitamin A 30% | Vitamin C 10% | Calcium 18% | Iron 24%   EXCHANGES 3 Starch, 2 Medium-Fat Meat, 5 Fat   CARBOHYDRATE CHOICES 3

1 pound lean ground beef

1 large onion, chopped (about 1 cup)

1 envelope (1 1/4 ounces) taco seasoning mix

1 cup water

1 package (12 ounces) tortilla chips

1/2 head iceberg lettuce, shredded

2 medium tomatoes, chopped (1 1/2 cups)

1 can (2 1/4 ounces) sliced ripe olives, drained

1 cup shredded Cheddar or Monterey Jack cheese (4 ounces)

2/3 cup sour cream

BETTY'S TIP

Kids will find this dinner much easier to eat than regular tacos because there are no crumbly taco shells to contend with, and the cook gets the benefit of not having to heat the taco shells—everyone wins! Set out bowls of toppings so everyone can top their taco dinner as they like.

Skillet Lasagna

1 pound lean ground beef

1 medium onion, chopped
(1/2 cup)

1 medium bell pepper,
chopped (1 cup)

3 cups uncooked mafalda
(mini-lasagna noodle) pasta
or wide egg noodles
(6 ounces)

2 1/2 cups water

1/2 teaspoon Italian
seasoning

1 jar (26 to 30 ounces)
tomato pasta sauce (any
variety) or marinara sauce

1 jar (4 1/2 ounces) sliced
mushrooms, drained

PREP **10 min**   COOK **22 min**   SERVINGS **8**

1. Cook beef, onion and bell pepper in 4-quart Dutch oven
    over medium heat 8 to 10 minutes, stirring occasion-
    ally, until beef is brown; drain.

2. Stir in remaining ingredients. Heat to boiling, stirring
    occasionally; reduce heat to low. Simmer uncovered
    10 to 12 minutes or until pasta is tender.

1 SERVING Calories 320 (Calories from Fat 115) | Fat 13g (Saturated 4g) |
Cholesterol 50mg | Sodium 600mg | Carbohydrate 36g (Dietary Fiber 3g) |
Protein 15g   %DAILY VALUE Vitamin A 14% | Vitamin C 24% | Calcium 4% |
Iron 14%   EXCHANGES 2 Starch, 1 Vegetable, 1 High-Fat Meat, 1 Fat
CARBOHYDRATE CHOICES 2 1/2

Skillet-Pizza Lasagna Substitute two 15-ounce cans of
pizza sauce for the pasta sauce and add 1/2 cup diced
pepperoni.

BETTY'S TIP

If you have leftover broken lasagna noodles on hand, you can use
those instead of the mafalda pasta in this Italian favorite.

Penne with Beef and Sun-Dried Tomatoes

PREP **10 min**   COOK **20 min**   SERVINGS **4**

1. Cook and drain pasta as directed on package.

2. While pasta is cooking, spray 12-inch nonstick skillet with cooking spray; heat over medium-high heat. Add beef to skillet; sprinkle with peppered seasoned salt. Cook 2 to 3 minutes, stirring occasionally, just until brown.

3. Stir tomatoes, 1 tablespoon of the oil and the onions into beef. Cook 1 to 2 minutes, stirring frequently, until hot. Stir in artichoke hearts, pasta and the remaining 1 tablespoon oil. Cook 1 to 2 minutes, stirring constantly, until hot. Sprinkle with basil.

1 SERVING Calories 395 (Calories from Fat 125) | Fat 14g (Saturated 3g) | Cholesterol 60mg | Sodium 390mg | Carbohydrate 42g (Dietary Fiber 5g) | Protein 31g   %DAILY VALUE Vitamin A 10% | Vitamin C 16% | Calcium 4% | Iron 26%   EXCHANGES 2 1/2 Starch, 1 Vegetable, 3 Lean Meat   CARBOHYDRATE CHOICES 3

1 1/2 cups uncooked penne pasta (6 ounces)

1 pound beef boneless sirloin steak, cut into thin strips

1/2 teaspoon peppered seasoned salt

1/2 cup sun-dried tomatoes packed in olive oil and herbs, drained and cut into thin strips

2 tablespoons oil from sun-dried tomatoes

4 medium green onions, sliced (1/4 cup)

1 jar (6 to 6 1/2 ounces) marinated artichoke hearts, drained

2 tablespoons chopped fresh basil leaves

BETTY'S TIP

Don't throw out the leftover sun-dried tomato oil. It adds pizzazz when added to salad dressings or drizzled over French bread.

Mexican Steak Stir-Fry

PREP **15 min**   COOK **10 min**   SERVINGS **4**

3/4-pound beef boneless sirloin steak, about 3/4 inch thick

1 medium onion, chopped (1/2 cup)

1/2 cup chopped green bell pepper

1 cup frozen whole kernel corn (from 1-pound bag)

1/2 cup salsa

1 medium zucchini, sliced (2 cups)

1 can (15 to 16 ounces) pinto beans, rinsed and drained

1 can (14 1/2 ounces) no-salt-added whole tomatoes, undrained

1. Trim fat from beef. Cut beef with grain into 2-inch strips; cut strips across grain into 1/8-inch slices.

2. Spray 12-inch nonstick skillet with cooking spray; heat over medium-high heat. Cook beef, onion and bell pepper 4 to 5 minutes, stirring frequently, until beef is brown.

3. Stir in remaining ingredients, breaking up tomatoes. Cook about 5 minutes, stirring occasionally, until zucchini is tender and mixture is hot.

1 SERVING Calories 295 (Calories from Fat 35) | Fat 4g (Saturated 1g) | Cholesterol 45mg | Sodium 360mg | Carbohydrate 49g (Dietary Fiber 13g) | Protein 29g   %DAILY VALUE Vitamin A 22% | Vitamin C 38% | Calcium 10% | Iron 32%   EXCHANGES 3 Starch, 1 Vegetable, 2 Very Lean Meat   CARBOHYDRATE CHOICES 3

BETTY'S TIP

If you're watching your sodium intake, make sure you rinse the canned beans—it helps get rid of some of the excess salt.

Stir-Fried Beef and Broccoli

PREP **15 min**   COOK **10 min**   SERVINGS **4**

1. Mix water, cornstarch and soy sauce; set aside. Trim fat from beef. Cut beef with grain into 2-inch strips; cut strips across grain into 1/8-inch slices.

2. Heat 12-inch skillet or wok over medium-high heat. Add oil; rotate skillet to coat bottom. Add beef, ginger and garlic powder; stir-fry about 3 minutes or until beef is brown. Add broccoli; stir-fry 2 minutes.

3. Stir in orange juice; heat to boiling. Stir in cornstarch mixture; cook and stir about 1 minute or until thickened. Serve beef mixture with rice.

1/2 cup cold water

2 tablespoons cornstarch

2 tablespoons soy sauce

1 pound beef boneless sirloin steak

2 tablespoons vegetable oil

1/4 teaspoon ground ginger

1/4 teaspoon garlic powder

1 bag (1 pound) frozen chopped broccoli, thawed and drained

1 cup orange juice

4 cups hot cooked rice

1 SERVING Calories 460 (Calories from Fat 100) | Fat 11g (Saturated 2g) | Cholesterol 55mg | Sodium 530mg | Carbohydrate 62g (Dietary Fiber 4g) | Protein 28g   **%DAILY VALUE** Vitamin A 36% | Vitamin C 50% | Calcium 8% | Iron 28%   **EXCHANGES** 3 1/2 Starch, 1 Vegetable, 2 Lean Meat, 1 Fat   **CARBOHYDRATE CHOICES** 4

BETTY'S TIP

A fresh spinach salad with sliced red onion and mushrooms nicely complements this citrus-kissed stir-fry. For added zip, top the salad with crumbled Gorgonzola or blue cheese.

Beef Stroganoff

PREP **15 min**   COOK **30 min**   SERVINGS **6**

1 1/2 pounds beef boneless top loin steak, about 1 inch thick

2 tablespoons butter or margarine

1 1/2 cups beef broth

2 tablespoons ketchup

1 teaspoon salt

1 clove garlic, finely chopped

1 medium onion, chopped (1/2 cup)

1 package (8 ounces) sliced mushrooms (3 cups)

3 tablespoons all-purpose flour

1 container (8 ounces) sour cream or plain yogurt

3 cups cooked egg noodles

1. Trim fat from beef. Cut beef with grain into 2-inch strips; cut strips across grain into 1/8-inch slices. Cut longer slices in half. Melt butter in 10-inch skillet over medium-high heat. Cook beef in butter 8 to 10 minutes, stirring occasionally, until brown.

2. Reserve 1/3 cup broth. Stir remaining broth, the ketchup, salt and garlic into beef. Heat to boiling; reduce heat to low. Cover and simmer about 10 minutes or until beef is tender. Stir in onion and mushrooms. Cover and simmer about 5 minutes or until onion is tender.

3. Shake the reserved 1/3 cup broth and the flour in tightly covered jar or container. Gradually stir into beef mixture. Heat to boiling. Boil about 1 minute, stirring constantly, until thickened. Reduce heat to low.

4. Stir in sour cream. Heat until hot. (Do not boil or mixture will curdle.) Serve beef over noodles.

1 SERVING Calories 435 (Calories from Fat 190) | Fat 21g (Saturated 10g) | Cholesterol 125mg | Sodium 820mg | Carbohydrate 29g (Dietary Fiber 2g) | Protein 32g %DAILY VALUE Vitamin A 12% | Vitamin C 2% | Calcium 6% | Iron 22% EXCHANGES 2 Starch, 4 Lean Meat, 1 Fat CARBOHYDRATE CHOICES 2

BETTY'S TIP

Try stretching the flavor boundaries of this classic dish by using chanterelle, morel or shiitake mushrooms instead of regular white mushrooms.

Cheesy Meatballs and Vegetables

PREP **5 min**   COOK **25 min**   SERVINGS **6**

1. Cook rice as directed on package.

2. While rice is cooking, cover and cook meatballs in 12-inch skillet over medium-high heat 4 minutes, stirring once. Stir in half-and-half, scraping skillet to remove any browned bits of meat.

3. Add blocks of frozen vegetables and sauce to skillet, placing vegetable sides down. Cover and cook 10 to 12 minutes, stirring occasionally, until vegetables and meatballs are hot. Serve over rice.

1 1/2 cups uncooked regular long-grain rice

1 package (16 ounces) frozen cooked meatballs

2/3 cup half-and-half

2 packages (10 ounces each) frozen broccoli, cauliflower and carrots in cheese-flavored sauce

1 SERVING Calories 465 (Calories from Fat 155) | Fat 17g (Saturated 8g) | Cholesterol 90mg | Sodium 520mg | Carbohydrate 54g (Dietary Fiber 3g) | Protein 24g   **%DAILY VALUE** Vitamin A 52% | Vitamin C 24% | Calcium 14% | Iron 22%   **EXCHANGES** 3 Starch, 2 Vegetable, 1 1/2 Medium-Fat Meat, 1 1/2 Fat **CARBOHYDRATE CHOICES** 3 1/2

BETTY'S TIP

Give this dish an extra dash of flavor by using fragrant jasmine rice or basmati rice instead of regular long-grain rice.

Parmesan Orzo and Meatballs

PREP **10** min   COOK **20** min   SERVINGS **4**

1 1/2 cups frozen stir-fry bell peppers and onions (from 1-pound bag)

2 tablespoons Italian dressing

1 can (14 ounces) beef broth

1 cup uncooked orzo or rosamarina pasta (6 ounces)

1 bag (10 1/2 ounces) frozen cooked Italian meatballs (16 meatballs)

1 large tomato, chopped (1 cup)

2 tablespoons chopped fresh parsley

1/4 cup shredded Parmesan cheese

1. Cook stir-fry vegetables and dressing in 12-inch non-stick skillet over medium-high heat 2 minutes. Stir broth into vegetables; heat to boiling. Stir in pasta and meatballs. Heat to boiling; reduce heat to low. Cover and simmer 10 minutes, stirring occasionally.

2. Stir in tomato. Cover and simmer 3 to 5 minutes or until most of the liquid has been absorbed and pasta is tender. Stir in parsley. Sprinkle with cheese.

1 SERVING Calories 425 (Calories from Fat 165) | Fat 18g (Saturated 6g) | Cholesterol 80mg | Sodium 1060mg | Carbohydrate 41g (Dietary Fiber 3g) | Protein 25g   %DAILY VALUE Vitamin A 16% | Vitamin C 32% | Calcium 16% | Iron 22%   EXCHANGES 2 1/2 Starch, 1 Vegetable, 2 Medium-Fat Meat, 1 Fat   CARBOHYDRATE CHOICES 3

BETTY'S TIP

Orzo is a rice-shaped pasta that cooks fairly quickly. It's kid-friendly because it's easier to fork up than spaghetti. (It's also less messy, making it parent-friendly as well!)

Easy Weeknight Beef-Veggie Mix

PREP 20 min   **COOK** 10 min   **SERVINGS** 5

1. Melt butter in 10-inch skillet over low heat. Stir in corn-starch. Stir tomatoes, bell pepper, onion and garlic into butter mixture. Cook about 5 minutes, stirring frequently, until hot.

2. Stir beef, raisins and salt into vegetable mixture. Cook about 5 minutes, stirring frequently, until beef and raisins are hot.

1 SERVING Calories 160 (Calories from Fat 45) | Fat 5g (Saturated 1g) | Cholesterol 45mg | Sodium 300mg | Carbohydrate 11g (Dietary Fiber 1g) | Protein 18g   **%DAILY VALUE** Vitamin A 12% | Vitamin C 20% | Calcium 0% | Iron 10%   **EXCHANGES** 2 Vegetable, 2 Lean Meat   **CARBOHYDRATE CHOICES** 1

1 tablespoon butter or margarine

1 teaspoon cornstarch

2 medium tomatoes, chopped (1 1/2 cups)

1 small green bell pepper, chopped (1/2 cup)

1 small onion, chopped (1/4 cup)

1 clove garlic, finely chopped

2 cups bite-size pieces cooked beef

3 tablespoons raisins

1/2 teaspoon salt

BETTY'S TIP

Get ahead of the game by chopping the tomatoes, bell pepper, onion and garlic the night before. Store in a tightly sealed container in the refrigerator.

Chicken and Ravioli Carbonara

2 tablespoons Italian dressing

1 pound boneless, skinless chicken breasts, cut into 1/2-inch strips

3/4 cup chicken broth

1 package (9 ounces) refrigerated cheese-filled ravioli

1/2 cup half-and-half

4 slices bacon, crisply cooked and crumbled

Shredded Parmesan cheese, if desired

Chopped fresh parsley, if desired

PREP **10 min**   COOK **16 min**   SERVINGS **4**

1. Heat dressing in 10-inch skillet over high heat. Cook chicken in dressing 2 to 4 minutes, turning occasionally, until brown.

2. Add broth and ravioli to skillet. Heat to boiling; reduce heat to medium. Cook uncovered about 4 minutes or until ravioli are tender and almost all broth has evaporated. Stir in half-and-half; reduce heat to low. Simmer uncovered 3 to 5 minutes or until sauce is hot and desired consistency. Sprinkle with bacon, cheese and parsley.

1 SERVING Calories 265 (Calories from Fat 170) | Fat 19g (Saturated 7g) | Cholesterol 150mg | Sodium 960mg | Carbohydrate 13g | (Dietary Fiber 0g) | Protein 36g   %DAILY VALUE Vitamin A 6% | Vitamin C 0% | Calcium 18% | Iron 10%   EXCHANGES 1 Starch, 5 Lean Meat   CARBOHYDRATE CHOICES 1

BETTY'S TIP

Like things saucy? You can determine the thinness or the thickness of the sauce by varying the cook time. The less time the mixture simmers, the thinner the sauce. Cooking the mixture longer thickens the sauce.

Mandarin Chicken Stir-Fry

PREP **20 min** COOK **8 min** SERVINGS **4**

2 tablespoons rice vinegar

2 tablespoons soy sauce

1 tablespoon honey

1 tablespoon cornstarch

1/8 teaspoon ground
red pepper (cayenne)

1 can (11 ounces) mandarin
orange segments, drained
and 2 tablespoons syrup
reserved

1 can (8 ounces) pineapple
chunks, drained and juice
reserved

1 tablespoon vegetable oil

1 pound boneless, skinless
chicken breasts, cut into
1-inch pieces

1 teaspoon finely chopped
gingerroot

1 clove garlic, finely
chopped

1 package (6 ounces)
frozen snow (Chinese) pea
pods, thawed and drained

2 medium green onions,
sliced (2 tablespoons)

Hot cooked Chinese
noodles or rice, if desired

1. Mix vinegar, soy sauce, honey, cornstarch, red pepper, reserved orange syrup and pineapple juice in small bowl; set aside.

2. Heat oil in 10-inch skillet over medium-high heat. Cook chicken, gingerroot and garlic 3 to 4 minutes, stirring frequently, until chicken is no longer pink in center. Stir soy sauce mixture into chicken. Heat to boiling. Boil 1 minute, stirring constantly.

3. Stir in pea pods, onions and pineapple; heat through. Fold in orange segments. Serve over noodles.

1 SERVING Calories 315 (Calories from Fat 65) | Fat 7g (Saturated 2g) | Cholesterol 70mg | Sodium 530mg | Carbohydrate 38g (Dietary Fiber 2g) | Protein 27g   **%DAILY VALUE** Vitamin A 10%, Vitamin C 32% | Calcium 4% | Iron 14%   **EXCHANGES** 3 1/2 Very Lean Meat, 2 Fruit, 1 Vegetable, 1 Fat   **CARBOHY-DRATE CHOICES** 2 1/2

Mandarin Pork Stir-Fry Substitute 1 pound boneless pork loin, shoulder or tenderloin for the chicken.

BETTY'S TIP

Rice vinegar is made from fermented rice and has a slightly sweet, mild flavor. You'll find it stocked with the other vinegars or with the Asian ingredients in your supermarket.

Caesar Chicken with Orzo

PREP **5 min**   COOK **27 min**   SERVINGS **4**

1 tablespoon vegetable oil

4 boneless, skinless chicken breast halves (about 1 1/4 pounds)

1 can (14 ounces) chicken broth

1 cup water

1 cup uncooked orzo or rosamarina pasta (6 ounces)

1 bag (1 pound) frozen baby whole carrots, green beans and yellow beans (or other combination)

3 tablespoons Caesar dressing

1/8 teaspoon coarsely ground pepper

1. Heat oil in 10-inch skillet over medium-high heat. Cook chicken in oil about 10 minutes, turning once, until brown. Remove chicken from skillet; keep warm.

2. Add broth and water to skillet; heat to boiling. Stir in pasta; heat to boiling. Cook uncovered 8 to 10 minutes, stirring occasionally, until pasta is tender. Stir in frozen vegetables and dressing. Add chicken. Sprinkle with pepper.

3. Heat to boiling; reduce heat to low. Simmer uncovered about 5 minutes or until vegetables are crisp-tender and juice of chicken is no longer pink when centers of thickest pieces are cut.

1 SERVING Calories 405 (Calories from Fat 125) | Fat 14g (Saturated 3g) | Cholesterol 75mg | Sodium 670mg | Carbohydrate 49g (Dietary Fiber 6g) | Protein 39g   %DAILY VALUE Vitamin A 100% | Vitamin C 22% | Calcium 10% | Iron 26%   EXCHANGES 2 Starch, 1 Vegetable, 4 Lean Meat   CARBOHYDRATE CHOICES 3

BETTY'S TIP

Warmed purchased focaccia bread and fresh pear slices or clusters of red grapes make tasty sides to this dish.

Sweet-and-Sour Chicken

PREP **10 min**   COOK **7 min**   SERVINGS **4**

1. Spray 12-inch nonstick skillet with cooking spray; heat over medium-high heat. Cook chicken 3 to 4 minutes, stirring frequently, until no longer pink in center.

2. Add vegetables; cook about 2 minutes or until vegetables are crisp-tender. Stir in pineapple and sweet-and-sour sauce; cook and stir 1 minute. Serve over noodles.

1 SERVING Calories 235 (Calories from Fat 45) | Fat 5g (Saturated 1g) | Cholesterol 70mg | Sodium 200mg | Carbohydrate 25g (Dietary Fiber 3g) | Protein 26g   %DAILY VALUE Vitamin A 100% | Vitamin C 60% | Calcium 4% | Iron 10%   EXCHANGES 1 Fruit, 1 Vegetable, 2 1/2 Lean Meat   CARBOHYDRATE CHOICES 1 1/2

1 pound boneless, skinless chicken breasts, cut into 1-inch pieces

4 cups cut-up assorted vegetables (bell peppers, carrots, tomatoes)

1 can (8 ounces) pineapple chunks in juice, drained

1/2 cup sweet-and-sour sauce

Chow mein noodles, if desired

BETTY'S TIP

Chow mein noodles are crispy because they're deep-fried. Unfortunately this also causes them to be high in fat. If you're counting calories, you may want to cut down on the amount you use.

Pesto Ravioli with Chicken

PREP **15** min   COOK **15** min   SERVINGS **4**

2 teaspoons olive or vegetable oil

1 pound boneless, skinless chicken breast strips for stir-fry

3/4 cup chicken broth

1 package (9 ounces) refrigerated cheese-filled ravioli

3 small zucchini, cut into 1/4-inch slices

1 large red bell pepper, thinly sliced

1/4 cup basil pesto

1. Heat oil in 12-inch skillet over medium-high heat. Cook chicken in oil about 4 minutes, turning occasionally, until brown. Remove chicken from skillet.

2. Add broth and ravioli to skillet. Heat to boiling; reduce heat to low. Cover and simmer about 4 minutes or until ravioli are tender.

3. Stir zucchini, bell pepper and chicken into ravioli. Cook over medium-high heat about 3 minutes, stirring occasionally, until vegetables are crisp-tender and chicken is no longer pink in center. Toss with pesto.

1 SERVING Calories 375 (Calories from Fat 180) | Fat 20g (Saturated 5g) | Cholesterol 130mg | Sodium 910mg | Carbohydrate 17g (Dietary Fiber 2g) | Protein 34g   **% DAILY VALUE** Vitamin A 66% | Vitamin C 72% | Calcium 20% | Iron 14%   **EXCHANGES** 1 Starch, 1 Vegetable, 4 Lean Meat, 1 Fat   **CARBOHYDRATE CHOICES** 1

Sausage Ravioli with Pesto Omit the chicken and use sausage-filled ravioli. Decrease the pesto to 3 tablespoons.

BETTY'S TIP

For an extra-special touch, sprinkle freshly grated Parmesan cheese or toasted pine nuts over the top of this skillet dish before serving.

Chicken and Veggie Pasta Alfredo

PREP **25 min**   COOK **20 min**   SERVINGS **4**

1. Heat oil in 12-inch skillet over medium-high heat. Cook chicken in oil 6 to 7 minutes, stirring frequently, just until chicken is no longer pink in center.

2. Stir water and frozen pasta-vegetable mixture into chicken. Cover and cook 4 to 5 minutes, stirring occasionally, until vegetables are hot. Stir in whipping cream. Cook 2 to 3 minutes or until hot.

3. Turn off heat. Stir in cheese. Let stand 2 to 3 minutes or until cheese is melted. Sprinkle with basil. Serve with additional shredded Parmesan cheese.

1 tablespoon olive or vegetable oil

1 pound boneless, skinless chicken breast strips for stir-fry

1/3 cup water

1 bag (1 pound) frozen vegetables and pasta in garlic-flavored sauce

1/3 cup whipping (heavy) cream

1/2 cup shredded Parmesan cheese

Chopped fresh basil leaves, if desired

1 SERVING Calories 385 (Calories from Fat 170) | Fat 19g (Saturated 8g) | Cholesterol 100mg | Sodium 470mg | Carbohydrate 24g (Dietary Fiber 2g) | Protein 30g %DAILY VALUE Vitamin A 24% | Vitamin C 12% | Calcium 4% | Iron 10% EXCHANGES 1 1/2 Starch, 3 1/2 Lean Meat, 1 1/2 Fat CARBOHYDRATE CHOICES 1 1/2

Shrimp and Veggie Pasta Alfredo Substitute shrimp or scallops for the chicken in this recipe. Reduce the cooking time in step 1 to 4 to 5 minutes.

BETTY'S TIP

To save a few grams of fat, use reduced-fat half-and-half instead of the whipping cream in this rich and creamy pasta dish.

Chicken Penne
à la Marengo

1 pound boneless, skinless chicken breasts, cut into 1-inch pieces

1 can (14 ounces) chicken broth

2 cups uncooked penne pasta (6 ounces)

1 medium green bell pepper, cut into 1-inch pieces (1 cup)

1 can (14 1/2 ounces) Italian-style stewed tomatoes, undrained

1/4 cup dry white wine or chicken broth

1 tablespoon tomato paste

1 can (2 1/4 ounces) sliced ripe olives, drained

1. Spray 12-inch nonstick skillet with cooking spray; heat over medium-high heat. Cook chicken 2 to 3 minutes, stirring frequently, until brown.

2. Stir broth into chicken; heat to boiling. Stir in pasta and bell pepper. Heat to boiling; reduce heat to medium. Cover and cook 10 minutes, stirring occasionally.

3. Stir in tomatoes, wine and tomato paste. Cook uncovered 5 to 10 minutes, stirring occasionally, until chicken is no longer pink in center and pasta is tender. Stir in olives.

1 SERVING Calories 365 (Calories from Fat 65) | Fat 7g (Saturated 2g) | Cholesterol 70mg | Sodium 1080mg | Carbohydrate 45g (Dietary Fiber 4g) | Protein 34g **%DAILY VALUE** Vitamin A 10% | Vitamin C 34% | Calcium 66% | Iron 22% **EXCHANGES** 2 1/2 Starch, 2 Vegetable, 3 Very Lean Meat **CARBOHYDRATE CHOICES** 3

BETTY'S TIP

Napoleon's chef is believed to have created this famous dish after the Battle of Marengo in 1800. In this version, the pasta is cooked right in the sauce for an easy one-dish meal.

Everyday Cassoulet

PREP 15 min   COOK 20 min   SERVINGS 4

1. Spray 12-inch nonstick skillet with cooking spray; heat over medium-high heat. Cook chicken 3 to 5 minutes, stirring occasionally, until brown.

2. Stir remaining ingredients except onions into chicken. Cook uncovered over medium-low heat 8 to 10 minutes, stirring occasionally, until chicken is no longer pink in center.

3. Stir in onions. Cook 3 to 5 minutes, stirring occasionally, until onions are crisp-tender.

1 SERVING Calories 410 (Calories from Fat 170) | Fat 19g (Saturated 4g) | Cholesterol 100mg | Sodium 320mg | Carbohydrate 31g (Dietary Fiber 2g) | Protein 29g **%DAILY VALUE** Vitamin A 28% | Vitamin C 30% | Calcium 14% | Iron 20% **EXCHANGES** 2 Starch, 3 Medium-Fat Meat, 1/2 Fat **CARBOHYDRATE CHOICES** 2

1/2 pound boneless, skinless chicken breasts, cut into 1/2-inch pieces

1/2 pound fully cooked Polish sausage, cut into 1/2-inch slices

1 can (15 to 16 ounces) great northern beans, rinsed and drained

1 can (15 to 16 ounces) dark red kidney beans, rinsed and drained

1 can (14 1/2 ounces) chunky tomatoes with olive oil, garlic and spices, undrained

1 tablespoon packed brown sugar

4 medium green onions, sliced (1/4 cup)

BETTY'S TIP

The term *cassoulet* usually refers to a covered dish that is cooked over a long period of time to blend flavors. This speedy dish packs in many of the flavors of a traditional cassoulet, but it's ready to eat in a fraction of the time.

Fettuccine with Chicken and Vegetables

1 package (9 ounces) refrigerated fettuccine

2 cups small broccoli flowerets

1/3 cup Italian dressing

1 pound boneless, skinless chicken breast strips for stir-fry

1 medium red onion, cut into thin wedges

1/4 teaspoon garlic pepper

1/2 cup sliced drained roasted red bell peppers (from 7-ounce jar)

Shredded Parmesan cheese, if desired

1. Cook and drain fettuccine and broccoli as directed on fettuccine package. Toss with 2 tablespoons of the dressing. Keep warm.

2. While fettuccine and broccoli are cooking, spray 12-inch nonstick skillet with cooking spray; heat over medium-high heat. Add chicken and onion to skillet; sprinkle with garlic pepper. Cook 4 to 6 minutes, stirring occasionally, until chicken is no longer pink in center.

3. Stir bell pepper and remaining dressing into chicken mixture. Cook 2 to 3 minutes, stirring occasionally, until warm. Serve chicken mixture over fettuccine and broccoli. Sprinkle with cheese.

1 SERVING Calories 470 (Calories from Fat 135) | Fat 15g (Saturated 2g) | Cholesterol 125mg | Sodium 260mg | Carbohydrate 49g (Dietary Fiber 4g) | Protein 35g   %DAILY VALUE Vitamin A 66% | Vitamin C 100% | Calcium 8% | Iron 22%   EXCHANGES 3 Starch, 1 Vegetable, 3 1/2 Lean Meat   CARBOHYDRATE CHOICES 3

Fettuccine with Chicken and Spinach Omit the broccoli, and add 4 cups fresh baby spinach leaves after warming the roasted peppers and dressing in step 3. Cook 1 to 2 minutes or just until the spinach wilts.

BETTY'S TIP

This recipe calls for garlic pepper, but if you don't have any on hand, use a combination of coarsely ground pepper and garlic powder instead.

Chicken Cacciatore

PREP **10 min**   COOK **30 min**   SERVINGS **4**

1 tablespoon olive or vegetable oil

1 pound boneless, skinless chicken breasts, cut into 1-inch pieces

1 cup sliced mushrooms (3 ounces)

1 medium green bell pepper, chopped (1 cup)

2 tablespoons finely chopped onion

2 cloves garlic, finely chopped

1/2 cup dry white wine or chicken broth

1 teaspoon red or white wine vinegar

1 jar (14 ounces) spaghetti sauce

4 cups hot cooked spaghetti

1. Heat oil in 10-inch skillet over medium-high heat. Cook chicken in oil, stirring occasionally, until brown. Stir mushrooms, bell pepper, onion and garlic into chicken. Cook 6 to 8 minutes, stirring occasionally, until bell pepper and onion are crisp-tender and chicken is no longer pink in center.

2. Stir in wine and vinegar. Cook 3 minutes. Stir in spaghetti sauce. Simmer uncovered 10 to 12 minutes to blend flavors. Serve sauce over spaghetti.

1 SERVING Calories 505 (Calories from Fat 110) | Fat 12g (Saturated 2g) | Cholesterol 70mg | Sodium 610mg | Carbohydrate 64g | (Dietary Fiber 4g) | Protein 35g %DAILY VALUE Vitamin A 16% | Vitamin C 36% | Calcium 6% | Iron 22% EXCHANGES 4 Starch, 1 Vegetable, 3 Lean Meat CARBOHYDRATE CHOICES 4

BETTY'S TIP

Cacciatore comes from *cacciatore*, the Italian word for hunter. If a food is prepared "hunter-style," it means it contains mushrooms, onions, tomatoes, herbs and sometimes wine.

Asparagus-Dijon-Chicken Fettuccine

1 tablespoon butter or margarine

1 pound boneless, skinless chicken breasts, cut into 1-inch pieces

1 can (4 ounces) mushroom pieces and stems, drained

1 medium onion, chopped (1/2 cup)

1 package (6.8 ounces) fettuccine Alfredo skillet-dinner mix for chicken

1 cup milk

2 1/2 cups water

2 tablespoons Dijon mustard

1 package (10 ounces) frozen asparagus cuts, thawed and drained

PREP **10 min**   COOK **17 min**   STAND **5 min**   SERVINGS **5**

1. Melt butter in 10-inch skillet over high heat. Cook chicken, mushrooms and onion in butter 3 to 5 minutes, stirring occasionally, until chicken is white.

2. Stir Sauce Mix from skillet-dinner mix, the milk, water and mustard into chicken mixture. Heat to boiling, stirring occasionally. Stir in uncooked Pasta; reduce heat to low. Cover and simmer about 10 minutes, stirring occasionally, until pasta is tender.

3. Stir in asparagus. Cover and simmer 2 minutes, stirring occasionally; remove from heat. Uncover and let stand about 5 minutes or until sauce thickens. Stir before serving.

1 SERVING Calories 290 (Calories from Fat 90) | Fat 10g (Saturated 3g) | Cholesterol 60mg | Sodium 1030mg | Carbohydrate 34g (Dietary Fiber 3g) | Protein 29g %DAILY VALUE Vitamin A 10% | Vitamin C 10% | Calcium 10% | Iron 12% EXCHANGES 2 Starch, 1 Vegetable, 3 Very Lean Meat CARBOHYDRATE CHOICES 2

Dijon-Chicken Fettuccine with Green Peas Use a 10-ounce package of frozen green peas, thawed and drained, instead of the asparagus cuts.

BETTY'S TIP

A tossed salad with mandarin orange segments and vinaigrette dressing would taste great with this delicious entrée.

Southwest Chicken and Couscous

PREP **10 min**   COOK **10 min**   STAND **5 min**   SERVINGS **4**

1. Spray 12-inch nonstick skillet with cooking spray; heat over medium-high heat. Cook stir-fry vegetables in skillet 2 to 3 minutes, stirring frequently, until crisp-tender.

2. Stir beans, salsa, chicken and corn into vegetable mixture. Heat to boiling; reduce heat to low. Cover and simmer about 5 minutes, stirring occasionally, until chicken is hot, breaking up large pieces of chicken.

3. While chicken mixture is cooking, heat water to boiling. Stir in couscous; remove from heat. Cover and let stand 5 minutes. Fluff with fork.

4. Spoon couscous onto serving plates. Top with chicken mixture. Sprinkle with cilantro.

1 SERVING Calories 505 (Calories from Fat 35) | Fat 4g (Saturated 1g) | Cholesterol 55mg | Sodium 610mg | Carbohydrate 90g (Dietary Fiber 12g) | Protein 39g   %DAILY VALUE Vitamin A 10% | Vitamin C 34% | Calcium 12% | Iron 26%   EXCHANGES 6 Starch, 2 Very Lean Meat   CARBOHYDRATE CHOICES 6

1 cup frozen stir-fry bell peppers and onions (from 1-pound bag)

1 can (15 ounces) black beans with cumin and chili spices, undrained

1/2 cup thick-and-chunky salsa

1 package (9 ounces) frozen cooked Southwest-seasoned chicken breast strips

1/2 cup frozen whole kernel corn (from 1-pound bag)

2 cups water

1 1/2 cups uncooked couscous

1/4 cup chopped fresh cilantro

BETTY'S TIP

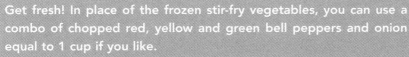

Get fresh! In place of the frozen stir-fry vegetables, you can use a combo of chopped red, yellow and green bell peppers and onion equal to 1 cup if you like.

Chicken-Vegetable Stroganoff

1 1/2 cups (from 1-pound bag) frozen broccoli, cauliflower and carrots (or other combination)

1 1/2 cups sliced mushrooms (4 ounces)

1 large onion, sliced

2 cups chicken broth

1 tablespoon chopped fresh or 1 teaspoon dried marjoram leaves

1/4 teaspoon pepper

3 to 3 3/4 cups uncooked egg noodles (6 to 7 ounces)

2 cups cut-up cooked chicken or turkey

1 container (8 ounces) sour cream

1/3 cup water

2 tablespoons all-purpose flour

PREP **15 min**   COOK **15 min**   SERVINGS **4**

1. Heat broccoli mixture, mushrooms, onion, broth, marjoram, pepper and noodles to boiling in 10-inch skillet; reduce heat to low.

2. Cover and simmer about 8 minutes, stirring occasionally, until noodles and vegetables are tender.

3. Stir in chicken. Mix sour cream, water and flour; stir into chicken mixture. Heat to boiling. Boil and stir 1 minute.

1 SERVING Calories 445 (Calories from Fat 170) | Fat 19g (Saturated 9g) | Cholesterol 135mg | Sodium 620mg | Carbohydrate 40g (Dietary Fiber 3g) | Protein 31g   %DAILY VALUE Vitamin A 22% | Vitamin C 12% | Calcium 10% | Iron 20%   EXCHANGES 2 Starch, 2 Vegetable, 3 Medium-Fat Meat   CARBOHYDRATE CHOICES 2 1/2

BETTY'S TIP

For a health twist, use low-sodium chicken broth and reduced-fat sour cream in this stroganoff.

Teriyaki Chicken Stir-Fry

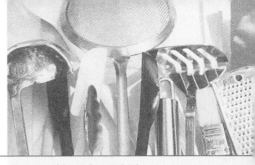

1. Spray 12-inch nonstick skillet with cooking spray; heat over medium-high heat. Cook chicken 3 to 4 minutes, stirring frequently, until chicken is no longer pink in center.

2. Stir remaining ingredients except rice into chicken. Heat to boiling, stirring constantly; reduce heat to low. Cover and simmer about 6 minutes or until vegetables are crisp-tender. Serve with rice.

1 pound boneless, skinless chicken breast strips for stir-fry

1/2 cup teriyaki baste and glaze

3 tablespoons lemon juice

1 bag (1 pound) frozen broccoli, carrots, water chestnuts and red peppers (or other combination)

Hot cooked rice, couscous, or noodles, if desired

1 SERVING Calories 215 (Calories from Fat 45) | Fat 5g (Saturated 1g) | Cholesterol 70mg | Sodium 1850mg | Carbohydrate 15g (Dietary Fiber 3g) | Protein 30g   %DAILY VALUE Vitamin A 26% | Vitamin C 32% | Calcium 6% | Iron 14%   EXCHANGES 3 Very Lean Meat, 3 Vegetable, 1 Fat   CARBOHYDRATE CHOICES 1

BETTY'S TIP

Take care not to confuse teriyaki baste and glaze with teriyaki sauce or marinade. The first is a thick and brown-colored sauce, while the second has a watery consistency. Both can be found in the Asian foods section of your supermarket.

Country-French Turkey and Red Potatoes

1/4 cup all-purpose flour

1/8 teaspoon pepper

1 pound uncooked turkey breast slices, about 1/4 inch thick

1 pound mushrooms, cut in half

8 large shallots, cut into fourths

8 small red potatoes (about 3/4 pound), cut into 6 wedges

1/3 cup dry white wine or chicken broth

1/2 teaspoon dried rosemary leaves

PREP **10 min**   COOK **18 min**   SERVINGS **4**

1. Mix flour and pepper in shallow dish or resealable plastic food-storage bag. Toss turkey with flour mixture. Spray 12-inch nonstick skillet with cooking spray; heat over medium heat. Cook turkey in skillet about 5 minutes, turning once, until brown. Remove turkey from skillet; keep warm.

2. Add mushrooms and shallots to skillet. Cook about 3 minutes, stirring frequently, until shallots are tender. Stir in remaining ingredients. Heat to boiling, stirring constantly. Boil and stir 2 minutes. Add turkey; reduce heat to low. Cover and simmer about 6 minutes, stirring occasionally, until turkey is no longer pink in center.

1 SERVING Calories 290 (Calories from Fat 20) | Fat 2g (Saturated 1g) | Cholesterol 75mg | Sodium 150mg | Carbohydrate 32g (Dietary Fiber 5g) | Protein 34g   **%DAILY VALUE** Vitamin A 8% | Vitamin C 18% | Calcium 6% | Iron 26%   **EXCHANGES** 2 Starch, 4 Very Lean Meat   **CARBOHYDRATE CHOICES** 2

BETTY'S TIP

Shallots look like mini onions and taste like a mild mix of garlic and onion. You can usually find them near the onions in the produce section of the supermarket.

Pesto Turkey and Pasta

PREP **5** min   COOK **20** min   SERVINGS **4**

3 cups uncooked farfalle (bow-tie) pasta or wide egg noodles (6 ounces)

2 cups cubed cooked turkey breast

1/2 cup basil pesto

1/2 cup coarsely chopped drained roasted red bell peppers (from 7-ounce jar)

Sliced ripe olives, if desired

1. Cook and drain pasta as directed on package in 3-quart saucepan.

2. Mix hot cooked pasta, turkey, pesto and bell peppers in same saucepan. Heat over low heat, stirring constantly, until hot. Garnish with olives.

1 SERVING Calories 410 (Calories from Fat 170) | Fat 19g (Saturated 4g) | Cholesterol 100mg | Sodium 320mg | Carbohydrate 31g (Dietary Fiber 2g) | Protein 29g   %DAILY VALUE Vitamin A 28% | Vitamin C 30% | Calcium 14% | Iron 20%   EXCHANGES 2 Starch, 3 Medium-Fat Meat, 1/2 Fat   CARBOHYDRATE CHOICES 2

BETTY'S TIP

This recipe makes good use of any turkey you may have left over from the holidays. Or looked for cooked turkey breast cubes in the deli section of your supermarket. You can also switch gears completely and use chicken breast instead of the turkey breast.

Glazed Turkey and Pea Pods

PREP **15** min   COOK **10** min   SERVINGS **4**

1 pound uncooked turkey breast slices, about 1/4 inch thick

1 teaspoon cornstarch

3/4 cup chicken broth

1 tablespoon cornstarch

3 tablespoons hoisin sauce

2 teaspoons chopped gingerroot or 1 teaspoon ground ginger

1/8 teaspoon pepper

2 tablespoons vegetable oil

2 cups snow (Chinese) pea pods, strings removed

1 large red or green bell pepper, cut into 3/4-inch pieces

2 cups frozen small whole onions (from 1-pound bag), thawed and drained

2 cups chow mein noodles

1/2 cup coarsely chopped cashews or peanuts

1. Cut turkey breast slices into bite-size pieces. Toss turkey and 1 teaspoon cornstarch. Mix broth, 1 tablespoon cornstarch, the hoisin sauce, gingerroot and pepper; set aside.

2. Heat 12-inch skillet or wok over medium-high heat. Add 1 tablespoon of the oil to skillet; rotate skillet to bottom. Add turkey; stir-fry about 4 minutes or until turkey is white. Remove turkey from skillet.

3. Add remaining 1 tablespoon oil to skillet; rotate skillet to bottom. Add pea pods, bell pepper and onions; stir-fry 4 to 5 minutes or until vegetables are crisp-tender. Stir in hoisin sauce mixture. Cook and stir about 1 minute or until thickened. Stir in turkey; heat through. Stir in noodles and cashews. Serve immediately.

1 SERVING Calories 495 (Calories from Fat 215) | Fat 24g (Saturated 4g) | Cholesterol 75mg | Sodium 640mg | Carbohydrate 35g (Dietary Fiber 5g) | Protein 35g   %DAILY VALUE Vitamin A 55% | Vitamin C 80% | Calcium 6% | Iron 24%   EXCHANGES 2 Starch, 1 Vegetable, 4 Lean Meat, 2 Fat   CARBOHYDRATE CHOICES 2

BETTY'S TIP

You can use a 6-ounce package of frozen snow (Chinese) pea pods, thawed and drained, instead of the fresh pea pods, if you have them on hand.

Smoked Turkey Lo Mein

1. Soak mushrooms in hot water about 20 minutes or until soft; drain. Rinse with warm water; drain. Squeeze out excess moisture. Remove and discard stems; cut caps into thin strips.

2. Spray 12-inch nonstick skillet or nonstick wok with cooking spray; heat over medium-high heat. Add turkey; stir-fry about 1 minute or until brown. Stir in mushrooms, peas, contents of Sauce Packet from noodles, water and oyster sauce. Add noodles; separate and stir-fry about 2 minutes or until heated through. Sprinkle with onions.

1 SERVING Calories 190 (Calories from Fat 45) | Fat 5g (Saturated 2g) | Cholesterol 30mg | Sodium 1080mg | Carbohydrate 21g (Dietary Fiber 3g) | Protein 15g   **%DAILY VALUE** Vitamin A 8% | Vitamin C 4% | Calcium 6% | Iron 10%   **EXCHANGES** 1 Starch, 1 Vegetable, 1 1/2 Lean Meat   **CARBOHYDRATE CHOICES** 1 1/2

6 dried black (shiitake) mushrooms

1/2 pound fully cooked smoked 97%-fat-free turkey breast, cut into 1/2-inch cubes (1 1/2 cups)

1 cup frozen green peas (from 1-pound bag)

1 package (about 7.31 ounces) fresh (refrigerated) stir-fry noodles with soy sauce–flavored sauce

3/4 cup water

1 tablespoon oyster sauce

2 green onions, chopped (2 tablespoons)

BETTY'S TIP

Instead of throwing away the mushroom stems, save them for future use in sautés, soups and sauces. They can be kept for up to three days when covered and stored in the fridge, or they can be frozen for up to six months.

Cheesy Turkey, Rice and Broccoli

1 pound turkey breast tenderloins, cut into 1-inch pieces

1 package (10 ounces) frozen broccoli with low-fat cheese-flavored sauce

1 2/3 cups uncooked instant brown rice

1 cup sliced mushrooms (3 ounces)

1/2 cup sliced water chestnuts

1 1/2 cups fat-free chicken broth

1 teaspoon chopped fresh or 1/2 teaspoon dried thyme leaves

1/2 teaspoon salt

5 medium green onions, sliced (1/3 cup)

PREP 10 min   COOK 17 min   STAND 5 min   SERVINGS 4

1. Spray 12-inch skillet with cooking spray; heat over medium heat. Cook turkey in skillet about 5 minutes, stirring occasionally, until no longer pink in center.

2. While turkey is cooking, microwave broccoli in pouch on High 1 minute to easily remove from package.

3. Add broccoli mixture to turkey. Stir in remaining ingredients. Heat to boiling; reduce heat to low. Cover and simmer about 10 minutes, stirring occasionally, until most of liquid is absorbed. Let stand 5 minutes before serving.

1 SERVING Calories 305 (Calories from Fat 25) | Fat 3g (Saturated 1g) | Cholesterol 60mg | Sodium 600mg | Carbohydrate 43g (Dietary Fiber 5g) | Protein 31g   %DAILY VALUE Vitamin A 12% | Vitamin C 14% | Calcium 12% | Iron 4%   EXCHANGES 2 Starch, 2 Vegetable, 3 Very Lean Meat   CARBOHYDRATE CHOICES 3

BETTY'S TIP

Regardless of whether it's fresh or frozen, one-half cup of chopped broccoli provides 90 percent of your RDA for vitamin A and 100 percent of vitamin C. With this tasty recipe, it's easy to go green.

Oriental Turkey and Rice

PREP **5 min**   COOK **30 min**   SERVINGS **4**

1 pound ground turkey breast

1 package (7.3 ounces) rice Oriental skillet-dinner mix for hamburger

4 cups water

1 can (16 ounces) chow mein vegetables, drained

1 can (8 ounces) sliced water chestnuts, drained

2 cups chow mein noodles

1. Cook turkey in 10-inch skillet over medium heat, stirring frequently, until no longer pink; drain.

2. Stir uncooked Rice and Sauce Mix from skillet-dinner mix, the water, vegetables and water chestnuts into turkey. Heat to boiling, stirring occasionally; reduce heat to low.

3. Cover and simmer about 25 minutes or until rice is tender. Uncover and cook until desired consistency. Serve over noodles.

1 SERVING Calories 490 (Calories from Fat 100) | Fat 11g (Saturated 2g) | Cholesterol 50mg | Sodium 1150mg | Carbohydrate 68g (Dietary Fiber 4g) | Protein 30g   %DAILY VALUE Vitamin A 8% | Vitamin C 10% | Calcium 4% | Iron 28%   EXCHANGES 4 Starch, 1 Vegetable, 2 Lean Meat   CARBOHYDRATE CHOICES 4 1/2

BETTY'S TIP

If you'd like to serve this dish with a side, grab a bag of Oriental salad greens and top the salad with drained canned mandarin orange segments and toasted slivered almonds.

Turkey-Pasta Primavera

1 package (9 ounces) refrigerated fettuccine or linguine

2 tablespoons Italian dressing

1 bag (1 pound) frozen broccoli, cauliflower and carrots (or other combination), thawed and drained

2 cups cut-up cooked turkey or chicken

1 teaspoon salt

2 large tomatoes, seeded and chopped (2 cups)

1/4 cup freshly grated Parmesan cheese

2 tablespoons chopped fresh parsley

1.   Cook and drain fettuccine as directed on package.

2.   While fettuccine is cooking, heat dressing in 10-inch skillet over medium-high heat. Cook vegetables in dressing, stirring occasionally, until crisp-tender.

3.   Stir turkey, salt and tomatoes into vegetables. Cook about 3 minutes or just until turkey is hot. Spoon turkey mixture over fettuccine. Sprinkle with cheese and parsley.

1 SERVING Calories 435 (Calories from Fat 115) | Fat 13g (Saturated 3g) | Cholesterol 120mg | Sodium 880mg | Carbohydrate 52g (Dietary Fiber 6g) | Protein 34g   %DAILY VALUE Vitamin A 80% | Vitamin C 46% | Calcium 16% | Iron 26%   EXCHANGES 3 Starch, 1 Vegetable, 3 Lean Meat   CARBOHYDRATE CHOICES 3 1/2

BETTY'S TIP

Need to thaw veggies in a hurry? Place them in a colander and run cool water over them until thawed but still cold.

Smoked Turkey and Couscous

PREP **10 min**   COOK **6 min**   STAND **10 min**   SERVINGS **4**

1 can (14 ounces) chicken broth

2 cups broccoli flowerets

1 cup cut-up fully cooked smoked turkey

1 1/2 teaspoons chopped fresh or 1/2 teaspoon dried tarragon leaves

1/2 cup uncooked couscous

1/2 cup shredded Cheddar cheese (2 ounces)

1. Heat broth to boiling in 10-inch skillet. Stir broccoli, turkey and tarragon into broth. Cover and cook 3 to 4 minutes or until broccoli is crisp-tender.

2. Stir in couscous; remove from heat. Cover and let stand about 5 minutes or until liquid is absorbed.

3. Fluff couscous mixture with fork. Sprinkle with cheese. Cover and let stand 3 to 5 minutes or until cheese is melted.

1 SERVING Calories 195 (Calories from Fat 65) | Fat 7g (Saturated 4g) | Cholesterol 35mg | Sodium 880mg | Carbohydrate 19g (Dietary Fiber 2g) | Protein 16g   **%DAILY VALUE** Vitamin A 12% | Vitamin C 8% | Calcium 10% | Iron 8%   **EXCHANGES** 1 Starch, 2 Lean Meat   **CARBOHYDRATE CHOICES** 1

BETTY'S TIP

Love bratwurst? Fully cooked smoked bratwurst, cut into 1-inch slices, makes a tasty substitute for the smoked turkey.

Peppery Cajun Pork Pasta

8 ounces uncooked fettuccine

1 pound pork tenderloin

4 teaspoons Cajun seasoning

1 tablespoon vegetable oil

1 large red onion, chopped (1 1/2 cups)

2 large zucchini, chopped (2 1/2 cups)

1/4 teaspoon salt

3 medium roma (plum) tomatoes, chopped (1 cup)

1 can (15 to 16 ounces) black-eyed peas, rinsed and drained

1/4 cup lemon juice

1 teaspoon dried oregano leaves

1/4 teaspoon freshly ground pepper

Red pepper sauce, if desired

1. Cook and drain fettuccine as directed on package.

2. While fettuccine is cooking, cut pork into 1/4-inch slices; sprinkle with Cajun seasoning. Heat oil in 12-inch non-stick skillet over medium-high heat. Cook pork in oil 4 to 6 minutes, turning occasionally, until pork is no longer pink in center. Remove from skillet; keep warm.

3. Spray same skillet with cooking spray; heat over medium-high heat. Cook onion in skillet about 4 minutes, stirring frequently, until onion begins to brown. Stir in zucchini and salt. Cook about 4 minutes, stirring frequently, until vegetables are tender. Stir in remaining ingredients. Cook about 1 minute, stirring frequently, until hot.

4. Toss vegetable mixture and fettuccine. Serve pork over fettuccine mixture, or toss pork with fettuccine mixture.

1 SERVING Calories 290 (Calories from Fat 65) | Fat 7g (Saturated 2g) | Cholesterol 80mg | Sodium 300mg | Carbohydrate 46g (Dietary Fiber 8g) | Protein 29g   %DAILY VALUE Vitamin A 20% | Vitamin C 16% | Calcium 6% | Iron 26%   EXCHANGES 2 1/2 Starch, 2 Vegetable, 2 Very Lean Meat   CARBOHYDRATE CHOICES 3

BETTY'S TIP

Black-eyed peas, a common staple in the South, are actually a legume. They are available dried, canned or frozen. If you like, substitute a 10-ounce package of frozen black-eyed peas for the canned; just thaw before cooking.

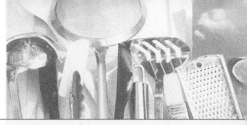

Sausage with Fettuccine

PREP **10 min**   COOK **8 min**   SERVINGS **4**

1. Cook and drain fettuccine as directed on package; keep warm.

2. Heat tomato sauce, bell pepper mixture and sausage to boiling in same saucepan. Serve sauce over fettuccine, or toss fettuccine with sauce mixture. Serve with cheese.

1 SERVING Calories 380 (Calories from Fat 25) | Fat 3g (Saturated 3g) | Cholesterol 110mg | Sodium 2310mg | Carbohydrate 67g (Dietary Fiber 7g) | Protein 29g %DAILY VALUE Vitamin A 36% | Vitamin C 70% | Calcium 8% | Iron 30% EXCHANGES 4 Starch, 1 Vegetable, 2 Very Lean Meat CARBOHYDRATE CHOICES 4 1/2

Fettuccine Alfredo with Sausage Use Alfredo pasta sauce instead of the chunky garlic-and-herb tomato sauce. Check Alfredo pasta sauce label for heating instructions; some should not be boiled.

1 package (9 ounces) refrigerated spinach or regular fettuccine

2 cans (15 ounces each) chunky garlic-and-herb tomato sauce

1 bag (1 pound) frozen stir-fry bell peppers and onions, thawed and drained

1 ring (1 pound) fully cooked fat-free Polish or kielbasa sausage, cut into 1/2-inch pieces

Finely shredded Parmesan cheese, if desired

BETTY'S TIP

A slice of crusty garlicky bread complements this Italian dish. To make your own, brush cut sides of French bread with olive oil and sprinkle with garlic powder or garlic salt, then sprinkle with grated Parmesan cheese. Broil on a cookie sheet until edges of bread are golden brown and bread is hot.

Pork Chop Dinner with Rice and Veggies

6 pork boneless loin chops, 1/2 inch thick (about 1 1/4 pounds)

2 cans (10 3/4 ounces each) condensed reduced-fat cream of mushroom soup

1 bag (1 pound) frozen baby peas, carrots, pea pods and corn (or other combination), thawed and drained

1 can (14 ounces) chicken broth

2 cups uncooked instant brown rice

PREP **5 min**   COOK **25 min**   SERVINGS **6**

1. Spray 12-inch nonstick skillet with cooking spray; heat over medium heat. Cook pork in skillet about 5 minutes, turning once, until brown. Remove pork from skillet; keep warm.

2. Heat soup, vegetables and broth to boiling in same skillet, stirring occasionally. Stir in rice; reduce heat to low. Cover and simmer 5 minutes.

3. Top with pork. Cover and simmer 10 to 15 minutes longer or until pork is no longer pink in center and rice is tender.

1 SERVING Calories 485 (Calories from Fat 115) | Fat 13g (Saturated 4g) | Cholesterol 70mg | Sodium 1160mg | Carbohydrate 65g (Dietary Fiber 6g) | Protein 33g   **%DAILY VALUE** Vitamin A 80% | Vitamin C 8% | Calcium 6% | Iron 14%   **EXCHANGES** 4 Starch, 1 Vegetable, 2 1/2 Lean Meat   **CARBOHYDRATE CHOICES** 4

BETTY'S TIP

Because brown rice contains oil in its bran, it should be used within six months of purchasing.

Italian Sausage with Tomatoes and Penne

PREP **15 min** COOK **20 min** SERVINGS **4**

1. Cut sausage crosswise into 1/4-inch slices. Spray 12-inch nonstick skillet with cooking spray; heat over medium-high heat. Cook sausage in skillet 4 to 6 minutes or until brown. Stir in broth; reduce heat to medium. Cover and cook 5 minutes.

2. Stir squash, tomatoes and 2 tablespoons of the basil into skillet. Heat to boiling; reduce heat to low. Cover and simmer 5 minutes, stirring occasionally. Stir in onions. Simmer uncovered 1 minute.

3. While sausage mixture is cooking, cook and drain pasta as directed on package. Toss pasta, oil and remaining 2 tablespoons basil. Divide pasta among bowls. Top with sausage mixture.

1 pound uncooked Italian sausage links

1/2 cup beef broth

1 medium yellow summer squash, cut lengthwise in half, then cut crosswise into 1/4-inch slices

2 cups grape or cherry tomatoes, cut lengthwise in half

1/4 cup chopped fresh or 1 tablespoon dried basil leaves

6 green onions, cut into 1/2-inch pieces (1/2 cup)

3 cups uncooked penne pasta (9 ounces)

2 tablespoons olive or vegetable oil

1 SERVING Calories 600 (Calories from Fat 270) | Fat 30g (Saturated 9g) | Cholesterol 65mg | Sodium 910mg | Carbohydrate 60g (Dietary Fiber 5g) | Protein 27g %DAILY VALUE Vitamin A 22% | Vitamin C 24% | Calcium 6% | Iron 26% EXCHANGES 3 1/2 Starch, 1 Vegetable, 2 High-Fat Meat, 2 Fat CARBOHYDRATE CHOICES 4

BETTY'S TIP

Sprinkle fresh Parmesan cheese shavings over this pasta dish or, if you are in a hurry, use purchased shredded or grated Parmesan cheese.

Penne and Ham Primavera

2 cups uncooked penne or mostaccioli pasta (6 ounces)

1 cup sliced zucchini

1 cup sliced yellow summer squash

2 cups cubed fully cooked ham

1/2 cup reduced-fat Italian dressing

1/4 cup chopped fresh basil leaves

1/3 cup shredded Parmesan cheese

Coarsely ground pepper, if desired

PREP **10 min**   COOK **15 min**   SERVINGS **4**

1. Cook pasta as directed on package, adding zucchini and yellow squash during last 3 to 4 minutes of cooking; drain.

2. Return pasta mixture to saucepan; add ham and dressing. Cook over medium heat, stirring occasionally, until hot. Sprinkle with basil, cheese and pepper.

1 SERVING Calories 365 (Calories from Fat 115) | Fat 13g (Saturated 4g) | Cholesterol 45mg | Sodium 1360mg | Carbohydrate 37g (Dietary Fiber 2g) | Protein 25g   %DAILY VALUE Vitamin A 10% | Vitamin C 6% | Calcium 14% | Iron 16%   EXCHANGES 2 Starch, 1 Vegetable, 2 1/2 Lean Meat, 1 Fat CARBOHYDRATE CHOICES 2 1/2

BETTY'S TIP

When shopping for zucchini, choose small zucchini that tend to be younger, more tender and have thinner skins. The skin should be a vibrant color and be free of blemishes.

Creamy Bow-Ties with Ham and Vegetables

PREP 10 min   COOK 15 min   SERVINGS 4

1. Cook and drain pasta as directed on package.

2. While pasta is cooking, mix cream cheese and half-and-half in 12-inch nonstick skillet. Cook over medium heat 2 to 3 minutes, stirring constantly, until melted and smooth.

3. Stir in carrots. Cook 4 minutes, stirring occasionally. Stir in asparagus. Cover and cook 4 to 5 minutes, stirring occasionally, until vegetables are crisp-tender.

4. Stir in ham, pasta and marjoram. Cook, stirring occasionally, just until hot.

2 cups uncooked farfalle (bow-tie) pasta or wide egg noodles (4 ounces)

1/2 cup soft cream cheese with chives and onion

3/4 cup half-and-half

1 cup baby-cut carrots, cut lengthwise in half if large

8 ounces asparagus, cut into 1 1/2-inch pieces

1 1/2 cups cooked ham strips (1 × 1/4-inch)

1/4 teaspoon dried marjoram leaves

1 SERVING Calories 425 (Calories from Fat 180) | Fat 20g (Saturated 11g) | Cholesterol 75mg | Sodium 860mg | Carbohydrate 40g (Dietary Fiber 3g) | Protein 21g   %DAILY VALUE Vitamin A 100% | Vitamin C 8% | Calcium 10% | Iron 16%   EXCHANGES 2 Starch, 2 Lean Meat, 2 Vegetable, 2 1/2 Fat   CARBOHYDRATE CHOICES 2 1/2

BETTY'S TIP

Fresh asparagus is easy to prepare. Just rinse the stalks with cool water to remove any grit in the tips, and snap off the ends where they naturally break. Then cut into pieces of the desired size. Or to save time, use frozen asparagus cuts.

Pork and Julienne Potatoes

2 tablespoons butter
or margarine

4 pork boneless loin chops,
about 3/4 inch thick (about
1 1/4 pounds)

1 medium onion, cut in half
and sliced

2 teaspoons dried sage
leaves

1 package (4.6 ounces)
julienne potato mix

2 1/3 cups boiling water

1/3 cup milk

PREP **15 min**   COOK **32 min**   SERVINGS **4**

1. Melt butter in 12-inch skillet over medium-high heat. Cook pork, onion and sage in butter 9 minutes, turning pork once.

2. Mix Potatoes and Sauce Mix from potato mix, the boiling water and milk in medium bowl. Reduce skillet heat to medium. Pour potato mixture over pork. Cover and cook 19 to 23 minutes, stirring occasionally, until pork is no longer pink in center. If potatoes are too saucy, cook uncovered 4 to 5 minutes longer, stirring occasionally, until desired consistency.

1 SERVING Calories 335 (Calories from Fat 145) | Fat 16g (Saturated 7g) | Cholesterol 80mg | Sodium 650mg | Carbohydrate 22g (Dietary Fiber 2g) | Protein 26g %DAILY VALUE Vitamin A 6% | Vitamin C 2% | Calcium 6% | Iron 4% EXCHANGES 1 1/2 Starch, 3 Lean Meat, 1 Fat CARBOHYDRATE CHOICES 1 1/2

Chicken and Julienne Potatoes Boneless, skinless chicken breasts can be used instead of the pork.

BETTY'S TIP

A side salad of sliced tomatoes and cucumber sprinkled with a squeeze of fresh lemon juice, salt and pepper adds color and crunch to this meat-and-potatoes meal.

Pork with Squash and Onions

PREP **15 min**   COOK **22 min**   SERVINGS **4**

4 lean pork loin or rib chops, about 1/2 inch thick (about 1 pound)

1 teaspoon dried sage leaves

1/2 teaspoon salt

1/4 teaspoon pepper

2 cloves garlic, finely chopped

1 medium onion, cut into 1/4-inch slices

1/2 cup chicken broth

1 acorn squash (about 1 1/2 pounds)

1 medium unpeeled cooking apple, cored and cut into eighths

1/4 teaspoon salt

1/4 teaspoon pepper

1. Trim fat from pork. Mix sage, 1/2 teaspoon salt, 1/4 teaspoon pepper and garlic; rub on both sides of pork.

2. Cook pork in 10-inch nonstick skillet over medium heat about 3 minutes on each side until brown. Place onion on pork. Pour broth around pork. Heat to boiling; reduce heat to low.

3. Cut squash crosswise into 1-inch slices; remove seeds and fibers. Cut each slice into fourths. Place squash and apple on pork; sprinkle with 1/4 teaspoon salt and 1/4 teaspoon pepper. Cover and simmer about 15 minutes or until pork is no longer pink when cut near bone and squash is tender.

1 SERVING Calories 255 (Calories from Fat 80) | Fat 9g (Saturated 3g) | Cholesterol 65mg | Sodium 620mg | Carbohydrate 25g (Dietary Fiber 6g) | Protein 25g   %DAILY VALUE Vitamin A 8% | Vitamin C 12% | Calcium 6% | Iron 10%   EXCHANGES 1 Starch, 2 Vegetable, 2 Lean Meat   CARBOHYDRATE CHOICES 1 1/2

BETTY'S TIP

If you like, you can leave out the fresh acorn squash and serve the squash on the side instead. Just microwave frozen cooked squash as directed on the package, and serve it alongside the pork, onion and apple.

Shrimp Scampi Fettuccine

PREP **10 min**   COOK **12 min**   SERVINGS **2 or 3**

3/4 pound uncooked peeled deveined medium shrimp, thawed if frozen and tails peeled

4 ounces uncooked fettuccine

1 tablespoon olive or vegetable oil

1 medium green onion, sliced (1 tablespoon)

1 clove garlic, finely chopped

2 teaspoons chopped fresh or 1/2 teaspoon dried basil leaves

2 teaspoons chopped fresh parsley or 3/4 teaspoon dried parsley flakes

1 tablespoon lemon juice

1/8 teaspoon salt

Grated Parmesan cheese, if desired

1. Rinse shrimp with cold water; pat dry with paper towels. Set aside.

2. Cook and drain fettuccine as directed on package. Keep warm.

3. While fettuccine is cooking, heat oil in 10-inch skillet over medium heat. Cook shrimp, onion, garlic, basil, parsley, lemon juice and salt in oil 2 to 3 minutes, stirring frequently, just until shrimp are pink and firm. (Do not overcook.) Remove skillet from heat.

4. Add fettuccine to skillet; toss fettuccine and shrimp mixture in skillet. Sprinkle with cheese.

1 SERVING Calories 375 (Calories from Fat 90) | Fat 10g (Saturated 2g) | Cholesterol 290mg | Sodium 440mg | Carbohydrate 38g (Dietary Fiber 2g) | Protein 33g   %DAILY VALUE Vitamin A 12% | Vitamin C 6% | Calcium 8% | Iron 36%   EXCHANGES 2 1/2 Starch, 4 1/2 Very Lean Meat, 1 Fat CARBOHYDRATE CHOICES 2 1/2

BETTY'S TIP

If you choose to use fresh fettuccine instead of dried, keep in mind it will cook much faster. Try to start the shrimp as soon as the fettuccine begins to cook.

Shrimp and Scallops in Wine Sauce

PREP **20** min   COOK **10** min   SERVINGS **4**

1. Heat oil in 12-inch nonstick skillet over medium heat. Cook garlic, onions, carrots and parsley in oil about 5 minutes, stirring occasionally, until carrots are crisp-tender.

2. Stir in remaining ingredients. Cook 4 to 5 minutes, stirring frequently, until shrimp are pink and firm and scallops are white.

1 SERVING Calories 220 (Calories from Fat 70) | Fat 8g (Saturated 1g) | Cholesterol 185mg | Sodium 350mg | Carbohydrate 6g (Dietary Fiber 1g) | Protein 31g %DAILY VALUE Vitamin A 100% | Vitamin C 6% | Calcium 12% | Iron 26% EXCHANGES 1 Vegetable, 4 Lean Meat, 1 Fat CARBOHYDRATE CHOICES 1/2

2 tablespoons olive or vegetable oil

1 clove garlic, finely chopped

2 medium green onions, sliced (2 tablespoons)

2 medium carrots, thinly sliced (1 cup)

1 tablespoon chopped fresh parsley or 1 teaspoon parsley flakes

1 pound uncooked peeled deveined medium shrimp, thawed if frozen and tails peeled

1 pound sea scallops, cut in half

1/2 cup dry white wine or chicken broth

1 tablespoon lemon juice

1/4 to 1/2 teaspoon crushed red pepper

BETTY'S TIP

For this recipe, pick up sea scallops, the larger ones that measure up to 2 inches, and cut in half. You can also use bay scallops, which are much smaller (only 1/2 inch), but don't cut them. Sea scallops will have a more tender texture for this dish.

Honey-Garlic Shrimp and Linguine

1 package (9 ounces) refrigerated linguine

1 tablespoon water

1 bag (1 pound) frozen baby peas, carrots, pea pods and corn (or other combination)

1/2 cup coarsely chopped red bell pepper

1 pound uncooked peeled deveined medium or large shrimp, thawed if frozen and tails peeled

1/2 cup roasted garlic and herbs marinade (from 14-ounce bottle)

1 tablespoon honey

PREP **10** min   COOK **15** min   SERVINGS **4**

1. Cook and drain linguine as directed on package; keep warm.

2. Heat water in 12-inch nonstick skillet over medium-high heat. Add frozen vegetables and bell pepper. Cook 2 to 3 minutes, stirring frequently.

3. Stir in shrimp. Cook 5 to 7 minutes, stirring frequently, until vegetables are crisp-tender and shrimp are pink and firm. Stir in marinade and honey. Cook, stirring frequently, until hot. Serve over linguine.

1 SERVING Calories 430 (Calories from Fat 20) | Fat 2g (Saturated 0g) | Cholesterol 160mg | Sodium 1650mg | Carbohydrate 77g (Dietary Fiber 8g) | Protein 33g %DAILY VALUE Vitamin A 38% | Vitamin C 38% | Calcium 8% | Iron 40% EXCHANGES 5 Starch, 2 Very Lean Meat CARBOHYDRATE CHOICES 5

BETTY'S TIP

Whole-grain rolls and sliced watermelon make great side dishes to this light shrimp dish.

Ginger-Peanut-Shrimp Stir-Fry

PREP 15 min   STAND 15 min   COOK 12 min   SERVINGS 4

1. Mix soy sauce, gingerroot, pepper sauce and garlic in large resealable plastic food-storage bag. Add shrimp; seal bag. Let stand 15 minutes.

2. Heat 2 tablespoons oil in 10-inch skillet or wok over medium-high heat. Add spaghetti, onions and pea pods; stir-fry until onions are crisp-tender. Remove mixture from skillet.

3. Heat 1 tablespoon oil in skillet. Add shrimp; stir-fry until shrimp are pink and firm. Stir in spaghetti mixture. Stir in peanut butter until mixture is coated; cook until hot. Sprinkle with peanuts.

1 SERVING Calories 400 (Calories from Fat 200) | Fat 22g (Saturated 4g) | Cholesterol 120mg | Sodium 930mg | Carbohydrate 31g (Dietary Fiber 5g) | Protein 25g   **%DAILY VALUE** Vitamin A 10% | Vitamin C 28% | Calcium 8% | Iron 28%   **EXCHANGES** 2 Starch, 2 1/2 Lean Meat, 2 Fat   **CARBOHYDRATE CHOICES** 2

3 tablespoons soy sauce

3 teaspoons grated gingerroot

1/4 teaspoon red pepper sauce

1 clove garlic, finely chopped

3/4 pound uncooked peeled deveined medium shrimp, thawed if frozen and tails peeled

2 tablespoons vegetable oil

2 cups cooked spaghetti or vermicelli

6 medium green onions, cut into 1-inch pieces

9 ounces snow (Chinese) pea pods, strings removed

1 tablespoon vegetable oil

3 tablespoons creamy peanut butter

1/4 cup chopped peanuts

BETTY'S TIP

This sassy stir-fry tastes great with mugs of icy-cold Chinese beer or freshly squeezed lemonade.

Italian Shrimp Linguine

PREP 15 min   COOK 15 min   SERVINGS 5

8 ounces uncooked linguine

3/4 cup reduced-calorie Italian dressing

1 1/2 teaspoons grated lemon peel

3 cloves garlic, finely chopped

3/4 pound uncooked peeled deveined medium shrimp, thawed if frozen and tails peeled

3 cups broccoli flowerets

1 medium yellow summer squash, cut lengthwise in half, then cut crosswise into slices (1 1/2 cups)

2 tablespoons water

8 cherry tomatoes, cut in half

12 extra-large pitted ripe olives, cut in half

1/4 cup chopped fresh basil leaves

Grated Parmesan cheese, if desired

1. Cook and drain linguine as directed on package; keep warm. Mix dressing, lemon peel and garlic; set aside.

2. Spray 12-inch nonstick skillet with cooking spray; heat over medium-high heat. Cook shrimp about 2 minutes, stirring frequently, until shrimp are pink and firm. Remove shrimp from skillet.

3. Spray skillet with cooking spray; heat over medium-high heat. Cook broccoli and squash in skillet about 1 minute, stirring frequently. Add water. Cover and cook about 3 minutes, stirring occasionally, until vegetables are crisp-tender (add water if necessary to prevent sticking).

4. Stir dressing mixture into skillet; cook 30 seconds. Stir in tomatoes, olives, basil, shrimp and linguine; heat until hot. Sprinkle with cheese.

1 SERVING Calories 310 (Calories from Fat 70) | Fat 8g (Saturated 1g) | Cholesterol 100mg | Sodium 660mg | Carbohydrate 45g (Dietary Fiber 4g) | Protein 19g   %DAILY VALUE Vitamin A 24% | Vitamin C 44% | Calcium 8% | Iron 24%   EXCHANGES 2 Starch, 3 Vegetable, 1 Medium-Fat Meat CARBOHYDRATE CHOICES 3

Italian Chicken Linguine Use 3/4 pound boneless, skinless chicken breasts, cut into 1-inch pieces. Cook the chicken 3 to 4 minutes, stirring frequently, or until no longer pink in center.

BETTY'S TIP

A sharp paring knife comes in handy when deveining shrimp. First, use the knife to make a shallow cut down the back of the shrimp. Then use the tip of the knife to pull out the dark vein. Rinse the shrimp under cold water.

Tuna Primavera

1. Mix uncooked Pasta and Sauce Mix from skillet-dinner mix, the butter, tuna, milk, water and carrots in 12-inch skillet. Heat to boiling, stirring occasionally; reduce heat. Cover and simmer 10 minutes, stirring occasionally.

2. Stir broccoli and mushrooms into tuna mixture. Cover and simmer about 10 minutes or until vegetables are tender.

1 SERVING Calories 325 (Calories from Fat 115) | Fat 13g (Saturated 3g) | Cholesterol 40mg | Sodium 1020mg | Carbohydrate 36g (Dietary Fiber 3g) | Protein 16g   %DAILY VALUE Vitamin A 100% | Vitamin C 14% | Calcium 10% | Iron 12%   EXCHANGES 2 Starch, 1 Vegetable, 1 Lean Meat, 2 Fat CARBOHYDRATE CHOICES 2 1/2

1 package (8.25 ounces) creamy pasta skillet-dinner mix for tuna

2 tablespoons butter or margarine

1 can (6 ounces) tuna in water, drained

1/2 cup milk

3 1/2 cups hot water

2 medium carrots, cut into 1/8-inch slices (1 cup)

1 cup frozen broccoli cuts (from 1-pound bag)

1 jar (4 1/2 ounces) sliced mushrooms, drained

BETTY'S TIP

If you're in a hurry, omit the fresh carrots and frozen broccoli cuts, and use 2 cups of a frozen broccoli blend instead.

Creamy Salmon with Gemelli and Vegetables

1 cup uncooked gemelli (twist) pasta (4 ounces)

1 salmon fillet (1 pound), skin removed and salmon cut into 1-inch pieces

1/4 teaspoon salt

1 1/2 cups refrigerated new potato wedges (from 1-pound 4-ounce bag)

1 cup fresh or frozen whole green beans

1 cup Parmesan and mozzarella pasta sauce (from 1-pound jar)

1/4 teaspoon coarsely ground pepper

2 tablespoons chopped fresh basil leaves

PREP **5** min   COOK **20** min   SERVINGS **4**

1. Cook and drain pasta as directed on package.

2. While pasta is cooking, spray 12-inch nonstick skillet with cooking spray. Place salmon in skillet; sprinkle with salt. Cook uncovered over medium-high heat 5 to 7 minutes, stirring frequently, until salmon flakes easily with fork. Remove salmon from skillet; keep warm.

3. Add potatoes, beans, pasta sauce and pepper to same skillet. Heat to boiling; reduce heat. Cover and cook 5 to 7 minutes, stirring occasionally, until vegetables are tender. Stir in pasta, salmon and basil. Cook 2 to 3 minutes, stirring occasionally, just until hot.

1 SERVING Calories 495 (Calories from Fat 135) | Fat 15g (Saturated 5g) | Cholesterol 90mg | Sodium 390mg | Carbohydrate 51g (Dietary Fiber 4g) | Protein 39g   %DAILY VALUE Vitamin A 16% | Vitamin C 8% | Calcium 24% | Iron 18%   EXCHANGES 3 Starch, 1 Vegetable, 4 Lean Meat   CARBOHYDRATE CHOICES 3 1/2

BETTY'S TIP

Salmon steaks will work just as well as the fillet in this Tuscan-inspired potatoes and pasta dish. Or try tuna steaks for a change.

Lemony Fish over Vegetables and Rice

PREP **10 min**   COOK **25 min**   SERVINGS **4**

2 tablespoons butter
or margarine

1 package (6.2 ounces) fried
rice (rice and vermicelli mix
with almonds and Oriental
seasonings)

2 cups water

1/2 teaspoon grated
lemon peel

1 bag (1 pound) frozen corn,
broccoli and red peppers
(or other combination)

1 pound mild-flavored fish
fillets, about 1/2 inch thick

1/2 teaspoon lemon pepper

1 tablespoon lemon juice

2 tablespoons chopped
fresh parsley

1.   Melt butter in 12-inch nonstick skillet over medium heat. Cook Rice from rice mix in butter 2 to 3 minutes, stirring occasionally, until golden brown. Stir water, Seasoning Packet from rice mix and lemon peel into skillet. Heat to boiling; reduce heat to low. Cover and simmer 10 minutes.

2.   Stir in vegetables. Heat to boiling, stirring occasionally. Cut fish into 4 serving pieces; arrange on rice mixture. Sprinkle fish with lemon pepper; drizzle with lemon juice. Reduce heat to low. Cover and simmer 8 to 10 minutes or until fish flakes easily with fork and vegetables are tender. Sprinkle with parsley.

1 SERVING Calories 240 (Calories from Fat 65) | Fat 7g (Saturated 1g) |
Cholesterol 70mg | Sodium 320mg | Carbohydrate 22g (Dietary Fiber 3g) |
Protein 25g   %DAILY VALUE Vitamin A 62% | Vitamin C 72% | Calcium 4% |
Iron 8%   EXCHANGES 1 Starch, 1 Vegetable, 2 1/2 Very Lean Meat, 1 Fat
CARBOHYDRATE CHOICES 1 1/2

BETTY'S TIP

Puzzled as to the type of mild-flavored fish you should use? Good
choices include cod, flounder, haddock, halibut, orange roughy
and sole.

Snapper with Sautéed Tomato Pepper Sauce

1 pound red snapper, cod
or other mild-flavored fish
fillets

1/4 teaspoon salt

1 large tomato, chopped
(1 cup)

1 small green bell pepper,
chopped (1/2 cup)

1 small onion, sliced

2 tablespoons finely
chopped fresh cilantro
or parsley

2 cups chicken broth

1/4 teaspoon salt

2 cups uncooked instant
white rice

Additional chopped
fresh cilantro or paprika,
if desired

PREP 10 min   COOK 15 min   STAND 5 min   SERVINGS 4

1. If fish fillets are large, cut into 4 serving pieces; sprinkle with 1/4 teaspoon salt. Spray 10-inch nonstick skillet with cooking spray; heat over medium heat. Arrange fish in single layer in skillet. Cook uncovered 4 to 6 minutes, turning once, until fish flakes easily with fork. Remove fish to warm platter; keep warm.

2. Cook tomato, bell pepper, onion, and cilantro in same skillet over medium heat 3 to 5 minutes, stirring frequently, until bell pepper and onion are crisp-tender. Stir in broth and 1/4 teaspoon salt; heat to boiling.

3. Stir in rice. Cover; remove from heat and let stand 5 minutes. Sprinkle fish and rice with additional cilantro.

1 SERVING Calories 340 (Calories from Fat 25) | Fat 3g (Saturated 1g) | Cholesterol 60mg | Sodium 900mg | Carbohydrate 52g (Dietary Fiber 2g) | Protein 29g %DAILY VALUE Vitamin A 10% | Vitamin C 22% | Calcium 4% | Iron 16%   EXCHANGES 3 Starch, 1 Vegetable, 2 1/2 Very Lean Meat CARBOHYDRATE CHOICES 3 1/2

BETTY'S TIP
For a slightly different flavor, try substituting 1/2 cup dry white wine for 1/2 cup of the chicken broth.

Easy Macaroni and Cheese

PREP **5 min**   COOK **20 min**   SERVINGS **4**

2 cups uncooked small pasta shells or elbow macaroni (about 8 ounces)

1 cup milk

1 1/2 cups shredded Cheddar cheese (6 ounces) or 8 ounces process American cheese loaf, cut into cubes

1/2 teaspoon salt

1/2 teaspoon ground mustard

1/4 teaspoon pepper

1 tablespoon butter or margarine, if desired

1. Cook and drain pasta as directed on package.

2. Return pasta to saucepan; stir in remaining ingredients. Cook over low heat about 5 minutes, stirring occasionally, until cheese is melted and sauce is desired consistency.

1 SERVING Calories 455 (Calories from Fat 155) | Fat 17g (Saturated 10g) | Cholesterol 50mg | Sodium 590mg | Carbohydrate 54g (Dietary Fiber 2g) | Protein 21g   %DAILY VALUE Vitamin A 12% | Vitamin C 0% | Calcium 30% | Iron 16%   EXCHANGES 3 1/2 Starch, 1 1/2 High-Fat Meat, 1/2 Fat CARBOHYDRATE CHOICES 3 1/2

BETTY'S TIP

Changing the flavor of this mac and cheese is as easy as changing the type of cheese. Monterey Jack, Colby or a mixture of different kinds of cheese will all give this classic dish a twist.

Southwest Cheese 'n Pasta

1 1/2 cups milk

1 cup green salsa
(salsa verde)

1 can (15 ounces)
cream-style corn

1 can (11 ounces) whole
kernel corn with red and
green peppers, drained

3 cups uncooked cavatappi
pasta or elbow macaroni
(8 ounces)

8 ounces process American
cheese loaf, cut into cubes

PREP **5** min   COOK **17** min   SERVINGS **6**

1. Mix all ingredients except cheese in 12-inch nonstick skillet. Heat to boiling, stirring occasionally; reduce heat. Cover and cook 10 to 14 minutes, stirring frequently, until pasta is tender.

2. Add cheese to pasta mixture; stir until cheese is melted.

1 SERVING Calories 420 (Calories from Fat 135) | Fat 15g (Saturated 8g) | Cholesterol 40mg | Sodium 960mg | Carbohydrate 54g (Dietary Fiber 5g) | Protein 18g   %DAILY VALUE Vitamin A 18% | Vitamin C 16% | Calcium 30% | Iron 14%   EXCHANGES 3 1/2 Starch, 1 High-Fat Meat, 1 Fat   CARBOHYDRATE CHOICES 3 1/2

Southwest Ham 'n Cheese Pasta Stir 2 cups of cubed fully cooked ham into the pasta in skillet; heat through.

BETTY'S TIP
Round out this meal with coleslaw and crusty rolls and finish with slices of cool, refreshing watermelon.

Vegetable Paella

1. Heat oil in 12-inch nonstick skillet over medium-high heat. Cook garlic and onion in oil, stirring frequently, until onion is tender.

2. Stir in remaining ingredients. Heat to boiling; reduce heat to medium-low. Cover and cook 5 minutes, stirring occasionally; remove from heat. Let stand covered 5 minutes.

1 SERVING Calories 335 (Calories from Fat 80) | Fat 9g (Saturated 1g) | Cholesterol 0mg | Sodium 590mg | Carbohydrate 62g (Dietary Fiber 8g) | Protein 9g   %DAILY VALUE Vitamin A 100% | Vitamin C 24% | Calcium 8% | Iron 14%   EXCHANGES 3 1/2 Starch, 1 Vegetable, 1/2 Fat   CARBOHYDRATE CHOICES 4

Vegetable Chicken Paella Remove half of the paella from the skillet; keep warm. Stir 1/2 cup of cubed cooked chicken or turkey into the remaining paella in skillet; heat through.

2 tablespoons olive or vegetable oil

2 cloves garlic, finely chopped

1 large red onion, cut into thin wedges

1 cup uncooked quick-cooking brown rice

1 cup vegetable or chicken broth

1/2 teaspoon saffron threads, crushed

1 bag (1 pound) frozen petite peas, baby whole carrots, snow peas and baby cob corn (or other combination)

1 can (14 1/2 ounces) stewed tomatoes, undrained

BETTY'S TIP

Saffron gives paella its characteristic bright yellow color and distinct flavor, but it can be a bit pricey. If you like, the same amount of turmeric can be substituted for the saffron.

Red Beans and Rice

2 tablespoons butter or margarine

1 medium green bell pepper, chopped (1 cup)

1 medium onion, chopped (1/2 cup)

1 cup uncooked regular long grain rice

2 cups water

1 teaspoon salt

1 can (15 to 16 ounces) red kidney beans, rinsed and drained

1/4 cup bacon flavor bits

PREP **10 min**   COOK **15 min**   STAND **10 min**   SERVINGS **4**

1. Melt butter in 3-quart saucepan over medium heat. Cook bell pepper and onion in butter, stirring occasionally, until onion is tender.

2. Stir in remaining ingredients except bacon bits. Heat to boiling, stirring once or twice; reduce heat to low. Cover and simmer 14 minutes. (Do not lift cover or stir.)

3. Remove saucepan from heat. Stir bacon bits into rice mixture. Cover and let stand 5 to 10 minutes.

1 SERVING Calories 395 (Calories from Fat 70) | Fat 8g (Saturated 1g) | Cholesterol 0mg | Sodium 1000mg | Carbohydrate 74g (Dietary Fiber 9g) | Protein 16g %DAILY VALUE Vitamin A 10% | Vitamin C 48% | Calcium 6% | Iron 30% EXCHANGES 5 Starch CARBOHYDRATE CHOICES 5

BETTY'S TIP

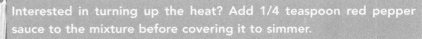

Interested in turning up the heat? Add 1/4 teaspoon red pepper sauce to the mixture before covering it to simmer.

Swiss Potato and Cheese Skillet

PREP **10 min**   COOK **26 min**   SERVINGS **4**

1 tablespoon butter or margarine

1 cup chopped onions

1 package (28 ounces) frozen chunky–style seasoned hash–brown potatoes

1/4 cup water

2 cups shredded Swiss or Gruyère cheese (8 ounces)

Dash nutmeg, if desired

1. Melt butter in 12-inch nonstick skillet over medium heat. Cook onions in butter 2 to 3 minutes, stirring frequently, until tender. Stir potatoes and water into skillet. Cover and cook 15 to 20 minutes, stirring occasionally, until potatoes are tender.

2. Sprinkle potatoes with cheese; reduce heat to low. Cover and cook 2 to 3 minutes or until cheese is melted. Sprinkle with nutmeg.

1 SERVING Calories 500 (Calories from Fat 170) | Fat 19g (Saturated 11g) | Cholesterol 50mg | Sodium 960mg | Carbohydrate 61g (Dietary Fiber 6g) | Protein 21g   **%DAILY VALUE** Vitamin A 14% | Vitamin C 18% | Calcium 58% | Iron 6%   **EXCHANGES** 4 Starch, 2 High-Fat Meat, 2 Fat   **CARBOHYDRATE CHOICES** 4

BETTY'S TIP

A fresh spinach salad with chopped hard-cooked eggs makes a tasty accompaniment to this skillet meal.

Niçoise Skillet Supper

PREP **15** min   COOK **27** min   SERVINGS **4**

2 tablespoons olive or vegetable oil

1/2 small red onion, coarsely chopped (1/2 cup)

4 or 5 small red potatoes, sliced (2 cups)

1 cup 1-inch pieces green beans (4 ounces)

1/2 teaspoon Italian seasoning

1/2 teaspoon garlic salt

2 roma (plum) tomatoes, thinly sliced

1 hard-cooked egg, chopped

1. Heat oil in 12-inch skillet over medium-high heat. Cook onion in oil 2 minutes, stirring frequently. Stir in potatoes; reduce heat to medium-low. Cover and cook 10 to 12 minutes, stirring occasionally, until potatoes are tender.

2. Stir green beans, Italian seasoning and garlic salt into potatoes. Cover and cook 6 to 8 minutes, stirring occasionally, until beans are tender and potatoes are light golden brown.

3. Stir in tomatoes. Cook 3 to 5 minutes, stirring occasionally and gently, just until hot. Sprinkle each serving with egg.

1 SERVING Calories 95 (Calories from Fat 70) | Fat 8g (Saturated 1g) | Cholesterol 55mg | Sodium 140mg | Carbohydrate 20g (Dietary Fiber 1g) | Protein 2g   %DAILY VALUE Vitamin A 8% | Vitamin C 4% | Calcium 2% | Iron 2%   EXCHANGES 1 Starch, 1 Vegetable, 1 1/2 Fat   CARBOHYDRATE CHOICES 1

BETTY'S TIP

To hard-cook an egg, place in a saucepan and cover with cold water. Heat the water to boiling, then remove the pan from heat, cover and let stand 18 minutes. Immediately cool in cold water.

Comforting Casseroles, Gratins and Stratas

Wild Rice and Beef Casserole

1 pound lean ground beef

1 package (6.2 ounces) fast-cooking long-grain and wild rice mix

1 can (10 3/4 ounces) condensed tomato soup

1/4 cup milk

1/4 teaspoon pepper

1 cup shredded Cheddar cheese (4 ounces)

PREP **5 min**   COOK **10 min**   BAKE **40 min**   SERVINGS **4**

1. Heat oven to 350°. Spray 2-quart casserole with cooking spray. Cook beef in 10-inch skillet over medium heat 8 to 10 minutes, stirring occasionally, until brown; drain.

2. While beef is cooking, make rice mix as directed on package—except omit butter. Stir rice mixture, soup, milk and pepper into beef. Spoon into casserole.

3. Cover and bake 30 minutes. Sprinkle with cheese. Bake uncovered 5 to 10 minutes longer or until cheese is melted and mixture is hot.

1 SERVING Calories 460 (Calories from Fat 240) | Fat 27g (Saturated 13g) | Cholesterol 95mg | Sodium 850mg | Carbohydrate 24g | (Dietary Fiber 1g) | Protein 31g %DAILY VALUE Vitamin A 14% | Vitamin C 8% | Calcium 18% | Iron 16% EXCHANGES 1 1/2 Starch, 4 Medium-Fat Meat, 1 Fat CARBOHYDRATE CHOICES 1 1/2

Wild Rice and Turkey Casserole Substitute 1 pound ground turkey breast for the ground beef.

BETTY'S TIP

Did you know you can purchase precooked ground beef crumbles? Just stir them into the remaining ingredients and knock 10 minutes off your prep time. Look for plain and flavored varieties in the meat or freezer section of your grocery store.

Texas Tater Casserole

PREP **10 min**   COOK **10 min**   BAKE **50 min**   SERVINGS **6**

1 pound lean ground beef

1 large onion, chopped (1 cup)

1 medium stalk celery, chopped (1/2 cup)

2 cloves garlic, finely chopped

2 cans (10 3/4 ounces each) condensed Cheddar cheese soup

1 can (11 ounces) whole kernel corn with red and green peppers, drained

1/2 cup picante sauce

2 teaspoons chili powder

1/4 teaspoon pepper

1 package (16 ounces) frozen potato nuggets

1/2 cup shredded taco-seasoned cheese (2 ounces)

1. Heat oven to 375°. Cook beef, onion, celery and garlic in 10-inch skillet over medium heat 8 to 10 minutes, stirring occasionally, until beef is brown; drain.

2. Stir soup, corn, picante sauce, chili powder and pepper into beef mixture. Spoon into ungreased 2 1/2-quart casserole. Top with potato nuggets.

3. Bake uncovered 40 minutes. Sprinkle with cheese. Bake 5 to 10 minutes longer or until bubbly and cheese is melted.

1 SERVING Calories 540 (Calories from Fat 280) | Fat 31g (Saturated 14g) | Cholesterol 70mg | Sodium 1680mg | Carbohydrate 45g (Dietary Fiber 5g) | Protein 25g   %DAILY VALUE Vitamin A 50% | Vitamin C 14% | Calcium 16% | Iron 18%   EXCHANGES 2 Starch, 3 Vegetable, 2 Medium-Fat Meat, 4 Fat   CARBOHYDRATE CHOICES 3

BETTY'S TIP

There's no need to peel garlic cloves when you're putting them through a garlic press. Just pop the clove—skin and all—into the press, then squeeze. The garlic flesh will be forced through the mesh, while the skin stays in the press.

Quick Lasagna

1/2 pound lean ground beef

1 clove garlic, finely chopped

1 teaspoon Italian seasoning

1 cup spaghetti sauce

6 frozen precooked lasagna noodles (each about 8 × 2 1/2 inches)

1 container (12 ounces) reduced-fat cottage cheese (1 1/2 cups)

1 cup shredded mozzarella cheese (4 ounces)

2 tablespoons grated Parmesan cheese

PREP **15 min**   COOK **7 min**   BAKE **40 min**   STAND **10 min**   SERVINGS **4**

1. Heat oven to 400°. Cook beef and garlic in 10-inch skillet over medium-high heat 5 to 7 minutes, stirring occasionally, until beef is brown; drain. Stir Italian seasoning and spaghetti sauce into beef. Spread 1/4 cup meat sauce in ungreased square pan, 8 × 8 × 2 inches.

2. Arrange 2 noodles on sauce, so they do not overlap or touch sides of pan. Spread about 1/2 cup of the remaining sauce over noodles. Spread about 1/2 cup cottage cheese over sauce. Sprinkle with about 1/3 cup mozzarella cheese.

3. Repeat step 2 two times, using remaining noodles, sauce, cottage cheese and mozzarella cheese. Sprinkle with Parmesan cheese.

4. Spray piece of aluminum foil large enough to cover square pan with cooking spray. Tightly cover pan with foil, sprayed side down. Bake 30 minutes. Carefully remove foil. Bake about 10 minutes longer or until lasagna is hot and bubbly. Let stand 10 minutes before cutting.

1 SERVING Calories 460 (Calories from Fat 160) | Fat 18g (Saturated 8g) | Cholesterol 55mg | Sodium 890mg | Carbohydrate 39g (Dietary Fiber 2g) | Protein 36g %DAILY VALUE Vitamin A 14% | Vitamin C 8% | Calcium 32% | Iron 14% EXCHANGES 2 1/2 Starch, 4 1/2 Lean Meat CARBOHYDRATE CHOICES 2 1/2

BETTY'S TIP

If you're out of cottage cheese but have some ricotta cheese in the fridge, you can use that instead.

Mexican Beef and Bean Casserole

1 pound lean ground beef

2 cans (15 to 16 ounces each) pinto beans, rinsed and drained

1 can (8 ounces) tomato sauce

1/2 cup mild chunky-style salsa

1 teaspoon chili powder

1 cup shredded Monterey Jack cheese (4 ounces)

1. Heat oven to 375°. Cook beef in 10-inch skillet over medium heat 8 to 10 minutes, stirring occasionally, until beef is brown; drain. Mix beef, beans, tomato sauce, salsa and chili powder in ungreased 2-quart casserole.

2. Cover and bake 40 to 45 minutes, stirring once or twice, until hot and bubbly. Sprinkle with cheese. Bake uncovered about 5 minutes longer or until cheese is melted.

1 SERVING Calories 585 (Calories from Fat 235) | Fat 26g (Saturated 12g) | Cholesterol 90mg | Sodium 1060mg | Carbohydrate 61g (Dietary Fiber 14g) | Protein 46g   %DAILY VALUE Vitamin A 20% | Vitamin C 14% | Calcium 34% | Iron 46%   EXCHANGES 4 Starch, 5 Lean Meat   CARBOHYDRATE CHOICES 4

BETTY'S TIP

To add more zip to this Mexican dish, use Monterey Jack cheese with jalapeño peppers or, as it's also known, pepper Jack cheese.

Curried Beef Casserole

PREP **10** min   COOK **15** min   BAKE **45** min   SERVINGS **4**

2 1/2 cups uncooked wagon wheel pasta (about 6 ounces)

1 pound lean ground beef

1 medium onion, chopped (1/2 cup)

2 tablespoons butter or margarine

2 tablespoons all-purpose flour

1 tablespoon curry powder

1/2 teaspoon salt

1/4 teaspoon crushed red pepper

2 cups milk

1 container (8 ounces) sour cream

1/2 cup dry-roasted peanuts

1 package (10 ounces) frozen mixed vegetables, thawed and drained

1. Heat oven to 350°. Spray 2-quart casserole with cooking spray. Cook and drain pasta as directed on package.

2. While pasta is cooking, cook ground beef and onion in 10-inch skillet over medium heat 8 to 10 minutes, stirring frequently, until beef is brown and onion is tender; drain. Remove beef mixture from skillet.

3. Melt butter in same skillet over medium heat. Stir flour, curry powder, salt and red pepper into butter. Cook, stirring constantly, until smooth and bubbly; remove from heat. Stir in milk. Heat to boiling, stirring constantly. Boil and stir 1 minute; remove from heat. Stir in sour cream and peanuts.

4. Mix pasta, beef mixture, vegetables and sour cream mixture in casserole. Cover and bake about 45 minutes or until hot.

1 SERVING Calories 750 (Calories from Fat 405) | Fat 45g (Saturated 17g) | Cholesterol 110mg | Sodium 680mg | Carbohydrate 53g (Dietary Fiber 6g) | Protein 39g   %DAILY VALUE Vitamin A 72% | Vitamin C 10% | Calcium 28% | Iron 36%   EXCHANGES 2 1/2 Starch, 1 Vegetable, 1 Milk, 3 High-Fat Meat, 3 Fat   CARBOHYDRATE CHOICES 3 1/2

BETTY'S TIP

Curry powder tends to be a love-it or leave-it type of seasoning. If you're not sure if your family will like this Indian blend of spices, herbs and seeds, you may not want to use a whole tablespoon the first time you make this beefy casserole.

Spinach-Lasagna Casserole

1. Heat oven to 375°. Rinse spinach with cold water to separate; drain thoroughly. Mix mozzarella, cottage and Parmesan cheeses; set aside.

2. Cook beef and garlic in 10-inch skillet over medium heat 8 to 10 minutes, stirring occasionally, until beef is brown; drain.

3. Mix beef mixture, spinach, uncooked Pasta and Sauce Mix from skillet-dinner mix and water in ungreased 2-quart casserole or rectangular baking dish, 11 × 7 × 1 1/2 inches. Spoon cheese mixture evenly over top.

4. Bake uncovered 40 to 50 minutes or until top is golden brown and sauce is bubbly.

1 package (10 ounces) frozen chopped spinach

1 cup shredded mozzarella cheese (4 ounces)

1/2 cup small curd creamed cottage cheese

1/4 cup grated Parmesan cheese

1 pound lean ground beef

1 clove garlic, finely chopped

1 package (6.4 ounces) lasagna skillet-dinner mix for hamburger

3 cups hot water

1 SERVING Calories 305 (Calories from Fat 125) | Fat 14g (Saturated 6g) | Cholesterol 50mg | Sodium 920mg | Carbohydrate 24g (Dietary Fiber 2g) | Protein 23g %DAILY VALUE Vitamin A 50% | Vitamin C 2% | Calcium 22% | Iron 10% EXCHANGES 1 Starch, 2 Medium-Fat Meat, 2 Vegetable, 1 Fat CARBOHYDRATE CHOICES 1 1/2

BETTY'S TIP

To get out as much moisture as you possibly can from the spinach, squeeze the spinach in a paper towel or two after you drain it.

Beef Enchiladas

1 pound lean ground beef

1 medium onion, chopped (1/2 cup)

1/2 cup sour cream

1 cup shredded Cheddar cheese (4 ounces)

2 tablespoons chopped fresh parsley

1/4 teaspoon pepper

1/3 cup chopped green bell pepper

2/3 cup water

1 tablespoon chili powder

1 1/2 teaspoons chopped fresh or 1/2 teaspoon dried oregano leaves

1/4 teaspoon ground cumin

1 can (4.5 ounces) chopped green chiles, drained, if desired

1 clove garlic, finely chopped

1 can (15 ounces) tomato sauce

8 corn tortillas (5 or 6 inches in diameter)

Shredded cheese, sour cream and chopped onions, if desired

PREP 15 min   COOK 20 min   BAKE 20 min   SERVINGS 4

1. Heat oven to 350°. Cook beef in 10-inch skillet over medium heat 8 to 10 minutes, stirring occasionally, until brown; drain. Stir onion, sour cream, cheese, parsley and pepper into beef. Cover and remove from heat.

2. Heat bell pepper, water, chili powder, oregano, cumin, chiles, garlic and tomato sauce to boiling in 2-quart saucepan, stirring occasionally; reduce heat to low. Simmer uncovered 5 minutes. Pour into ungreased pie plate, 9 × 1 1/4 inches.

3. Dip each tortilla into sauce in pie plate to coat both sides. Spoon about 1/4 cup beef mixture onto each tortilla; roll tortilla around filling. Place seam side down in ungreased rectangular baking dish, 11 × 7 × 1 1/2 inches. Pour remaining sauce over enchiladas.

4. Bake uncovered about 20 minutes or until bubbly. Garnish with shredded cheese, sour cream and chopped onions.

1 SERVING Calories 520 (Calories from Fat 290) | Fat 32g (Saturated 16g) | Cholesterol 115mg | Sodium 670mg | Carbohydrate 26g (Dietary Fiber 4g) | Protein 32g   %DAILY VALUE Vitamin A 24% | Vitamin C 18% | Calcium 26% | Iron 18%   EXCHANGES 2 Starch, 4 Medium-Fat Meat, 1 1/2 Fat   CARBOHYDRATE CHOICES 2

Cheese Enchiladas Use 2 cups shredded Monterey Jack cheese (8 ounces) and 1 cup shredded Cheddar cheese (4 ounces) in place of the ground beef. Mix cheeses, onion, sour cream, parsley and pepper in step 1 and set aside. Continue with step 2.

BETTY'S TIP

If you're watching the fat in your diet, use low-fat sour cream and reduced-fat Cheddar cheese in this Mexican favorite.

Garlic Shepherd's Pie

PREP **10 min**   COOK **15 min**   BAKE **30 min**   SERVINGS **6**

1 pound lean ground beef

1 medium onion, chopped (1/2 cup)

2 cups (from 1-pound bag) frozen baby beans and carrots (or other combination)

1 cup sliced mushrooms (3 ounces)

1 can (14 1/2 ounces) diced tomatoes, undrained

1 jar (12 ounces) beef gravy

2 tablespoons chili sauce

1/2 teaspoon dried basil leaves

1/8 teaspoon pepper

1/2 package (7.2-ounce size) roasted garlic mashed potato mix (1 pouch)

Water, milk, margarine or butter called for on potato mix package

2 teaspoons shredded Parmesan cheese

1. Heat oven to 350°. Cook beef and onion in 12-inch non-stick skillet over medium heat 8 to 10 minutes, stirring occasionally, until beef is brown; drain well. Stir in frozen vegetables, mushrooms, tomatoes, gravy, chili sauce, basil and pepper. Heat to boiling; reduce heat. Cover and simmer about 10 minutes or until vegetables are tender.

2. Make potatoes as directed on package for 4 servings, using 1 pouch potatoes and seasoning, water, milk and margarine; let stand 3 to 5 minutes.

3. Spoon beef mixture into ungreased square baking dish, 8 × 8 × 2 inches, or 2-quart casserole. Spoon potatoes onto beef mixture around edge of dish. Sprinkle with cheese. Bake uncovered 25 to 30 minutes or until potatoes are firm and beef mixture is bubbly.

1 SERVING Calories 350 (Calories from Fat 155) | Fat 17g (Saturated 8g) | Cholesterol 60mg | Sodium 620mg | Carbohydrate 27g (Dietary Fiber 4g) | Protein 21g   %DAILY VALUE Vitamin A 98% | Vitamin C 22% | Calcium 10% | Iron 14%   EXCHANGES 1 1/2 Starch, 1 Vegetable, 2 Medium-Fat Meat, 1 1/2 Fat   CARBOHYDRATE CHOICES 2

BETTY'S TIP

Shepherd's Pie was originally created as a handy way to use up leftovers. If you'd prefer, you can use ground pork or ground turkey in place of the ground beef.

Fajita Lasagna

1 pound lean ground beef

1 can (29 ounces) tomato sauce

1 envelope (1.4 ounces) fajita seasoning mix

12 no-boil lasagna noodles (each about 6 to 7 inches long and 3 1/2 inches wide)

1 bag (1 pound) frozen stir-fry bell peppers and onions, thawed and drained

3 cups shredded Colby-Monterey Jack cheese (12 ounces)

1 can (2 1/4 ounces) sliced ripe olives, drained

PREP **15 min**   BAKE **30 min**   STAND **15 min**   SERVINGS **8**

1. Heat oven to 350°. Spray rectangular baking dish, $13 \times 9 \times 2$ inches, with cooking spray. Cook ground beef in 10-inch skillet over medium-high heat 5 to 7 minutes, stirring occasionally, until brown; drain. Stir tomato sauce and seasoning mix into beef; heat to boiling.

2. Spread 1/2 cup sauce mixture in baking dish. Arrange 4 noodles crosswise, slightly overlapping, on sauce. Spread 1 1/2 cups sauce over noodles, completely covering noodles. Spread bell pepper mixture evenly over sauce; sprinkle with 1 cup of the cheese.

3. Arrange 4 noodles crosswise, slightly overlapping, on cheese. Spread about 1 1/2 cups sauce over noodles, completely covering noodles. Sprinkle 1 cup of the cheese and the olives over sauce. Arrange 4 noodles crosswise, slightly overlapping, on olives. Spread remaining sauce over noodles, completely covering noodles. Sprinkle with remaining 1 cup cheese.

4. Spray piece of aluminum foil large enough to cover baking dish with cooking spray. Tightly cover baking dish with foil, sprayed side down. Bake about 30 minutes or until hot and bubbly. Let stand 15 minutes before cutting.

1 SERVING Calories 460 (Calories from Fat 205) | Fat 23g (Saturated 12g) | Cholesterol 75mg | Sodium 1220mg | Carbohydrate 40g | (Dietary Fiber 4g) | Protein 27g %DAILY VALUE Vitamin A 36% | Vitamin C 36% | Calcium 32% | Iron 20% EXCHANGES 2 1/2 Starch, 1 Vegetable, 2 1/2 Medium-Fat Meat, 1 Fat CARBOHYDRATE CHOICES 2 1/2

BETTY'S TIP

No-boil lasagna noodles are a great item to stock in your pantry. Most large grocery stores carry boxes of them right next to the regular lasagna noodles and other pastas.

Beef and Potatoes au Gratin

PREP **15 min**   COOK **15 min**   BAKE **30 min**   STAND **5 min**   SERVINGS **4**

1. Heat oven to 375°. Heat water and potatoes to boiling in 2 1/2-quart saucepan; reduce heat to medium. Cook uncovered 8 to 10 minutes or just until potatoes are tender; drain. Set aside.

2. While potatoes are cooking, cook ground beef and celery in 10-inch skillet over medium heat 8 to 10 minutes, stirring frequently, until beef is brown; drain. Remove beef mixture from skillet; set aside.

3. Melt 3 tablespoons butter in same skillet over medium heat. Stir flour, chervil, mustard, salt and pepper into butter. Cook, stirring constantly, until bubbly; remove from heat. Stir in milk. Heat to boiling, stirring constantly. Boil and stir 1 minute. Stir in cheese until melted. Stir in 3 tablespoons parsley.

4. Layer half of the potatoes in ungreased 2-quart casserole. Layer with beef mixture and remaining potatoes. Pour cheese sauce over potatoes. Bake uncovered 20 to 25 minutes or until bubbly.

5. Mix bread crumbs, 1 tablespoon parsley and 2 teaspoons melted butter; sprinkle over potatoes. Bake about 5 minutes longer or until crumbs are brown and crisp. Let stand 5 minutes before serving.

4 cups water

3 medium potatoes, cut into 1/4-inch slices (about 3 cups)

1 pound lean ground beef

1 medium stalk celery, thinly sliced (1/2 cup)

3 tablespoons butter or margarine

3 tablespoons all-purpose flour

1 tablespoon chopped fresh or 1 teaspoon dried chervil leaves

1 teaspoon yellow mustard

1/4 teaspoon salt

1/4 teaspoon pepper

2 cups milk

1 1/4 cups shredded sharp process American cheese (5 ounces)

3 tablespoons chopped fresh parsley

1/4 cup dry bread crumbs

1 tablespoon chopped fresh parsley

2 teaspoons butter or margarine, melted

1 SERVING Calories 675 (Calories from Fat 370) | Fat 41g (Saturated 17g) | Cholesterol 110mg | Sodium 1000mg | Carbohydrate 35g (Dietary Fiber 2g) | Protein 34g **%DAILY VALUE** Vitamin A 32% | Vitamin C 10% | Calcium 36% | Iron 18% **EXCHANGES** 1 1/2 Starch, 1 Milk, 3 Medium-Fat Meat, 5 Fat **CARBOHYDRATE CHOICES** 2

BETTY'S TIP

If you love kitchen gadgets, you may want to look into getting a mandoline. This hand-operated machine has blades that adjust for thin to thick slicing of firm vegetables and fruits. It works nicely for slicing the potatoes in this gratin.

Beef and Bulgur Casserole

1 pound lean ground beef or ground pork

1 small green bell pepper, chopped (about 1/2 cup)

1 medium onion, chopped (about 1/2 cup)

1 can (14 1/2 ounces) whole tomatoes, undrained

1/2 cup water

1/3 cup raisins

2 tablespoons chopped fresh or 2 teaspoons dried oregano leaves

1 tablespoon Worcestershire sauce

1/2 teaspoon salt

1/2 teaspoon red pepper sauce

1 cup uncooked bulgur

2 small yellow summer squash, cut lengthwise in half and sliced

1/3 cup coarsely chopped walnuts

PREP **15 min**   COOK **15 min**   BAKE **35 min**   SERVINGS **4**

1. Heat oven to 375°. Cook ground beef, bell pepper and onion in 10-inch skillet over medium heat 8 to 10 minutes, stirring frequently, until beef is brown; drain.

2. Stir tomatoes, water, raisins, oregano, Worcestershire sauce, salt and pepper sauce into beef mixture, breaking up tomatoes. Heat to boiling. Stir in bulgur; reduce heat to low. Cover and simmer 5 minutes. Stir in squash and walnuts. Spoon mixture into ungreased 2-quart casserole.

3. Cover and bake 20 minutes; stir. Cover and bake about 15 minutes longer or until bulgur is tender and mixture is heated through.

1 SERVING Calories 500 (Calories from Fat 225) | Fat 25g (Saturated 7g) | Cholesterol 65mg | Sodium 560mg | Carbohydrate 50g (Dietary Fiber 14g) | Protein 29g   %DAILY VALUE Vitamin A 12% | Vitamin C 36% | Calcium 10% | Iron 24%   EXCHANGES 3 Starch, 1 Vegetable, 2 1/2 Medium-Fat Meat, 1 Fat CARBOHYDRATE CHOICES 3

BETTY'S TIP

Bulgur is whole wheat that has been cooked, dried and then broken into coarse fragments. You may have tasted it before in a tabbouleh salad. You'll find it shelved along with the other grains at your grocery store.

Cheesy Pizza Casserole

PREP **15 min**   BAKE **35 min**   SERVINGS **6**

3 cups uncooked rigatoni pasta (9 ounces)

1/2 pound lean ground beef

1/4 cup sliced ripe olives

1 can (4 ounces) mushroom pieces and stems, drained

1 jar (26 to 28 ounces) vegetable primavera pasta sauce

1 cup shredded mozzarella cheese (4 ounces)

1.   Heat oven to 350°. Cook and drain pasta as directed on package.

2.   While pasta is cooking, cook beef in 10-inch skillet over medium-high heat 5 to 7 minutes, stirring occasionally, until beef is brown; drain. Mix pasta, beef and remaining ingredients except cheese in ungreased 2 1/2-quart casserole.

3.   Cover and bake about 30 minutes or until hot and bubbly. Sprinkle with cheese. Bake uncovered about 5 minutes longer or until cheese is melted.

1 SERVING Calories 455 (Calories from Fat 135) | Fat 15g (Saturated 5g) | Cholesterol 30mg | Sodium 920mg | Carbohydrate 60g (Dietary Fiber 4g) | Protein 20g **%DAILY VALUE** Vitamin A 20% | Vitamin C 16% | Calcium 18% | Iron 20% **EXCHANGES** 4 Starch, 1 Medium-Fat Meat **CARBOHYDRATE CHOICES** 4

Cheesy Italian Sausage Casserole Use bulk Italian sausage instead of ground beef.

BETTY'S TIP

Try serving this yummy pizza and pasta casserole with toasted garlic bread and a tossed salad. A fruit-flavored sorbet or ice does the trick for dessert.

Deep-Dish Spaghetti Pie

6 ounces uncooked spaghetti

2 eggs, slightly beaten

1/4 cup grated Parmesan cheese

1 pound lean ground beef

1/4 cup chopped onion

1 jar (14 ounces) spaghetti sauce

1 can (11 ounces) vacuum-packed whole kernel corn, drained

1 small green bell pepper, cut into rings

1 cup shredded mozzarella cheese (4 ounces)

PREP 15 min   COOK 15 min   BAKE 30 min   STAND 5 min   SERVINGS 6

1. Heat oven to 350°. Spray pie plate, 10 × 1 1/2 inches, or square pan, 9 × 9 × 2 inches, with cooking spray.

2. Cook spaghetti as directed on package; drain. Rinse with hot water; drain. Mix spaghetti, eggs and Parmesan cheese. Press spaghetti mixture evenly over bottom and up sides of pie plate to form crust; set aside.

3. Cook ground beef and onion in 12-inch skillet over medium heat 8 to 10 minutes, stirring occasionally, until beef is brown; drain. Stir spaghetti sauce and corn into beef mixture. Spoon evenly over spaghetti crust. Top with bell pepper; sprinkle with cheese.

4. Bake 25 to 30 minutes. Let stand 5 minutes before serving.

1 SERVING Calories 440 (Calories from Fat 170) | Fat 19g (Saturated 8g) | Cholesterol 130mg | Sodium 700mg | Carbohydrate 39g (Dietary Fiber 3g) | Protein 27g   **%DAILY VALUE** Vitamin A 10% | Vitamin C 15% | Calcium 24% | Iron 20%   **EXCHANGES** 2 1/2 Starch, 3 Medium-Fat Meat   **CARBOHYDRATE CHOICES** 2 1/2

BETTY'S TIP

This kid-friendly casserole will serve up smiles when you add bread-sticks and some carrot sticks on the side. If your kids don't like green bell peppers, feel free to leave them out.

Western Beef Casserole au Gratin

PREP **15 min**   COOK **10 min**   BAKE **35 min**   STAND **5 min**   SERVINGS **6**

1. Heat oven to 350°. Spray rectangular baking dish, 11 × 7 × 1 1/2, with cooking spray. Make mashed potatoes as directed on package using 1 1/2 cups water, 3/4 cup milk and 2 cups mashed potato flakes. Keep warm.

2. Cook ground beef and onion in 12-inch skillet over medium heat 8 to 10 minutes, stirring occasionally, until beef is brown; drain. Stir tomato sauce, garlic powder and pepper into beef mixture. Spoon into baking dish. Spoon corn evenly over beef mixture. Spread potatoes evenly over corn; sprinkle with cheese. Top with green chiles.

3. Bake 30 to 35 minutes or until bubbly around edges and cheese is melted. Let stand 5 minutes. Top with chopped tomato.

1 SERVING Calories 400 (Calories from Fat 180) | Fat 20g (Saturated 11g) | Cholesterol 65mg | Sodium 720mg | Carbohydrate 34g (Dietary Fiber 4g) | Protein 20g   %DAILY VALUE Vitamin A 20% | Vitamin C 24% | Calcium 34% | Iron 10%   EXCHANGES 2 Starch, 2 High-Fat Meat, 1 Fat   CARBOHYDRATE CHOICES 2

1 1/2 cups water

3/4 cup milk

2 cups mashed potato flakes

1/2 pound lean ground beef

1/3 cup chopped onion

1 can (8 ounces) tomato sauce

1/4 teaspoon garlic powder

1/8 teaspoon pepper

1 can (15 1/4 ounces) whole kernel corn, drained

2 cups shredded Cheddar cheese (8 ounces)

1 can (4.5 ounces) chopped green chiles, drained

1 medium tomato, chopped (3/4 cup)

BETTY'S TIP

Green chiles and corn give this casserole a southwestern flair. Pick up some corn bread muffins on the way home from work, and your meal is made.

Meatball Sandwich Casserole

18 slices French bread, about 1/4 inch thick

3 tablespoons olive or vegetable oil

1 package (18 ounces) frozen Italian-flavor or regular meatballs, 1 inch in diameter (36 meatballs), thawed

3 cups frozen stir-fry bell peppers and onions (from 1-pound bag), thawed and drained

1 1/2 cups tomato pasta sauce (any variety)

1 cup shredded mozzarella cheese (4 ounces)

1. Heat oven to 350°. Spray pie plate, 10 × 1 1/2 inches, with cooking spray. Brush one side of bread slices with olive oil. Line bottom and side of pie plate with bread, oil side up and slightly overlapping.

2. Bake about 5 minutes or until edges are light golden brown. Toss meatballs, bell pepper mixture and pasta sauce in large bowl. Spoon meatball mixture into baked crust.

3. Bake uncovered 30 to 35 minutes or until hot in center. Sprinkle with cheese. Bake about 5 minutes longer or until cheese is melted.

1 SERVING Calories 520 (Calories from Fat 250) | Fat 28g (Saturated 9g) | Cholesterol 105mg | Sodium 1090mg | Carbohydrate 42g | (Dietary Fiber 3g) | Protein 26g   %DAILY VALUE Vitamin A 16% | Vitamin C 26% | Calcium 24% | Iron 22%   EXCHANGES 2 1/2 Starch, 1 Vegetable, 2 1/2 Medium-Fat Meat, 2 Fat   CARBOHYDRATE CHOICES 3

BETTY'S TIP

If you have a mister for olive oil or olive oil–flavored cooking spray, use it to lightly spray one side of the bread slices for a quick coating of oil.

Baked Ravioli and Meatballs

PREP **15 min**   COOK **10 min**   BAKE **35 min**   SERVINGS **6**

1. Heat oven to 375°. Spray rectangular baking dish, 13 × 9 × 2 inches, with cooking spray.

2. Cook and drain ravioli as directed on package. Spoon ravioli into baking dish; top with meatballs and sauce. Sprinkle with cheese.

3. Bake 30 to 35 minutes or until cheese is melted and casserole is hot.

1 SERVING Calories 840 (Calories from Fat 400) | Fat 44g (Saturated 20g) | Cholesterol 165mg | Sodium 1060mg | Carbohydrate 68g (Dietary Fiber 8g) | Protein 43g   %DAILY VALUE Vitamin A 34% | Vitamin C 4% | Calcium 60% | Iron 30%   EXCHANGES 4 1/2 Starch, 4 High-Fat Meat, 2 Fat   CARBOHYDRATE CHOICES 4 1/2

1 package (25 ounces) frozen cheese-filled ravioli

1 package (20 ounces) frozen cooked meatballs, thawed

1 jar (28 ounces) low-sodium spaghetti sauce

1 1/2 cups shredded mozzarella cheese (6 ounces)

BETTY'S TIP

This is a great recipe for involving the kids. Depending on their age, they could spoon the ravioli and meatballs into the baking dish or sprinkle the cheese on top.

Beef, Bacon and Noodle Bake

4 slices bacon, cut into 3/4-inch pieces

1 1/2 pounds beef stew meat

1/2 teaspoon peppered seasoned salt

1 medium onion, chopped (1/2 cup)

1 1/2 cups baby-cut carrots

1 can (14 1/2 ounces) diced tomatoes with basil, garlic and oregano, undrained

1 jar (12 ounces) beef gravy

1 cup water

2 cups uncooked wide egg noodles (4 ounces)

1 1/2 cups frozen whole green beans (from 1-pound bag)

PREP **15 min**   COOK **15 min**   BAKE **1 hr 55 min**   SERVINGS **6**

1. Heat oven to 325°. Spray rectangular baking dish, 13 × 9 × 2 inches, with cooking spray.

2. Cook bacon in 12-inch nonstick skillet over medium-high heat 3 minutes, stirring occasionally. Stir beef, seasoned salt and onion into bacon. Cook, stirring occasionally, until beef is brown. Spoon beef mixture into baking dish. Stir in carrots, tomatoes, gravy and water.

3. Cover and bake 1 hour 30 minutes. Stir in noodles and green beans.

4. Cover and bake 20 to 25 minutes longer or until beef, noodles and beans are tender.

1 SERVING Calories 350 (Calories from Fat 155) | Fat 17g (Saturated 6g) | Cholesterol 85mg | Sodium 770mg | Carbohydrate 22g (Dietary Fiber 3g) | Protein 30g   %DAILY VALUE Vitamin A 100% | Vitamin C 10% | Calcium 6% | Iron 24%   EXCHANGES 1 Starch, 2 Vegetable, 3 Medium-Fat Meat   CARBOHYDRATE CHOICES 1 1/2

BETTY'S TIP
Not a green bean lover? Substitute your favorite frozen vegetable or frozen vegetable combo.

Cheesy Southwest Chicken Casserole

PREP **15 min** BAKE **55 min** SERVINGS **5**

3 cups uncooked mafalda (mini-lasagna noodle) pasta (6 ounces)

1 cup frozen whole kernel corn (from 1-pound bag)

1/4 cup sliced ripe olives

1/4 cup chopped fresh cilantro

1/3 cup milk

8 medium green onions, sliced (1/2 cup)

1 large roma (plum) tomato, chopped (1/2 cup)

1 jar (16 ounces) double Cheddar cheese pasta sauce

1 package (9 ounces) frozen cooked smoke-flavor chicken breast strips

1 cup shredded Colby-Monterey Jack cheese (4 ounces)

1. Heat oven to 350°. Spray rectangular baking dish, 11 × 7 × 1 1/2 inches, with cooking spray. Cook and drain pasta as directed on package.

2. Mix pasta and remaining ingredients except cheese in large bowl. Spoon into baking dish.

3. Cover and bake 45 minutes. Sprinkle with cheese. Bake uncovered 5 to 10 minutes longer or until cheese is melted and casserole is bubbly.

1 SERVING Calories 490 (Calories from Fat 215) | Fat 24g (Saturated 11g) | Cholesterol 100mg | Sodium 790mg | Carbohydrate 40g (Dietary Fiber 3g) | Protein 31g %DAILY VALUE Vitamin A 30% | Vitamin C 6% | Calcium 48% | Iron 14% EXCHANGES 2 1/2 Starch, 3 1/2 Medium-Fat Meat, 1 Fat CARBOHYDRATE CHOICES 2 1/2

BETTY'S TIP

Mafalda looks like mini-lasagna noodles and can come in long ribbons or short pieces. The short variety works best for this recipe. If you don't have mafalda on hand, use another pasta of a similar size, such as gemelli, rotini or mostaccioli.

California Chicken Bake

2 cups shredded taco-seasoned cheese (8 ounces)

3/4 cup uncooked regular long-grain rice

1/4 cup chopped fresh cilantro

1 cup salsa

1 cup water

4 boneless, skinless chicken breast halves (about 1 1/4 pounds)

PREP **15 min**   BAKE **1 hr 10 min**   SERVINGS **4**

1. Heat oven to 350°. Spray rectangular baking dish, 11 × 7 × 1 1/2 inches, with cooking spray.

2. Reserve 1/2 cup cheese. Mix remaining cheese, the rice, cilantro, salsa and water in large bowl. Spread evenly in baking dish. Arrange chicken on rice mixture.

3. Bake 55 to 65 minutes or until juice of chicken is no longer pink when centers of thickest pieces are cut and rice is tender. Sprinkle with reserved 1/2 cup cheese. Bake uncovered 5 minutes longer or until cheese is melted.

1 SERVING Calories 500 (Calories from Fat 200) | Fat 22g (Saturated 14g) | Cholesterol 130mg | Sodium 970mg | Carbohydrate 34g (Dietary Fiber 0g) | Protein 42g **%DAILY VALUE** Vitamin A 20% | Vitamin C 0% | Calcium 40% | Iron 14% **EXCHANGES** 2 Starch, 5 Lean Meat, 1 1/2 Fat **CARBOHYDRATE CHOICES** 2

BETTY'S TIP

Here's a quick trick to test the rice for doneness. Remove a small amount from the casserole and let it cool slightly. Then taste it. It's done when the rice is tender in the center.

Lemon Chicken with Broccoli

PREP **5 min**   COOK **15 min**   BAKE **40 min**   SERVINGS **6**

1. Heat oven to 350°. Spray rectangular baking dish, 13 × 9 × 2 inches, with cooking spray. Cook and drain pasta as directed on package.

2. While pasta is cooking, mix crushed crackers and lemon peel in small bowl; set aside. Spray 10-inch nonstick skillet with cooking spray; heat over medium-high heat. Cook chicken and garlic in skillet 2 to 3 minutes, stirring frequently, until chicken is brown. Remove skillet from heat; stir in pasta and remaining ingredients. Spoon chicken mixture into baking dish. Sprinkle with crumb mixture.

3. Cover and bake 25 minutes. Uncover and bake 10 to 15 minutes longer or until hot and bubbly.

1 SERVING Calories 275 (Calories from Fat 70) | Fat 8g (Saturated 2g) | Cholesterol 50mg | Sodium 660mg | Carbohydrate 29g (Dietary Fiber 3g) | Protein 25g **%DAILY VALUE** Vitamin A 24% | Vitamin C 22% | Calcium 8% | Iron 12% **EXCHANGES** 1 1/2 Starch, 1 Vegetable, 3 Very Lean Meat, 1/2 Fat **CARBOHYDRATE CHOICES** 2

2 cups uncooked farfalle (bow-tie) pasta (4 ounces)

1/4 cup crushed butter-flavor crackers

1 teaspoon grated lemon peel

1 pound boneless, skinless chicken breasts, cut into 1/4-inch strips

2 cloves garlic, finely chopped

2 cups frozen broccoli flowerets or broccoli cuts (from 1-pound bag), thawed and drained

1 cup chicken broth

1/2 cup fat-free (skim) milk

2 tablespoons lemon juice

1/8 teaspoon pepper

1 can (10 3/4 ounces) condensed reduced-fat cream of chicken soup

BETTY'S TIP

If you don't have butter-flavor cracker crumbs, regular cracker crumbs or seasoned bread crumbs also work well in this recipe.

Chicken and Cashew Bake

2 medium stalks celery, thinly sliced (1 cup)

1/4 cup chopped onion

1 tablespoon water

3 cups cubed cooked chicken breast

1 1/2 cups frozen green peas (from 1-pound bag)

1/4 cup chopped salted cashews

1/4 cup water or chicken broth

1 can (10 3/4 ounces) condensed 98% fat–free cream of chicken soup with 30% less sodium

1 jar (2 ounces) sliced pimientos, drained

1/4 cup chow mein noodles

1/4 cup salted cashew halves

PREP **15 min**   COOK **5 min**   BAKE **40 min**   SERVINGS **4**

1. Heat oven to 350°. Spray 1 1/2-quart casserole and 3-quart saucepan with cooking spray. Heat saucepan over medium-high heat; add celery, onion and 1 tablespoon water. Cover and cook 3 to 4 minutes, stirring occasionally, until vegetables are crisp-tender.

2. Stir in remaining ingredients except chow mein noodles and cashew halves. Pour into casserole.

3. Bake 30 to 35 minutes. Sprinkle chow mein noodles and cashew halves evenly over casserole. Bake 5 minutes longer or until hot.

1 SERVING Calories 430 (Calories from Fat 150) | Fat 17g (Saturated 4g) | Cholesterol 90mg | Sodium 640mg | Carbohydrate 28g (Dietary Fiber 4g) | Protein 40g **%DAILY VALUE** Vitamin A 20% | Vitamin C 34% | Calcium 6% | Iron 20% **EXCHANGES** 1 1/2 Starch, 1 Vegetable, 5 Lean Meat **CARBOHYDRATE CHOICES** 2

BETTY'S TIP

If you'd like to decrease the fat and calories of this chow mein–like casserole, simply reduce the amount of cashews and chow mein noodles.

Super-Easy
Chicken Manicotti

PREP **20 min**   BAKE **1 hr 30 min**   SERVINGS **7**

3/4 cup water

1 jar (26 to 30 ounces) tomato pasta sauce (any variety)

1 teaspoon garlic salt

1 1/2 pounds chicken breast tenders (not breaded)

14 uncooked manicotti shells (8 ounces)

2 cups shredded mozzarella cheese (8 ounces)

Chopped fresh basil leaves, if desired

1. Heat oven to 350°. Mix water and pasta sauce in medium bowl. Spread about 1 cup of the pasta sauce mixture in ungreased rectangular baking dish, $13 \times 9 \times 2$ inches.

2. Sprinkle garlic salt over chicken. Fill uncooked pasta shells with chicken, stuffing chicken from each end of shell. Place filled shells on pasta sauce in baking dish. Pour remaining pasta sauce mixture evenly over shells, covering shells completely. Sprinkle with cheese.

3. Cover dish with aluminum foil and bake about 1 hour 30 minutes or until shells are tender. Sprinkle with basil.

1 SERVING Calories 460 (Calories from Fat 115) | Fat 13g (Saturated 5g) | Cholesterol 75mg | Sodium 940mg | Carbohydrate 48g (Dietary Fiber 3g) | Protein 36g   %DAILY VALUE Vitamin A 18% | Vitamin C 14% | Calcium 28% | Iron 16%   EXCHANGES 3 Starch, 4 Lean Meat   CARBOHYDRATE CHOICES 3

BETTY'S TIP

To make this dish ahead, tightly wrap the unbaked manicotti with aluminum foil (before adding cheese) and freeze up to 1 month. Thaw, wrapped, in the refrigerator 12 hours or until completely thawed. Sprinkle with cheese, and bake as directed.

Wild Rice and Chicken Casserole

2 cups cut-up cooked chicken or turkey

1/2 cup frozen green peas (from 1-pound bag)

2 1/4 cups boiling water

1/3 cup milk

1 small onion, chopped (1/4 cup)

1 can (10 3/4 ounces) condensed cream of mushroom soup

1 package (6 ounces) seasoned long-grain and wild rice

PREP **10 min**   BAKE **1 hr 5 min**   SERVINGS **6**

1. Heat oven to 350°.

2. Mix all ingredients including seasoning packet from rice mix in ungreased 2-quart casserole.

3. Cover and bake 45 to 50 minutes or until rice is tender. Uncover and bake 10 to 15 minutes longer or until liquid is absorbed.

1 SERVING Calories 210 (Calories from Fat 65) | Fat 7g (Saturated 2g) | Cholesterol 45mg | Sodium 440mg | Carbohydrate 19g (Dietary Fiber 1g) | Protein 17g   **%DAILY VALUE** Vitamin A 6% | Vitamin C 4% | Calcium 6% | Iron 10%   **EXCHANGES** 1 Starch, 2 Lean Meat, 1/2 Fat   **CARBOHYDRATE CHOICES** 1

Wild Rice and Ham Casserole Substitute 2 cups cut-up ham for the chicken.

BETTY'S TIP

Mushroom lovers may like to add a small can of sliced mushrooms, drained, to this wild rice casserole.

Ranch Potatoes and Chicken Casserole

PREP **15 min**   BAKE **43 min**   STAND **5 min**   SERVINGS **4 to 6**

1. Heat oven to 400°. Spray 2-quart casserole with cooking spray.

2. Layer uncooked Potatoes from potato mix, the American cheese, chicken and broccoli in casserole. Mix boiling water, Sauce Mix from potato mix and cream cheese; pour over broccoli.

3. Bake uncovered 35 to 40 minutes or until potatoes are tender. Sprinkle with Topping from potato mix. Bake 3 minutes longer. Let stand 5 minutes before serving.

1 package (5.1 ounces) ranch potato mix

4 slices process American cheese

2 cups cut-up cooked chicken

1 package (10 ounces) frozen chopped broccoli, thawed and drained

2 1/4 cups boiling water

1 package (3 ounces) cream cheese, cut into cubes and softened

1 SERVING Calories 415 (Calories from Fat 180) | Fat 20g (Saturated 10g) | Cholesterol 105mg | Sodium 1140mg | Carbohydrate 33g (Dietary Fiber 4g) | Protein 30g   %DAILY VALUE Vitamin A 24% | Vitamin C 20% | Calcium 18% | Iron 8%   EXCHANGES 2 Starch, 3 Medium-Fat Meat, 1 Fat   CARBOHYDRATE CHOICES 2

BETTY'S TIP

For the sake of convenience, you may want to use a 9-ounce package of frozen diced cooked chicken, thawed, in place of the 2 cups cut-up chicken.

Country Chicken and Pasta Bake

2 cups uncooked radiatore (nugget) pasta (6 ounces)

3 cups cubed cooked chicken

2 jars (12 ounces each) chicken gravy

1 bag (1 pound) frozen broccoli, carrots and cauliflower (or other combination)

1/4 teaspoon dried thyme leaves

1/4 teaspoon salt

1/2 cup herb-seasoned stuffing crumbs

2 tablespoons butter or margarine, melted

PREP 10 min   COOK 15 min   BAKE 30 min   SERVINGS 6

1. Heat oven to 375°. Cook and drain pasta as directed on package.

2. Mix pasta and remaining ingredients except stuffing and butter. Spread in ungreased rectangular baking dish, 11 × 7 × 1 1/2 inches. Sprinkle with stuffing; drizzle with butter.

3. Cover and bake about 30 minutes or until hot.

1 SERVING Calories 390 (Calories from Fat 115) | Fat 16g (Saturated 6g) | Cholesterol 75mg | Sodium 900mg | Carbohydrate 37g (Dietary Fiber 4g) | Protein 37g %DAILY VALUE Vitamin A 60% | Vitamin C 20% | Calcium 6% | Iron 16% EXCHANGES 2 Starch, 1 Vegetable, 3 Lean Meat, 1 Fat CARBOHYDRATE CHOICES 2 1/2

BETTY'S TIP

When cooking pasta to be used in a casserole, cook only the minimum amount of time listed on the package because the pasta will continue to cook and absorb liquid while baking in the casserole.

Chicken Pot Pie with Herb Crust

1. Heat oven to 350°. Spread chicken and vegetables in ungreased rectangular pan, 13 × 9 × 2 inches.

2. Mix soup and broth; pour into pan. Mix remaining ingredients except parsley; pour evenly over soup mixture (crust will rise during baking).

3. Bake uncovered 50 to 60 minutes or until golden brown. Sprinkle with parsley.

1 SERVING Calories 350 (Calories from Fat 135) | Fat 15g (Saturated 5g) | Cholesterol 70mg | Sodium 1260mg | Carbohydrate 29g (Dietary Fiber 2g) | Protein 27g   %DAILY VALUE Vitamin A 18% | Vitamin C 10% | Calcium 14% | Iron 14%   EXCHANGES 2 Starch, 3 Medium-Fat Meat   CARBOHYDRATE CHOICES 2

Turkey Pot Pie with Herb Crust Substitute cut-up roasted turkey in place of the chicken.

4 cups cut-up cooked chicken

1 package (10 ounces) frozen mixed vegetables, thawed and drained

2 cans (10 3/4 ounces each) condensed cream of chicken soup

1 1/2 cups chicken broth

2 cups Original Bisquick® mix

1 1/2 cups milk

1/2 teaspoon dried thyme leaves

1/4 teaspoon dried sage leaves

Chopped fresh parsley, if desired

BETTY'S TIP

For 10 grams of fat and 310 calories per serving, prepare this recipe using reduced-fat cream of chicken soup, Reduced Fat Bisquick® mix and fat-free (skim) milk.

Chicken-Vegetable Strata

4 to 5 slices whole wheat or rye bread

1 1/2 cups cut-up cooked chicken or turkey

1 1/2 cups (from 1-pound bag) frozen broccoli, green beans, onions and red pepper (or other combination)

1 cup shredded Cheddar cheese (4 ounces)

4 eggs, slightly beaten

2 cups milk

1 1/2 teaspoons chopped fresh or 1/2 teaspoon dried oregano leaves

1 1/2 teaspoons chopped fresh or 1/2 teaspoon dried thyme leaves

1 teaspoon onion powder

1/4 teaspoon pepper

PREP **15 min**   CHILL **2 hr**   BAKE **1 hr 15 min**   STAND **10 min**   SERVINGS **4**

1. Trim crust edges from bread slices; cut each bread slice diagonally into 4 triangles. Arrange half of the bread in ungreased square pan, $8 \times 8 \times 2$ inches. Top with chicken and vegetables. Sprinkle with cheese. Top with remaining bread.

2. Mix remaining ingredients; pour over bread. Cover and refrigerate at least 2 hours but no longer than 24 hours, occasionally pressing bread down into egg mixture.

3. Heat oven to 325°. Cover pan with aluminum foil; bake 30 minutes. Uncover and bake about 45 minutes longer or until knife inserted in center comes out clean. Let stand 10 minutes before serving.

1 SERVING Calories 435 (Calories from Fat 190) | Fat 21g (Saturated 10g) | Cholesterol 300mg | Sodium 500mg | Carbohydrate 25g (Dietary Fiber 3g) | Protein 37g   **%DAILY VALUE** Vitamin A 38% | Vitamin C 26% | Calcium 36% | Iron 14%   **EXCHANGES** 1 1/2 Starch, 1 Vegetable, 4 Medium-Fat Meat   **CARBOHYDRATE CHOICES** 1 1/2

BETTY'S TIP

This is a great dish to turn to when you want a make-ahead meal that's ready to bake without last-minute fuss. If you like, you can also leave your bread untrimmed.

Chicken and Rice Bake

PREP **15 min**　BAKE **1 hr 30 min**　STAND **5 min**　SERVINGS **6**

1 package (6 ounces) long-grain and wild rice

3- to 3 1/2-pound cut-up broiler-fryer chicken, skinned if desired

2 medium stalks celery, sliced (1 cup)

1 jar (4.5 ounces) whole mushrooms, drained

2 cups water

1 can (10 3/4 ounces) condensed cream of chicken or cream of celery soup

Paprika

1. Heat oven to 350°. Spray rectangular baking dish, 13 × 9 × 2 inches, with cooking spray. Pour uncooked rice from rice mix evenly into baking dish. Sprinkle seasoning mix from rice mix evenly over rice. Arrange chicken over rice; arrange celery and mushrooms around chicken.

2. Mix water and soup in 2-quart saucepan; heat to boiling. Pour soup mixture evenly over chicken and vegetables. Sprinkle with paprika. Cover with aluminum foil.

3. Bake 1 hour; remove foil. Bake 20 to 30 minutes longer or until juice of chicken is no longer pink when centers of thickest pieces are cut. Let stand 5 minutes before serving.

1 SERVING Calories 390 (Calories from Fat 150) | Fat 17g (Saturated 5g) | Cholesterol 95mg | Sodium 910mg | Carbohydrate 26g (Dietary Fiber 1g) | Protein 33g %DAILY VALUE Vitamin A 8% | Vitamin C 0% | Calcium 4% | Iron 15% EXCHANGES 1 1/2 Starch, 4 Lean Meat, 1 Fat CARBOHYDRATE CHOICES 1 1/2

BETTY'S TIP

Chances are you've used paprika before, but do you know what it is? It's actually a powder made from grinding sweet red pepper pods. It's a good idea to store it in a cool, dark place for no longer than six months.

Chicken Tetrazzini Bake

1 package (7 ounces) uncooked spaghetti

1/4 cup butter or margarine

1 medium onion, sliced

1/4 cup all-purpose flour

1/2 teaspoon salt

1/2 teaspoon ground sage

1/4 teaspoon pepper

2 cups chicken broth

1 cup milk

1 jar (4.5 ounces) sliced mushrooms, drained

3 cups cubed cooked chicken or turkey

1/2 cup chopped fresh parsley

1/3 cup grated Parmesan cheese

1 jar (2 ounces) diced pimientos, drained

1/2 cup shredded Swiss cheese (2 ounces)

PREP 25 min   COOK 15 min   BAKE 30 min   SERVINGS 8

1. Heat oven to 350°. Cook and drain spaghetti as directed on package.

2. While spaghetti is cooking, melt butter in 3-quart saucepan over medium heat. Cook onion in butter, stirring occasionally, until onion is tender. Stir flour, salt, sage and pepper into onion mixture. Cook and stir until mixture is bubbly. Stir in broth, milk and mushrooms. Cook and stir until mixture boils and thickens slightly.

3. Stir in spaghetti and remaining ingredients except Swiss cheese. Pour into ungreased rectangular baking dish, 11 × 7 × 1 1/2 inches; sprinkle with Swiss cheese.

4. Bake 20 to 30 minutes or until hot and bubbly.

1 SERVING Calories 330 (Calories from Fat 130) | Fat 14g (Saturated 5g) | Cholesterol 60mg | Sodium 600mg | Carbohydrate 26g (Dietary Fiber 2g) | Protein 26g   %DAILY VALUE Vitamin A 14% | Vitamin C 20% | Calcium 20% | Iron 14%   EXCHANGES 1 1/2 Starch, 3 Lean Meat, 1 Fat   CARBOHYDRATE CHOICES 1 1/2

BETTY'S TIP

It's believed chicken tetrazzini is named for the opera singer Luisa Tetrazzini. Try serving this popular Italian dish with a tomato-mozzarella salad drizzled with olive oil.

Chicken Curry

PREP **10 min**   BAKE **30 min**   STAND **5 min**   SERVINGS **5**

1. Heat oven to 425°.

2. Mix uncooked Pasta and Sauce Mix from skillet-dinner mix and remaining ingredients except green onion in ungreased 2-quart casserole or rectangular baking dish, 11 × 7 × 1 1/2 inches.

3. Cover and bake about 30 minutes or until pasta is tender; stir. Let stand uncovered 5 minutes before serving. Sprinkle with green onion.

1 SERVING Calories 335 (Calories from Fat 135) | Fat 15g (Saturated 4g) | Cholesterol 50mg | Sodium 720mg | Carbohydrate 30g (Dietary Fiber 1g) | Protein 21g   %DAILY VALUE Vitamin A 14% | Vitamin C 0% | Calcium 2% | Iron 4%   EXCHANGES 2 Starch, 2 Medium-Fat Meat, 1/2 Fat   CARBOHYDRATE CHOICES 2

Tuna Curry Substitute a 12-ounce can of tuna for the chicken.

1 package (8.25 ounces) creamy pasta skillet-dinner mix for tuna

3 1/4 cups boiling water

1/4 cup milk

2 tablespoons butter or margarine

2 cups cut-up cooked chicken

1 to 2 teaspoons curry powder

Chopped green onion, flaked coconut or chopped peanuts, if desired

BETTY'S TIP

If you're a chutney fan, mango chutney would be a delicious condiment to serve with this simple-to-make curry dish.

Layered Chicken–Black Bean Enchiladas

2 cups chopped cooked chicken

2 tablespoons chopped fresh cilantro

1 can (15 ounces) black beans, rinsed and drained

1 can (4.5 ounces) chopped green chiles

1 can (10 ounces) enchilada sauce

8 corn tortillas (5 or 6 inches in diameter)

1 1/2 cups shredded Colby–Monterey Jack cheese (6 ounces)

1 container (8 ounces) sour cream

PREP **25 min**   BAKE **40 min**   STAND **10 min**   SERVINGS **6**

1. Heat oven to 375°. Spray rectangular baking dish, 11 × 7 × 1 1/2 inches, with cooking spray. Mix chicken, cilantro, black beans and chiles in medium bowl.

2. Spread 2 tablespoons of the enchilada sauce in bottom of baking dish. Place 4 tortillas over sauce, overlapping as necessary. Spoon half of the chicken mixture over tortillas; sprinkle with 1/2 cup cheese. Spoon half of the remaining enchilada sauce and half of the sour cream randomly over cheese. Repeat with remaining tortillas, chicken mixture, 1/2 cup cheese, the enchilada sauce and sour cream.

3. Cover with aluminum foil. Bake 30 to 35 minutes or until hot. Sprinkle remaining 1/2 cup cheese over casserole. Bake uncovered 5 minutes longer or until cheese is melted. Let stand 10 minutes before serving.

1 SERVING Calories 440 (Calories from Fat 210) | Fat 23g (Saturated 12g) | Cholesterol 85mg | Sodium 640mg | Carbohydrate 30g (Dietary Fiber 6g) | Protein 28g   %DAILY VALUE Vitamin A 14% | Vitamin C 8% | Calcium 34% | Iron 14%   EXCHANGES 2 Starch, 3 Lean Meat, 2 1/2 Fat   CARBOHYDRATE CHOICES 2

BETTY'S TIP

Spanish rice and a green salad tossed with jicama sticks and orange segments make tasty accompaniments to this Mexican specialty.

Chicken Drumstick Cacciatore Casserole

PREP **15 min**   BAKE **45 min**   SERVINGS **4**

1. Heat oven to 375°. Spray rectangular baking dish, $11 \times 7 \times 1 \ 1/2$ inches, with cooking spray.

2. Gently mix rice, zucchini, broth, tomatoes and mushrooms in baking dish. Arrange chicken over rice mixture. Sprinkle with paprika. Cover with aluminum foil.

3. Bake 30 minutes. Uncover and bake 10 to 15 minutes longer or until juice of chicken is no longer pink when centers of thickest pieces are cut.

1 cup uncooked regular long–grain rice

1 medium zucchini, sliced

1 can (14 ounces) chicken broth

1 can (14.5 ounces) diced tomatoes with Italian–style herbs, undrained

1 jar (4.5 ounces) sliced mushrooms, drained

8 chicken drumsticks, skin removed

1 teaspoon paprika

1 SERVING Calories 380 (Calories from Fat 55) | Fat 6g (Saturated 2g) | Cholesterol 80mg | Sodium 740mg | Carbohydrate 48g (Dietary Fiber 3g) | Protein 33g %DAILY VALUE Vitamin A 20% | Vitamin C 20% | Calcium 8% | Iron 24% EXCHANGES 3 Starch, 1 Vegetable, 3 Lean Meat CARBOHYDRATE CHOICES 3

BETTY'S TIP

Here's a quick trick to removing the skin from the drumsticks: Use a paper towel to grab the skin and pull it from the large end to the small end of the leg. The paper towel makes it easy to get a grip on the slippery skin.

Scalloped Chicken and Potatoes

1 package (4.8 ounces) sour cream 'n chives potato mix

2 1/4 cups boiling water

3/4 cup half-and-half or whole milk

3 cups cubed cooked chicken

1 cup frozen green peas (from 1-pound bag)

1 can (8 ounces) mushroom pieces and stems, drained

1/2 cup plain bread crumbs

1/4 cup butter or margarine, melted

1 tablespoon chopped fresh parsley

1. Heat oven to 450°. Mix Potatoes and Sauce Mix from potato mix, the water, half-and-half, chicken, peas and mushrooms in ungreased 2-quart casserole.

2. Bake uncovered 30 to 35 minutes, stirring once, until potatoes are tender.

3. Mix remaining ingredients in small bowl; sprinkle over potato mixture. Bake uncovered about 5 minutes longer or until light golden brown.

1 SERVING Calories 450 (Calories from Fat 200) | Fat 22g (Saturated 11g) | Cholesterol 110mg | Sodium 800mg | Carbohydrate 34g (Dietary Fiber 4g) | Protein 29g %DAILY VALUE Vitamin A 14% | Vitamin C 2% | Calcium 8% | Iron 14% EXCHANGES 2 Starch, 1 Vegetable, 3 Medium-Fat Meat, 1 Fat CARBOHYDRATE CHOICES 2

Scalloped Tuna and Potatoes Substitute a 12-ounce can of tuna, drained, for the chicken.

BETTY'S TIP

Cooked green beans sprinkled with grated carrots make a scrumptious side dish to this creamy comfort meal.

Baked Chicken Gumbo

PREP **35 min**   BAKE **45 min**   SERVINGS **4**

3 slices bacon, cut into
1-inch pieces

4 skinless chicken thighs
(about 1 1/4 pounds)

1 large green bell pepper,
chopped (about 1 1/2 cups)

1 large onion, chopped
(about 1 cup)

1 medium stalk celery,
chopped (about 1/2 cup)

3 cloves garlic, finely
chopped

1 package (10 ounces)
frozen cut okra, thawed
and drained

1 cup chicken broth

3/4 cup uncooked
quick-cooking brown rice

1/2 teaspoon pepper

1/4 teaspoon ground
red pepper (cayenne)

2 tablespoons chopped
fresh parsley

1. Cook bacon in 10-inch skillet over medium heat, stirring occasionally, until crisp. Remove bacon with slotted spoon and drain. Drain all but 1 tablespoon fat from skillet.

2. Heat oven to 350°. Cook chicken thighs in bacon fat over low heat about 15 minutes or until light brown on all sides. Remove chicken from skillet.

3. Cook bell pepper, onion, celery and garlic in drippings in skillet about 3 minutes, stirring frequently, until vegetables are crisp-tender. Stir in okra, broth, rice, pepper and red pepper. Heat to boiling; remove from heat. Pour rice mixture into ungreased rectangular baking dish, 11 × 7 × 1 1/2 inches. Place chicken on top.

4. Cover with aluminum foil. Bake 40 to 45 minutes or until juice of chicken is no longer pink when centers of thickest pieces are cut and rice is tender. Sprinkle with parsley and bacon.

1 SERVING Calories 320 (Calories from Fat 80) | Fat 9g (Saturated 3g) | Cholesterol 45mg | Sodium 390mg | Carbohydrate 38g (Dietary Fiber 6g) | Protein 22g %DAILY VALUE Vitamin A 8% | Vitamin C 38% | Calcium 10% | Iron 14% EXCHANGES 2 Starch, 2 Vegetable, 2 Very Lean Meat, 1 Fat CARBOHYDRATE CHOICES 2 1/2

BETTY'S TIP

Okra is a common ingredient in many southern dishes, especially gumbo. It serves to both thicken this stew-like dish and add flavor. In fact, *gumbo* is actually a derivation of the African word for "okra."

Maple-Glazed Turkey and Rice Casserole

1 package (6 ounces) long-grain and wild rice mix

1 1/2 cups water

2-pound bone-in skin-on turkey breast half

3 tablespoons maple-flavored syrup

1/2 teaspoon ground cinnamon

1/2 cup chopped walnuts

PREP **15 min**   BAKE **1 hr 15 min**   SERVINGS **4**

1. Heat oven to 350°. Mix Rice and Seasoning Packet from rice mix and water in ungreased square baking dish, 8 × 8 × 2 inches.

2. Place turkey breast half, skin side up, on rice mixture. Drizzle with maple syrup. Sprinkle with cinnamon. Insert meat thermometer so tip is in thickest part of turkey.

3. Cover and bake about 55 minutes. Sprinkle with walnuts. Bake uncovered 15 to 20 minutes longer or until rice is tender, thermometer reads 170° and juice of turkey is no longer pink when center is cut.

1 SERVING Calories 475 (Calories from Fat 180) | Fat 20g (Saturated 4g) | Cholesterol 105mg | Sodium 260mg | Carbohydrate 45g (Dietary Fiber 1g) | Protein 29g   %DAILY VALUE Vitamin A 2% | Vitamin C 0% | Calcium 4% | Iron 12%   EXCHANGES 3 Starch, 3 Lean Meat, 1 1/2 Fat   CARBOHYDRATE CHOICES 3

BETTY'S TIP

A green vegetable, such as Brussels sprouts or French green beans, would be a nice complement to this casserole. And why not pick up an apple pie from your favorite bakery for a special dessert?

Turkey Divan

PREP **25 min**   BAKE **20 min**   SERVINGS **6**

1. Heat oven to 425°. Place broccoli and water in rectangular microwavable dish, 11 × 7 × 1 1/2 inches. Cover with plastic wrap, folding back one edge or corner 1/4 inch to vent steam. Microwave on High 6 to 8 minutes or until tender; drain.

2. Meanwhile, melt butter in 2-quart saucepan over low heat. Stir flour and nutmeg into butter. Cook, stirring constantly, until smooth and bubbly; remove from heat. Stir in broth. Heat to boiling, stirring constantly. Boil and stir 1 minute; remove from heat. Stir in 1/2 cup cheese, the wine and whipping cream.

3. Arrange hot broccoli in ungreased rectangular baking dish, 13 × 9 × 2 inches. Top with turkey. Pour cheese sauce over turkey. Sprinkle with 2 tablespoons cheese.

4. Bake uncovered 15 to 20 minutes or until sauce is bubbly and cheese is light brown.

1 1/2 pounds fresh broccoli spears

2 tablespoons water

1/4 cup butter or margarine

1/4 cup all-purpose flour

1/8 teaspoon ground nutmeg

1 cup chicken broth

1/2 cup grated Parmesan cheese

2 tablespoons dry white wine or apple juice

1/2 cup whipping (heavy) cream

6 large slices cooked turkey breast, 1/8 to 1/4 inch thick (about 1 pound)

2 tablespoons grated Parmesan cheese

1 SERVING Calories 300 (Calories from Fat 160) | Fat 18g (Saturated 11g) | Cholesterol 100mg | Sodium 470mg | Carbohydrate 9g (Dietary Fiber 2g) | Protein 26g %DAILY VALUE Vitamin A 30% | Vitamin C 54% | Calcium 20% | Iron 10% EXCHANGES 2 Vegetable, 3 Lean Meat, 2 Fat CARBOHYDRATE CHOICES 1/2

BETTY'S TIP

Instead of fresh broccoli, two 10-ounce packages of frozen broccoli spears can be used instead. Cook as directed on the package, then continue with step 2.

Turkey, Carrot and Noodle Bake

2 cups uncooked egg noodles (4 ounces)

1 pound ground turkey

1 medium onion, chopped (1/2 cup)

3 medium carrots, thinly sliced (about 1 1/2 cups)

2 medium tomatoes, seeded and cut into bite-size pieces

1 jar (12 ounces) chicken or turkey gravy

1 container (8 ounces) sour cream

1 tablespoon chopped fresh or 1 teaspoon dried sage leaves

1 tablespoon chopped fresh or 1 teaspoon dried marjoram leaves

1/4 teaspoon pepper

1/2 cup buttery cracker crumbs

1/3 cup chopped pecans or walnuts

2 tablespoons butter or margarine, melted

PREP **15 min** COOK **10 min** BAKE **40 min** SERVINGS **4**

1. Heat oven to 375°. Cook and drain noodles as directed on package.

2. While noodles are cooking, cook turkey and onion in 10-inch skillet over medium heat, stirring frequently, until turkey is no longer pink; drain. Stir carrots, tomatoes, gravy, sour cream, sage, marjoram and pepper into turkey mixture. Place cooked noodles in ungreased rectangular pan, 11 × 7 × 1 1/2 inches. Gently fold in turkey mixture.

3. Cover with aluminum foil. Bake 30 minutes. Mix cracker crumbs, pecans and butter; sprinkle over turkey mixture. Bake uncovered 5 to 10 minutes longer or until hot.

1 SERVING Calories 660 (Calories from Fat 360) | Fat 40g (Saturated 12g) | Cholesterol 140mg | Sodium 880mg | Carbohydrate 42g (Dietary Fiber 2g) | Protein 34g %DAILY VALUE Vitamin A 100% | Vitamin C 14% | Calcium 12% | Iron 20% EXCHANGES 2 Starch, 2 Vegetable, 3 1/2 Medium-Fat Meat, 4 Fat CARBOHYDRATE CHOICES 3

Beef, Carrot and Noodle Bake Substitute 1 pound lean ground beef in place of the ground turkey.

BETTY'S TIP
To make quick work of seeding a tomato, cut the tomato in half along its equator, and squeeze each half to release the seeds.

Turkey with Italian Roasted Vegetables

1. Heat oven to 400°. Line jelly roll pan, 15 1/2 × 10 1/2 × 1 inch, with aluminum foil. Spray foil with cooking spray.

2. Toss all ingredients in large bowl or resealable plastic food-storage bag. Remove turkey and vegetables; place in pan. Discard remaining dressing.

3. Bake 30 to 40 minutes or until juice of turkey is no longer pink when centers of thickest pieces are cut and vegetables are tender.

1 SERVING Calories 380 (Calories from Fat 140) | Fat 15g (Saturated 2g) | Cholesterol 95mg | Sodium 300mg | Carbohydrate 25g (Dietary Fiber 3g) | Protein 37g %DAILY VALUE Vitamin A 2% | Vitamin C 34% | Calcium 4% | Iron 20% EXCHANGES 1 Starch, 2 Vegetable, 4 Lean Meat, 1/2 Fat CARBOHYDRATE CHOICES 1 1/2

Chicken with Italian Roasted Vegetables Substitute 1 pound boneless, skinless chicken breasts in place of the turkey tenderloins.

1 pound turkey breast tenderloins

1/2 cup Italian dressing

2 medium russet or Idaho baking potatoes, unpeeled, cut into 1-inch cubes

1 medium red or green bell pepper, cut into 8 pieces

1 medium onion, cut into wedges

1 package (8 ounces) whole mushrooms

1/2 teaspoon garlic pepper

BETTY'S TIP

Russet potatoes are also called baking potatoes. They are oval in shape and have skin that is brown and rough. In addition to roasting, russet potatoes are good for baking, mashing and frying because they are low in moisture and high in starch.

Turkey and Stuffing Bake

1 cup frozen cut green beans (from 1-pound bag)

1/2 cup uncooked instant rice

3 tablespoons butter or margarine

1 3/4 cups water

3 1/2 cups herb-seasoned cubed stuffing mix (from 14-ounce package)

2 cups chopped cooked turkey

1/2 cup sweetened dried cranberries

2 green onions, sliced (2 tablespoons)

1 can (10 3/4 ounces) condensed 98% fat–free cream of celery soup with 30% less sodium

PREP **25 min**　COOK **5 min**　BAKE **45 min**　SERVINGS **4**

1. Heat oven to 375°. Spray square baking dish, $8 \times 8 \times 2$ inches, with cooking spray. Mix green beans, rice, butter and water in 3-quart saucepan. Heat to boiling. Add stuffing mix. Stir in turkey, cranberries, onions and soup.

2. Spoon turkey mixture into baking dish. Spray piece of aluminum foil large enough to cover baking dish with cooking spray. Tightly cover baking dish with foil, sprayed side down.

3. Bake 30 minutes; remove foil. Bake uncovered 10 to 15 minutes longer or until casserole is light golden brown and edges start to bubble.

1 SERVING Calories 540 (Calories from Fat 135) | Fat 15g (Saturated 3g) | Cholesterol 55mg | Sodium 1160mg | Carbohydrate 73g (Dietary Fiber 6g) | Protein 28g %DAILY VALUE Vitamin A 10% | Vitamin C 4% | Calcium 20% | Iron 24% EXCHANGES 4 Starch, 2 Vegetable, 2 Medium-Fat Meat, 1/2 Fat CARBOHYDRATE CHOICES 5

BETTY'S TIP

Instant rice is available in both white and brown varieties; either can be used in this casserole. Brown rice has a nuttier, slightly chewy texture and is also slightly higher in fiber than white rice.

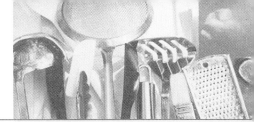

Easy Turkey Lasagna

PREP **25 min**   BAKE **45 min**   STAND **15 min**   SERVINGS **8**

3 cups chunky-style spaghetti sauce

2 cups chopped cooked turkey

1 small zucchini, shredded (1 cup)

6 uncooked lasagna noodles

1 cup ricotta cheese

1/4 cup grated Parmesan cheese

1 teaspoon dried oregano leaves

2 cups shredded mozzarella cheese (8 ounces)

1. Heat oven to 350°. Mix spaghetti sauce, turkey and zucchini. Spread 1 1/2 cups turkey mixture in ungreased rectangular baking dish, 11 × 7 × 1 1/2 inches. Top with 3 noodles.

2. Mix ricotta cheese, Parmesan cheese and oregano; spread over noodles in dish. Spread with 1 1/2 cups of the turkey mixture. Top with remaining noodles and turkey mixture. Sprinkle with mozzarella cheese.

3. Bake uncovered about 45 minutes or until hot and bubbly. Let stand 15 minutes before cutting.

1 Serving. Calories 315 (Calories from Fat 125) | Fat 14g (Saturated 6g) | Cholesterol 55mg | Sodium 870mg | Carbohydrate 23g (Dietary Fiber 2g) | Protein 26g %DAILY VALUE Vitamin A 14% | Vitamin C 4% | Calcium 36% | Iron 12% EXCHANGES 1 1/2 Starch, 3 Lean Meat, 1 Fat CARBOHYDRATE CHOICES 1 1/2

BETTY'S TIP

You may be tempted to start cutting into this cheesy lasagna right away instead of letting it stand for 15 minutes, but try to resist. If you don't let it stand, the lasagna will be too saucy and won't hold its shape.

Turkey and Corn Bread Stuffing Casserole

1 can (10 3/4 ounces) condensed cream of chicken or celery soup

1 1/4 cups milk

1 cup frozen green peas (from 1-pound bag)

1/2 cup dried cranberries

4 medium green onions, sliced (1/4 cup)

2 cups cut-up cooked turkey or chicken

1 1/2 cups corn bread stuffing mix

1 cup Original Bisquick mix

1/4 cup milk

2 eggs

PREP **10 min**   COOK **5 min**   BAKE **40 min**   SERVINGS **6**

1. Heat oven to 400°. Spray 3-quart casserole with cooking spray. Heat soup and milk to boiling in 3-quart saucepan, stirring frequently. Stir peas, cranberries and onions into soup mixture. Heat to boiling, stirring frequently; remove from heat. Stir in turkey and stuffing mix. Spoon into casserole.

2. Stir remaining ingredients until blended. Pour over stuffing mixture.

3. Bake uncovered 35 to 40 minutes or until knife inserted in center comes out clean.

1 SERVING Calories 410 (Calories from Fat 135) | Fat 15g (Saturated 4g) | Cholesterol 140mg | Sodium 1000mg | Carbohydrate 43g (Dietary Fiber 3g) | Protein 29g   %DAILY VALUE Vitamin A 12% | Vitamin C 4% | Calcium 16% | Iron 16%   EXCHANGES 3 Starch, 3 Lean Meat   CARBOHYDRATE CHOICES 3

BETTY'S TIP

No dried cranberries on hand? You can leave them out of the recipe, or use dried cherries or raisins instead.

Wild Rice and Turkey Casserole

1. Heat oven to 350°. Mix all ingredients, including seasoning packet from rice mix, except the sliced green onion in ungreased 2-quart casserole.

2. Cover and bake 45 to 50 minutes or until rice is tender. Uncover and bake 10 to 15 minutes longer or until liquid is absorbed. Sprinkle with green onion.

1 SERVING Calories 155 (Calories from Fat 45) | Fat 5g (Saturated 1g) | Cholesterol 40mg | Sodium 440mg | Carbohydrate 13g (Dietary Fiber 1g) | Protein 15g   %DAILY VALUE Vitamin A 2% | Vitamin C 2% | Calcium 4% | Iron 6%   EXCHANGES 1 Starch, 2 Very Lean Meat   CARBOHYDRATE CHOICES 1

2 cups cut-up cooked turkey or chicken

2 1/4 cups boiling water

1/3 cup fat-free (skim) milk

4 medium green onions, sliced (1/4 cup)

1 can (10 3/4 ounces) condensed 98% fat-free cream of mushroom soup

1 package (6 ounces) original-flavor long-grain and wild rice mix

Sliced green onion, if desired

BETTY'S TIP

If you don't have cream of mushroom soup available, you can also use cream of chicken or cream of celery.

Home-Style Turkey and Potato Bake

1/2 package (7.2-ounce size) roasted garlic mashed potato mix (1 pouch)

Water, milk, margarine or butter called for on potato mix package

4 medium green onions, sliced (1/4 cup)

2 cups chopped cooked turkey

1 bag (1 pound) frozen mixed vegetables, thawed and drained

1 jar (12 ounces) home-style turkey gravy

1/4 teaspoon poultry seasoning

1. Heat oven to 350°. Spray 2-quart casserole with cooking spray. Make potatoes as directed on package for 4 servings, using 1 pouch potatoes and seasoning, water, milk and margarine; let stand 3 to 5 minutes. Stir in onions.

2. Heat turkey, vegetables, gravy and poultry seasoning to boiling in 2-quart saucepan over medium-high heat. Pour turkey mixture into casserole. Spoon or pipe potatoes around edge of casserole.

3. Bake uncovered about 30 minutes or until heated through and potatoes are light brown.

1 SERVING Calories 280 (Calories from Fat 115) | Fat 13g (Saturated 3g) | Cholesterol 45mg | Sodium 720mg | Carbohydrate 22g (Dietary Fiber 6g) | Protein 19g   %DAILY VALUE Vitamin A 54% | Vitamin C 22% | Calcium 6% | Iron 8%   EXCHANGES 1 Starch, 1 Vegetable, 2 Medium-Fat Meat, 1/2 Fat   CARBOHYDRATE CHOICES 1 1/2

BETTY'S TIP

After spooning potatoes around edge of casserole, swirl the tops with the back of the spoon. For a fancier presentation, place potatoes in a pastry bag fitted with a large star tip and pipe onto the casserole; sprinkle with paprika.

Turkey and Tortilla Casserole

PREP **10 min**   BAKE **20 min**   SERVINGS **8**

1. Heat oven to 350°. Heat enchilada sauce in 12-inch skillet over medium heat, stirring occasionally, until warm. Dip each tortilla into warm enchilada sauce to coat both sides.

2. Place 4 of the tortillas in ungreased pie plate, 9 × 1 1/4 inches, with edges overlapping. Top with half of the remaining enchilada sauce, 1 cup of the turkey and 1 cup cheese. Arrange 4 tortillas over cheese. Repeat layers, using remaining enchilada sauce, turkey and cheese.

3. Bake uncovered about 20 minutes or until cheese is melted. Serve with guacamole or chopped tomato.

1 SERVING Calories 465 (Calories from Fat 125) | Fat 14g (Saturated 5g) | Cholesterol 45mg | Sodium 920mg | Carbohydrate 58g (Dietary Fiber 4g) | Protein 27g   %DAILY VALUE Vitamin A 12% | Vitamin C 6% | Calcium 34% | Iron 24%   EXCHANGES 4 Starch, 2 Medium-Fat Meat   CARBOHYDRATE CHOICES 4

2 cups green enchilada sauce or green taco sauce

8 flour tortillas (about 12 inches in diameter)

2 cups cut-up cooked turkey or chicken

2 cups shredded mozzarella cheese (8 ounces)

Guacamole, if desired

Chopped tomato, if desired

BETTY'S TIP

Instead of mozzarella cheese, try using one of the Mexican cheese blends available instead. They are usually combinations of some or all of the following: Monterey Jack, Cheddar, asadero or queso blanco cheeses and taco seasonings.

Ham and Brie Bake

1/4 cup milk

1 tablespoon butter
or margarine, melted

1 egg

6 slices rye bread, cut into
cubes (6 cups)

1 1/4 cups coarsely
chopped fully cooked ham
(8 ounces)

1 medium pear, peeled
and chopped

3 green onions, sliced
(3 tablespoons)

8 ounces Brie cheese,
peeled and cut into cubes

PREP **20 min**   BAKE **30 min**   SERVINGS **6**

1. Heat oven to 350°. Spray square baking dish, $8 \times 8 \times 2$ inches, with cooking spray.

2. Beat milk, butter and egg in medium bowl. Add bread cubes, ham, pear and onions; toss. Spread bread mixture in baking dish. Top with cheese.

3. Bake uncovered 25 to 30 minutes or until pears are tender and cheese is melted.

1 SERVING Calories 295 (Calories from Fat 155) | Fat 17g (Saturated 8g) | Cholesterol 85mg | Sodium 1100mg | Carbohydrate 13g (Dietary Fiber 1g) | Protein 17g   %DAILY VALUE Vitamin A 14% | Vitamin C 2% | Calcium 18% | Iron 8%   EXCHANGES 1 Starch, 2 1/2 Medium-Fat Meat, 1/2 Fat   CARBOHYDRATE CHOICES 1

Turkey and Brie Bake Substitute chopped smoked turkey for the ham.

BETTY'S TIP

This strata-like casserole is a great, hearty dish to serve for brunch. Keep things simple by serving it with steamed asparagus and a variety of fresh fruit.

Ham and Asparagus with Cashews

PREP **10 min**   BAKE **35 min**   SERVINGS **6**

1. Heat oven to 350°. Spray 2-quart casserole with cooking spray.

2. Mix soup, milk, sour cream and mustard in casserole. Stir in remaining ingredients except cashews. Sprinkle with cashews.

3. Bake uncovered 30 to 35 minutes or until asparagus is tender.

1 can (10 3/4 ounces) condensed reduced-fat cream of chicken soup

1/2 cup fat-free (skim) milk

1/2 cup reduced-fat sour cream

1/2 teaspoon ground mustard

2 cups chopped fully cooked lean ham

1 package (10 ounces) frozen asparagus cuts, thawed and drained

3 cups cooked brown or white rice

1/4 cup cashew pieces

1 SERVING Calories 305 (Calories from Fat 100) | Fat 11g (Saturated 3g) | Cholesterol 35mg | Sodium 1140mg | Carbohydrate 33g (Dietary Fiber 3g) | Protein 18g   %DAILY VALUE Vitamin A 14% | Vitamin C 8% | Calcium 8% | Iron 10%   EXCHANGES 2 Starch, 1 Vegetable, 1 1/2 Lean Meat, 1 Fat CARBOHYDRATE CHOICES 2

Chicken and Broccoli with Cashews Substitute 2 cups cooked chicken for the ham and 1 package frozen broccoli cuts for the asparagus.

BETTY'S TIP

Want to bulk up the fiber of this all-in-one casserole? Simply use brown rice instead of white and serve with slices of whole-grain bread.

Do-Ahead Sausage Lasagna

1 1/4 pounds bulk Italian sausage

1 jar (26 to 28 ounces) tomato pasta sauce (any variety)

1 package (25 to 27 1/2 ounces) frozen cheese-filled ravioli

2 1/2 cups shredded mozzarella cheese (10 ounces)

2 tablespoons grated Parmesan cheese

PREP **10 min**   COOK **10 min**   CHILL **8 hr**   BAKE **1 hr**   STAND **10 min**   SERVINGS **8**

1. Cook sausage in 10-inch skillet over medium heat 8 to 10 minutes, stirring occasionally, until no longer pink; drain.

2. Spread 1/2 cup of the pasta sauce in ungreased rectangular pan, 13 × 9 × 2 inches. Arrange single layer of frozen ravioli over sauce; pour 1 cup pasta sauce evenly over ravioli. Sprinkle evenly with 1 1/2 cups sausage and 1 cup of the mozzarella cheese. Repeat layers with remaining ravioli, pasta sauce and sausage.

3. Cover tightly with aluminum foil and refrigerate at least 8 hours but no longer than 24 hours.

4. Heat oven to 350°. Bake covered 45 minutes. Remove foil; sprinkle with remaining 1 1/2 cups mozzarella and the Parmesan cheese. Bake about 15 minutes longer or until cheese is melted and lasagna is hot in center. Let stand 10 minutes before cutting.

1 SERVING Calories 540 (Calories from Fat 280) | Fat 31g (Saturated 13g) | Cholesterol 150mg | Sodium 1920mg | Carbohydrate 35g (Dietary Fiber 2g) | Protein 32g   %DAILY VALUE Vitamin A 22% | Vitamin C 12% | Calcium 48% | Iron 14%   EXCHANGES 2 Starch, 1 Vegetable, 3 1/2 High-Fat Meat, 2 Fat   CARBOHYDRATE CHOICES 2

BETTY'S TIP

This easy, cheesy casserole is a crowd pleaser. Serve it with thick slices of garlic bread or buttered Vienna bread and a tossed green salad. If you still have room for dessert, offer scoops of raspberry and chocolate sorbet.

Sausage and Pizza Bake

1. Heat oven to 350°. Spray 3-quart casserole with cooking spray. Cook and drain pasta in 3-quart saucepan as directed on package. Return pasta to saucepan.

2. While pasta is cooking, cook sausage and onion in 10-inch skillet over medium heat 8 to 10 minutes, stirring occasionally, until sausage is no longer pink; drain. Stir sausage mixture, bell pepper, water, bacon, pizza sauce and mushrooms into pasta. Spoon pasta mixture into casserole. Sprinkle with cheese.

3. Cover and bake 30 to 35 minutes or until hot and cheese is melted.

1 SERVING Calories 560 (Calories from Fat 200) | Fat 22g (Saturated 8g) | Cholesterol 60mg | Sodium 1270mg | Carbohydrate 56g (Dietary Fiber 4g) | Protein 26g   %DAILY VALUE Vitamin A 12% | Vitamin C 20% | Calcium 14% | Iron 18%   EXCHANGES 4 Starch, 2 High-Fat Meat   CARBOHYDRATE CHOICES 4

3 cups uncooked rotini pasta (9 ounces)

1 pound bulk Italian sausage

1 medium onion, chopped (1/2 cup)

1 small bell pepper, chopped (1/2 cup)

1/4 cup water

4 ounces sliced Canadian-style bacon, cut into fourths

1 jar or can (14 or 15 ounces) pizza sauce

1 can (4 ounces) sliced mushrooms, drained

3/4 cup shredded pizza cheese blend (3 ounces)

BETTY'S TIP

Be sure to thoroughly drain the cooked pasta—a few hard shakes of the colander after the water drains should do it. Excess cooking water clinging to the pasta will dilute the sauce.

Smoked Sausage Baked Beans

2 cans (55 ounces each)
baked beans

1 ring (1 pound) fully
cooked smoked sausage,
cubed

2 jalapeño chilies, seeded
and finely chopped

1 tablespoon ground
cumin

1 tablespoon chili powder

PREP **10 min**   BAKE **1 hr**   SERVINGS **24**

1. Heat oven to 350°. Mix all ingredients in large bowl;
   spoon into ungreased 4-quart casserole.

2. Bake uncovered 45 to 60 minutes or until hot and bubbly.

1 SERVING Calories 180 (Calories from Fat 65) | Fat 7g (Saturated 3g) |
Cholesterol 20mg | Sodium 770mg | Carbohydrate 26g (Dietary Fiber 6g) |
Protein 9g   %DAILY VALUE Vitamin A 26% | Vitamin C 4% | Calcium 8% |
Iron 26%   EXCHANGES 2 Starch, 1/2 Medium-Fat Meat   CARBOHYDRATE
CHOICES 2

BETTY'S TIP

This dish makes for great potluck fare, especially when you make it in
a slow cooker. Mix all ingredients in a 3 1/2- to 6-quart slow cooker.
Cover and cook on Low heat setting 4 to 5 hours (or High heat setting
2 to 2 1/2 hours) or until desired consistency and flavors are blended.

Mashed Potato and Sausage Casserole

PREP **20 min**   COOK **10 min**   BAKE **57 min**   SERVINGS **5**

1 pound bulk pork sausage

1 bag (1 pound) frozen mixed vegetables

1 cup onion-seasoned beef broth (from 14-ounce can)

3 tablespoons all-purpose flour

1/2 package (7.2-ounce size) roasted garlic mashed potato mix (1 pouch)

Water, milk, margarine or butter called for on potato mix package

1. Heat oven to 425°. Spray square baking dish, 8 × 8 × 2 inches, with cooking spray. Cook sausage in 10-inch skillet over medium heat 8 to 10 minutes, stirring frequently, until no longer pink; drain. Mix sausage and frozen vegetables in baking dish. Mix broth and flour in small bowl. Pour over sausage mixture; gently stir.

2. Cover and bake 35 to 45 minutes, stirring occasionally, until mixture is hot, bubbly and slightly thickened.

3. Make potatoes as directed on package for 4 servings, using 1 pouch Potatoes and Seasoning, water, milk and margarine; let stand 3 to 5 minutes. Spoon onto sausage mixture. Bake uncovered 8 to 12 minutes or until potatoes start to brown.

1 SERVING Calories 400 (Calories from Fat 215) | Fat 24g (Saturated 7g) | Cholesterol 40mg | Sodium 950mg | Carbohydrate 30g (Dietary Fiber 4g) | Protein 16g   %DAILY VALUE Vitamin A 62% | Vitamin C 32% | Calcium 14% | Iron 8%   EXCHANGES 2 Starch, 1 1/2 High-Fat Meat, 2 Fat   CARBOHYDRATE CHOICES 2

BETTY'S TIP

You can substitute 1 pound fully cooked kielbasa or Polish sausage, cut into 1/2-inch slices, for the bulk pork sausage. Omit the cooking in step 1, and just mix the kielbasa with the vegetables.

Cajun Pork Tenderloin with Vegetables

2 teaspoons Cajun
or Creole seasoning

1-pound pork tenderloin

2 medium baking or Yukon
gold potatoes, peeled

4 small zucchini (1 pound)

1 1/2 cups frozen small
whole onions (from
1-pound bag)

2 tablespoons butter
or margarine, melted

1/2 teaspoon dried thyme
leaves

1/4 teaspoon salt

PREP 15 min   BAKE 35 min   STAND 10 min   SERVINGS 4

1. Heat oven to 425°. Rub Cajun seasoning into pork. Place pork in ungreased jelly roll pan, 15 1/2 × 10 1/2 × 1 inch. Insert meat thermometer horizontally into center of thickest part of pork.

2. Cut potatoes and zucchini lengthwise in half. Arrange potatoes, zucchini and onions around pork. Drizzle butter over vegetables; sprinkle with thyme and salt.

3. Bake uncovered about 35 minutes or until thermometer reads 155°. Loosely cover pan with aluminum foil and let stand about 10 minutes or until thermometer reads 160°. Cut pork into thin slices. Serve with vegetables.

1 SERVING Calories 260 (Calories from Fat 90) | Fat 10g (Saturated 5g) | Cholesterol 85mg | Sodium 240mg | Carbohydrate 18g (Dietary Fiber 3g) | Protein 28g %DAILY VALUE Vitamin A 22% | Vitamin C 16% | Calcium 4% | Iron 12% EXCHANGES 1/2 Starch, 2 Vegetable, 3 Lean Meat CARBOHYDRATE CHOICES 1

BETTY'S TIP
Serve this pork and veggie dish with creamy coleslaw and soft, tender dinner rolls.

Roasted Pork Chops and Vegetables

PREP **20 min**   BAKE **1 hr**   SERVINGS **4**

1. Heat oven to 425°. Spray jelly roll pan, 15 1/2 × 10 1/2 × 1 inch, with cooking spray. Remove fat from pork. Mix parsley, marjoram, thyme, garlic salt and pepper. Spray both sides of pork chops with cooking spray. Sprinkle with 1 to 1 1/2 teaspoons herb mixture. Place pork chop in each corner of pan.

2. Mix potatoes, mushrooms, bell pepper and onion in large bowl. Spray vegetables 2 or 3 times with cooking spray; stir. Sprinkle with remaining herb mixture; toss to coat. Spread evenly in center of pan.

3. Bake uncovered 45 minutes. Turn pork; stir vegetables. Place tomato wedges on vegetables. Bake uncovered 10 to 15 minutes longer or until pork is no longer pink when cut near bone and vegetables are tender.

1 SERVING Calories 265 (Calories from Fat 65) | Fat 7g (Saturated 2g) | Cholesterol 55mg | Sodium 170mg | Carbohydrate 28g (Dietary Fiber 4g) | Protein 23g %DAILY VALUE Vitamin A 6% | Vitamin C 40% | Calcium 2% | Iron 8% EXCHANGES 1 1/2 Starch, 1 Vegetable, 2 Lean Meat CARBOHYDRATE CHOICES 2

4 pork rib chops, 1/2 inch thick (1 pound)

2 teaspoons parsley flakes

1/2 teaspoon dried marjoram leaves

1/2 teaspoon dried thyme leaves

1/2 teaspoon garlic salt

1/4 teaspoon coarsely ground pepper

Olive oil–flavored cooking spray

6 new potatoes, cut into fourths (3 cups)

4 ounces mushrooms, cut in half (1 1/2 cups)

1 medium red bell pepper, cut into 1-inch pieces

1 medium onion, cut into thin wedges

1 medium tomato, cut into 8 wedges

BETTY'S TIP

Love veggies? Add sliced carrots, zucchini and red, yellow and green bell peppers to the vegetable mixture for a jolt of color, texture and flavor.

Lamb and Lentil Casserole

2 slices bacon, cut into 1-inch pieces

1 tablespoon vegetable oil

1 pound lamb boneless loin or shoulder, cut into 3/4-inch pieces

3 medium carrots, thinly sliced (about 1 1/2 cups)

1 large onion, cut in half and sliced

1 can (14 1/2 ounces) stewed tomatoes

1 can (8 ounces) tomato sauce

1 cup dried lentils, sorted and rinsed

1 cup water

1 tablespoon packed brown sugar

1 tablespoon chopped fresh or 1 teaspoon dried thyme leaves

1 tablespoon chopped fresh or 1 teaspoon dried savory leaves

1/4 teaspoon salt

1/4 teaspoon pepper

PREP 25 min   COOK 10 min   BAKE 55 min   SERVINGS 4

1. Heat oven to 350°. Cook bacon in 4-quart Dutch oven over medium heat, stirring occasionally, until bacon is crisp. Remove bacon with slotted spoon; drain. Drain fat from Dutch oven.

2. Heat oil in same Dutch oven over medium heat until hot. Cook lamb in oil, stirring frequently, until brown; drain fat. Stir bacon and remaining ingredients into lamb. Heat to boiling; remove from heat.

3. Spoon lamb mixture into ungreased 2-quart casserole. Cover and bake 50 to 55 minutes, stirring occasionally, until lamb and lentils are tender.

1 SERVING Calories 490 (Calories from Fat 125) | Fat 14g (Saturated 4g) | Cholesterol 85mg | Sodium 900mg | Carbohydrate 50g (Dietary Fiber 14g) | Protein 41g %DAILY VALUE Vitamin A 100% | Vitamin C 24% | Calcium 8% | Iron 42% EXCHANGES 3 Starch, 1 Vegetable, 4 Lean Meat CARBOHYDRATE CHOICES 3

Pork and Lentil Casserole Substitute pork boneless loin or shoulder for the lamb.

BETTY'S TIP

When buying lamb, let color be your guide: Look for lamb that's pinkish red with a velvety texture and a thin, firm layer of fat surrounding it. Keep in mind the darker the meat, the older the animal and stronger the flavor.

Parmesan-Shrimp Pasta Bake

PREP 15 min   COOK 5 min   BAKE 40 min   SERVINGS 8

1. Heat oven to 350°. Spray shallow 2-quart casserole with cooking spray. Cook and drain pasta as directed on package. Melt butter in 2-quart saucepan over medium heat. Cook garlic in butter 1 minute, stirring constantly. Stir in flour. Cook, stirring constantly with wire whisk, until smooth and bubbly.

2. Stir in vermouth. Stir in half-and-half, clam juice, tomato paste, salt and pepper. Cook over medium heat, stirring constantly, until thickened. Stir in shrimp, dill weed and 1/4 cup of the cheese.

3. Stir pasta into shrimp mixture. Pour into casserole. Sprinkle with remaining 1/2 cup cheese. Bake uncovered 35 to 40 minutes or until light brown and hot.

1 SERVING Calories 480 (Calories from Fat 100) | Fat 22g (Saturated 13g) | Cholesterol 115mg | Sodium 560mg | Carbohydrate 53g (Dietary Fiber 2g) | Protein 20g   %DAILY VALUE Vitamin A 18% | Vitamin C 2% | Calcium 22% | Iron 20%   EXCHANGES 3 Starch, 1 Vegetable, 1 Medium-Fat Meat, 3 Fat CARBOHYDRATE CHOICES 3 1/2

1 package (16 ounces) farfalle (bow-tie) pasta

6 tablespoons butter or margarine

3 cloves garlic, finely chopped

6 tablespoons all-purpose flour

1/3 cup dry vermouth

2 3/4 cups half-and-half

1/2 cup clam juice

1 tablespoon tomato paste

3/4 teaspoon salt

1/4 teaspoon pepper

1 pound uncooked peeled deveined medium shrimp, thawed if frozen and tails peeled

2 tablespoons chopped fresh or 2 teaspoons dried dill weed

3/4 cup freshly grated Parmesan cheese

BETTY'S TIP

Need some last-minute substitutions? You can use white wine, chicken broth or clam juice in place of the vermouth. Cocktail sauce or ketchup can be substituted for the tomato paste.

Tuna Twist
Casserole

PREP **10 min**   BAKE **20 min**   SERVINGS **6**

1/2 cup reduced-fat
Alfredo pasta sauce

2 eggs

1 clove garlic, finely
chopped

4 cups cooked tricolor
rotelle pasta

2 cups (from 1-pound bag)
frozen broccoli, carrots
and cauliflower (or other
combination), thawed and
drained

1 can (12 ounces) tuna
in water, drained

1 cup seasoned croutons

1. Heat oven to 350°.

2. Mix Alfredo sauce, eggs and garlic in ungreased square
   baking dish, $8 \times 8 \times 2$ inches. Stir in pasta, vegetables
   and tuna. Press lightly in baking dish.

3. Cover and bake about 20 minutes or until set. Sprinkle
   with croutons.

1 SERVING Calories 285 (Calories from Fat 35) | Fat 4g (Saturated 2g) |
Cholesterol 95mg | Sodium 380mg | Carbohydrate 34g (Dietary Fiber 3g) |
Protein 24g   %DAILY VALUE Vitamin A 22% | Vitamin C 8% | Calcium 8% |
Iron 14%   EXCHANGES 2 Starch, 1 Vegetable, 2 Lean Meat   CARBOHYDRATE
CHOICES 2

BETTY'S TIP

Feel free to use regular Alfredo sauce and tuna in oil, but you save
8 grams of fat per serving by using the reduced-fat version of
Alfredo sauce and tuna packed in water.

Tuna and Noodles with Mushroom Sauce

PREP **10 min**   COOK **15 min**   BAKE **40 min**   SERVINGS **6**

1. Heat oven to 350°. Cook and drain noodles as directed on package.

2. Mix noodles, tuna, mushrooms, sour cream, milk, chives, salt and pepper in ungreased 2-quart casserole or square baking dish, 8 × 8 × 2 inches. Mix bread crumbs, cheese and butter; sprinkle over tuna mixture.

3. Bake uncovered 35 to 40 minutes or until hot in center.

1 SERVING Calories 395 (Calories from Fat 170) | Fat 19g (Saturated 9g) | Cholesterol 95mg | Sodium 860mg | Carbohydrate 32g (Dietary Fiber 2g) | Protein 24g %DAILY VALUE Vitamin A 14% | Vitamin C 0% | Calcium 18% | Iron 16% EXCHANGES 2 Starch, 2 1/2 Lean Meat, 2 Fat CARBOHYDRATE CHOICES 2

4 cups uncooked egg noodles (8 ounces)

2 cans (6 ounces each) tuna, drained

1 cup sliced mushrooms (3 ounces)

1 1/2 cups sour cream

3/4 cup milk

1 tablespoon chopped fresh chives

1 teaspoon salt

1/4 teaspoon pepper

1/4 cup dry bread crumbs

1/4 cup grated Romano cheese

2 tablespoons butter or margarine, melted

BETTY'S TIP

Creamy and comforting, this dish is well partnered with a loaf of dilled herb bread and steamed asparagus spears topped with bread crumbs browned in butter.

Salmon Macaroni Casserole

1 1/3 cups uncooked medium pasta shells or elbow macaroni (4 ounces)

White Sauce (below right)

1 1/2 cups shredded sharp process American or Cheddar cheese (6 ounces)

1 tablespoon chopped fresh or 1 teaspoon dried marjoram leaves

2 cups cooked broccoli flowerets

1 can (6 ounces) skinless boneless pink salmon, drained and flaked

PREP 10 min   COOK 15 min   BAKE 30 min   SERVINGS 4

1. Heat oven to 350°. Cook and drain pasta as directed on package.

2. While pasta is cooking, make White Sauce. Stir 1 cup of the cheese and the marjoram into sauce until cheese is melted.

3. Mix pasta, broccoli, salmon and sauce in ungreased 2-quart casserole. Cover and bake 25 minutes. Sprinkle with remaining 1/2 cup cheese. Bake uncovered about 5 minutes longer or until heated through.

White Sauce

1/4 cup butter or margarine

1/4 cup all-purpose flour

1/2 teaspoon salt

1/4 teaspoon pepper

2 cups milk

Melt butter in 1 1/2-quart saucepan over low heat. Stir in flour, salt and pepper. Cook over medium heat, stirring constantly, until mixture is smooth and bubbly; remove from heat. Gradually stir in milk. Heat sauce to boiling, stirring constantly. Boil and stir 1 minute.

1 SERVING Calories 560 (Calories from Fat 280) | Fat 31g (Saturated 18g) | Cholesterol 110mg | Sodium 950mg | Carbohydrate 40g (Dietary Fiber 4g) | Protein 30g   %DAILY VALUE Vitamin A 50% | Vitamin C 26% | Calcium 50% | Iron 16%   EXCHANGES 1 1/2 Starch, 1 Milk, 1 Vegetable, 2 1/2 Medium-Fat Meat, 3 Fat   CARBOHYDRATE CHOICES 2 1/2

BETTY'S TIP

With so many pasta shapes available, why not experiment with a different shape next time you make this casserole? Be sure to use a pasta of similar size, though, such as wagon wheel, rotini, mini penne or farfalle.

Cheddar Strata with Onions

PREP **5 min**   COOK **8 min**   BAKE **1 hr**   STAND **10 min**   SERVINGS **6**

1 teaspoon vegetable oil

2 medium onions, sliced

8 slices rye bread

2 tablespoons Dijon
mustard

1 1/2 cups shredded
Cheddar cheese (6 ounces)

1 large tomato, seeded
and coarsely chopped
(1 cup)

1 1/2 cups milk

4 eggs

1.   Heat oven to 300°. Spray square baking dish, 8 × 8 × 2 inches, with cooking spray. Heat oil in 10-inch nonstick skillet over medium-high heat. Cook onions in oil 6 to 8 minutes, stirring frequently, until golden brown; remove from heat.

2.   Trim crusts from bread. Spread mustard on one side of each bread slice. Arrange 4 slices, mustard sides up, in baking dish. Layer 1 cup of the cheese, the tomato and onions on bread. Place remaining bread, mustard sides down, on onions. Beat milk and eggs until well blended. Pour evenly over bread.

3.   Bake uncovered about 1 hour or until center is set and bread is golden brown. Sprinkle with remaining 1/2 cup cheese. Let stand 10 minutes before cutting.

1 SERVING Calories 280 (Calories from Fat 145) | Fat 16g (Saturated 8g) | Cholesterol 175mg | Sodium 490mg | Carbohydrate 21g (Dietary Fiber 3g) | Protein 16g   %DAILY VALUE Vitamin A 16% | Vitamin C 6% | Calcium 26% | Iron 8%   EXCHANGES 1 Starch, 1 Vegetable, 1 1/2 High-Fat Meat, 1/2 Fat CARBOHYDRATE CHOICES 1 1/2

BETTY'S TIP

This dish can be assembled and refrigerated up to 24 hours before baking. You may need to add 5 to 10 minutes to the bake time.

Mozzarella and Pesto Strata

16 slices French bread, 3/4 inch thick (1/2-pound loaf)

1/2 cup basil pesto

1/2 cup sliced ripe olives

1 cup roasted red bell peppers (from 12-ounce jar), drained and sliced

2 cups shredded mozzarella cheese (8 ounces)

8 eggs

2 cups milk

1/4 teaspoon salt

1/8 teaspoon pepper

2 tablespoons freshly shredded Parmesan cheese

PREP **15 min**   CHILL **2 hr**   BAKE **1 hr**   STAND **5 min**   SERVINGS **8**

1. Spray rectangular baking dish, 13 × 9 × 2 inches, with cooking spray. Spread one side of each bread slice with pesto. Arrange bread, pesto sides up, in baking dish, cutting to fit if necessary. Sprinkle with olives, bell peppers and mozzarella cheese.

2. Beat eggs, milk, salt and pepper until well blended. Pour evenly over cheese in dish. Sprinkle with Parmesan cheese. Cover and refrigerate at least 2 hours but no longer than 24 hours.

3. Heat oven to 325°. Bake uncovered 55 to 60 minutes or until knife inserted in center comes out clean and top is golden brown. Let stand 5 minutes before cutting.

1 SERVING Calories 405 (Calories from Fat 200) | Fat 22g (Saturated 8g) | Cholesterol 235mg | Sodium 830mg | Carbohydrate 32g (Dietary Fiber 2g) | Protein 22g %DAILY VALUE Vitamin A 22% | Vitamin C 24% | Calcium 42% | Iron 16% EXCHANGES 2 Starch, 2 High-Fat Meat, 1 Fat CARBOHYDRATE CHOICES 2

BETTY'S TIP
Don't throw away that day-old bread! Slightly dried-out bread slices are great for soaking up all the wonderful flavors in this dish.

Lazy-Day Lasagna

PREP **15** min   BAKE **1** hr   STAND **15** min   SERVINGS **8**

1 container (15 ounces) ricotta cheese

1/2 cup grated Parmesan cheese

2 tablespoons chopped fresh parsley

1 tablespoon chopped fresh or 1 1/2 teaspoons dried oregano leaves

2 jars (28 ounces each) tomato pasta sauce

12 uncooked lasagna noodles (12 ounces)

2 cups shredded mozzarella cheese (8 ounces)

1/4 cup grated Parmesan cheese

Additional shredded mozzarella cheese, if desired

1. Heat oven to 350°. Mix ricotta cheese, 1/2 cup Parmesan cheese, the parsley and oregano.

2. Spread 2 cups of the pasta sauce in ungreased rectangular pan, 13 × 9 × 2 inches. Top with 4 uncooked noodles; spread ricotta mixture over noodles. Spread with 2 cups pasta sauce; top with 4 noodles. Repeat with 2 cups pasta sauce and 4 noodles. Sprinkle with 2 cups mozzarella cheese. Spread with remaining pasta sauce. Sprinkle with 1/4 cup Parmesan cheese.

3. Cover and bake 30 minutes. Uncover and bake about 30 minutes longer or until hot in center. Sprinkle with additional mozzarella cheese. Let stand 15 minutes before cutting.

1 SERVING Calories 500 (Calories from Fat 160) | Fat 19g (Saturated 8g) | Cholesterol 35mg | Sodium 1340mg | Carbohydrate 64g (Dietary Fiber 4g) | Protein 24g   %DAILY VALUE Vitamin A 26% | Vitamin C 26% | Calcium 50% | Iron 16%   EXCHANGES 4 Starch, 1 Vegetable, 1 1/2 Medium-Fat Meat, 1 Fat CARBOHYDRATE CHOICES 4

BETTY'S TIP

This lasagna can be covered with aluminum foil and refrigerated for up to 24 hours before baking. About 1 1/2 hours before serving, heat the oven to 350°. Bake the covered lasagna 45 minutes. Uncover and bake 15 to 20 minutes longer or until hot and bubbly. Sprinkle with additional mozzarella cheese. Let stand 15 minutes before cutting.

Vegetable Strata

8 slices whole wheat bread

1 bag (1 pound) frozen broccoli, green beans, pearl onions and red peppers (or other combination), thawed and drained

2 cups shredded sharp Cheddar cheese (8 ounces)

8 eggs, slightly beaten

4 cups milk

1/2 teaspoon salt

1/2 teaspoon ground mustard

1/4 teaspoon pepper

1/8 teaspoon ground red pepper (cayenne)

PREP **15 min**   CHILL **2 hr**   BAKE **1 hr 15 min**   STAND **10 min**   SERVINGS **8**

1. Cut each bread slice diagonally into 4 triangles. Arrange half of the bread in ungreased rectangular pan, $13 \times 9 \times 2$ inches. Top with vegetables. Sprinkle with cheese. Top with remaining bread.

2. Beat remaining ingredients until blended; pour over bread. Cover and refrigerate at least 2 hours but no longer than 24 hours.

3. Heat oven to 325°. Cover and bake 30 minutes. Uncover and bake about 45 minutes longer or until knife inserted in center comes out clean. Let stand 10 minutes before cutting.

1 SERVING Calories 325 (Calories from Fat 160) | Fat 18g (Saturated 9g) | Cholesterol 250mg | Sodium 600mg | Carbohydrate 23g (Dietary Fiber 3g) | Protein 21g   %DAILY VALUE Vitamin A 26% | Vitamin C 24% | Calcium 36% | Iron 10%   EXCHANGES 1 Starch, 1 Milk, 1 High-Fat Meat, 1 Fat   CARBOHYDRATE CHOICES 1 1/2

BETTY'S TIP

Instead of whole wheat bread, you can also use white or rye bread in this easy-to-whip-up veggie strata.

Macaroni and Cheese

PREP **15 min**   COOK **10 min**   BAKE **25 min**   SERVINGS **4**

2 cups uncooked elbow macaroni (7 ounces)

1/4 cup butter or margarine

1/4 cup all-purpose flour

1/2 teaspoon salt

1/4 teaspoon pepper

1/4 teaspoon ground mustard

1/4 teaspoon Worcestershire sauce

2 cups milk

2 cups shredded sharp Cheddar cheese (8 ounces)

1. Heat oven to 350°. Cook and drain macaroni as directed on package.

2. While macaroni is cooking, melt butter in 3-quart saucepan over low heat. Stir flour, salt, pepper, mustard and Worcestershire sauce into butter. Cook over low heat, stirring constantly, until mixture is smooth and bubbly; remove from heat. Stir in milk. Heat to boiling, stirring constantly. Boil and stir 1 minute; remove from heat. Stir in cheese until melted.

3. Gently stir macaroni into cheese sauce. Pour into ungreased 2-quart casserole. Bake uncovered 20 to 25 minutes or until bubbly.

1 SERVING Calories 615 (Calories from Fat 305) | Fat 34g (Saturated 21g) | Cholesterol 100mg | Sodium 790mg | Carbohydrate 51g (Dietary Fiber 2g) | Protein 26g   %DAILY VALUE Vitamin A 26% | Vitamin C 0% | Calcium 46% | Iron 14%   EXCHANGES 3 Starch, 2 High-Fat Meat, 4 Fat   CARBOHYDRATE CHOICES 3 1/2

Mexican Macaroni and Cheese Substitute shredded process cheese spread with jalapeño peppers for the sharp Cheddar cheese. Stir in 1/4 cup salsa. Top with crushed corn chips.

BETTY'S TIP

This mac and cheese recipe calls for sharp Cheddar cheese, but go ahead and use your family's favorite. You may want to try Monterey Jack, Colby, or experiment with a blend of several cheeses.

Three-Cheese Rigatoni

3 cups uncooked rigatoni pasta (9 ounces)

2 medium stalks celery, sliced (1 cup)

1 small carrot, shredded (1/2 cup)

1 container (8 ounces) sour cream-and-chive dip

1 cup shredded Colby cheese (4 ounces)

1 cup shredded brick cheese (4 ounces)

1/4 cup grated Parmesan cheese

1/4 cup milk

1 tablespoon chopped fresh or 1 teaspoon dried basil leaves

1/4 cup seasoned dry bread crumbs

1 tablespoon butter or margarine, melted

PREP 10 min   COOK 10 min   BAKE 30 min   SERVINGS 6

1. Heat oven to 375°. Cook and drain pasta as directed on package.

2. Mix pasta and remaining ingredients except bread crumbs and butter. Place pasta mixture in ungreased 2-quart casserole. Mix bread crumbs and butter; sprinkle around edge of casserole.

3. Bake uncovered 25 to 30 minutes or until hot and bubbly.

1 SERVING Calories 470 (Calories from Fat 205) | Fat 23g (Saturated 14g) | Cholesterol 60mg | Sodium 640mg | Carbohydrate 49g (Dietary Fiber 3g) | Protein 20g   %DAILY VALUE Vitamin A 48% | Vitamin C 0% | Calcium 36% | Iron 14%   EXCHANGES 3 Starch, 1 Vegetable, 1 High-Fat Meat, 2 1/2 Fat CARBOHYDRATE CHOICES 3

Three-Cheese Rigatoni with Shrimp Add 1 to 1 1/2 cups cooked shrimp.

BETTY'S TIP

Prepare the casserole as directed, but do not sprinkle on the bread crumbs. Cover the casserole and then refrigerate up to 48 hours. To bake, mix bread crumbs and butter and sprinkle around edge of casserole. Bake uncovered at 375° about 50 minutes or until hot and bubbly.

Easy Cheesy Manicotti

PREP **25 min**   BAKE **1 hr 20 min**   SERVINGS **7**

1 jar (28 ounces) chunky-style spaghetti sauce

2 packages (10 ounces each) frozen chopped spinach, thawed and squeezed to drain

1 container (12 ounces) small curd creamed cottage cheese (1 1/2 cups)

1/8 cup grated Parmesan cheese

1 teaspoon dried oregano leaves, crumbled

1/4 teaspoon pepper

1 package (8 ounces) manicotti shells (14 shells)

2 cups shredded mozzarella cheese (8 ounces)

1. Heat oven to 350°. Spread about one-third of the spaghetti sauce in ungreased rectangular baking dish, 13 × 9 × 2 inches.

2. Mix spinach, cottage cheese, Parmesan cheese, oregano and pepper. Fill manicotti shells with spinach mixture; place on spaghetti sauce in baking dish.

3. Pour remaining spaghetti sauce evenly over shells, covering completely. Cover and bake 1 hour. Sprinkle with mozzarella cheese. Cover and bake 15 to 20 minutes longer or until shells are tender.

2 SHELLS Calories 425 (Calories from Fat 115) | Fat 13g (Saturated 6g) | Cholesterol 25mg | Sodium 1060mg | Carbohydrate 54g (Dietary Fiber 4g) | Protein 23g   **%DAILY VALUE** Vitamin A 100% | Vitamin C 20% | Calcium 40% | Iron 16%   **EXCHANGES** 3 Starch, 2 Vegetable, 1 1/2 Medium-Fat Meat, 1/2 Fat   **CARBOHYDRATE CHOICES** 3 1/2

BETTY'S TIP

Try using a baby spoon to fill the manicotti shells—it works great! Or fill a resealable plastic food-storage bag with the spinach mixture, snip off a corner and pipe the mixture into the shells.

Chili con Queso Casserole

PREP 10 min   BAKE 40 min   SERVINGS 6

2 cans (4.5 ounces each) chopped green chiles, drained

2 large tomatoes, seeded and chopped (2 cups)

2 cups shredded Cheddar cheese (8 ounces)

1 cup Original Bisquick mix

1/2 cup sour cream

3 eggs

Salsa, if desired

1. Heat oven to 375°. Spray 2-quart casserole or square pan, 8 × 8 × 2 inches, with cooking spray. Sprinkle chiles and tomatoes evenly in casserole.

2. Beat remaining ingredients except salsa with wire whisk until blended. Pour over chiles and tomatoes.

3. Bake uncovered 35 to 40 minutes or until knife inserted in center comes out clean. Serve with salsa.

1 SERVING Calories 320 (Calories from Fat 200) | Fat 22g (Saturated 12g) | Cholesterol 160mg | Sodium 710mg | Carbohydrate 18g (Dietary Fiber 2g) | Protein 15g   %DAILY VALUE Vitamin A 26% | Vitamin C 20% | Calcium 28% | Iron 10%   EXCHANGES 1 Starch, 2 High-Fat Meat, 1 Fat   CARBOHYDRATE CHOICES 1

BETTY'S TIP

Garnish this cheesy Mexican bake with sour cream, cherry tomato wedges and cilantro, and sprinkle a little taco seasoning mix over the sour cream.

Roasted-Vegetable Lasagna

PREP 25 min   BAKE 1 hr 15 min   STAND 5 min   SERVINGS 8

1. Heat oven to 425°. Spray bottom and sides of jelly roll pan, 15 1/2 × 10 1/2 × 1 inch, with cooking spray. Place bell peppers, onion, zucchini, potatoes, mushrooms, oil, peppered seasoned salt and basil in large bowl; toss to coat. Spread vegetables in pan. Bake uncovered about 30 minutes or until crisp-tender. Cool slightly.

2. Reduce oven temperature to 350°. Spray bottom and sides of rectangular baking dish, 13 × 9 × 2 inches, with cooking spray. Cook and drain noodles as directed on package. Mix ricotta cheese, pesto and egg. Coarsely chop vegetables.

3. Place 3 noodles lengthwise in baking dish. Spread with half of the ricotta mixture. Top with 2 cups vegetables and 1 cup of the provolone cheese. Repeat layers, starting with noodles. Top with remaining 3 noodles and remaining vegetables. Sprinkle with mozzarella cheese.

4. Bake uncovered 40 to 45 minutes or until hot in center and top is golden brown. Let stand 5 minutes before cutting.

1 SERVING Calories 510 (Calories from Fat 250) | Fat 28g (Saturated 12g) | Cholesterol 80mg | Sodium 660mg | Carbohydrate 44g (Dietary Fiber 4g) | Protein 26g %DAILY VALUE Vitamin A 54% | Vitamin C 50% | Calcium 54% | Iron 18% EXCHANGES 2 Starch, 3 Vegetable, 2 High-Fat Meat, 2 Fat CARBOHYDRATE CHOICES 3

2 medium red, green or yellow bell peppers, each cut into 8 pieces

1 medium onion, cut into 8 wedges

1 large zucchini, cut into 2-inch pieces (2 cups)

6 small red potatoes, cut into fourths

1 package (8 ounces) whole mushrooms, cut in half

2 tablespoons olive or vegetable oil

1/2 teaspoon peppered seasoned salt

2 teaspoons chopped fresh or 1/2 teaspoon dried basil leaves

9 uncooked lasagna noodles (9 ounces)

1 container (15 ounces) ricotta cheese

1/2 cup basil pesto

1 egg, slightly beaten

2 cups shredded provolone cheese (8 ounces)

1 cup shredded mozzarella cheese (4 ounces)

BETTY'S TIP

Roasting vegetables takes some time, but the richly flavored results are definitely worth it. If you want to get a jump start, roast the vegetables up to 8 hours in advance and refrigerate.

Easy Cheese Strata

1/3 cup butter or margarine, softened

1/2 teaspoon ground mustard

1 clove garlic, finely chopped

10 slices white bread, crusts removed

2 cups shredded sharp Cheddar cheese (8 ounces)

2 tablespoons chopped fresh parsley

2 tablespoons chopped onion

1 teaspoon salt

1/2 teaspoon Worcestershire sauce

1/8 teaspoon pepper

Dash of ground red pepper (cayenne)

4 eggs

2 1/2 cups milk

PREP 15 min   **CHILL** 2 hr   **BAKE** 1 hr 15 min   **STAND** 10 min   **SERVINGS** 6

1. Mix butter, mustard and garlic. Spread over each slice bread. Cut each slice into thirds. Line bottom and sides of ungreased square baking dish, $8 \times 8 \times 2$ inches, with enough of the bread slices, buttered sides down.

2. Mix cheese, parsley, onion, salt, Worcestershire sauce, pepper and red pepper. Spread evenly over bread slices in dish. Top with remaining bread slices, buttered sides up. Beat eggs; stir in milk. Pour over bread. Cover and refrigerate at least 2 hours but no longer than 24 hours.

3. Heat oven to 325°. Bake uncovered about 1 hour 15 minutes or until knife inserted in center comes out clean. Let stand 10 minutes before cutting.

1 SERVING Calories 425 (Calories from Fat 260) | Fat 29g (Saturated 12g) | Cholesterol 190mg | Sodium 620mg | Carbohydrate 21g (Dietary Fiber 1g) | Protein 20g   **%DAILY VALUE** Vitamin A 28% | Vitamin C 2% | Calcium 38% | Iron 8%   **EXCHANGES** 1 Starch, 1/2 Milk, 2 High-Fat Meat, 2 Fat   **CARBOHYDRATE CHOICES** 1 1/2

BETTY'S TIP

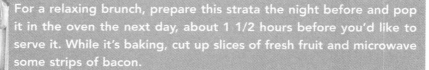

For a relaxing brunch, prepare this strata the night before and pop it in the oven the next day, about 1 1/2 hours before you'd like to serve it. While it's baking, cut up slices of fresh fruit and microwave some strips of bacon.

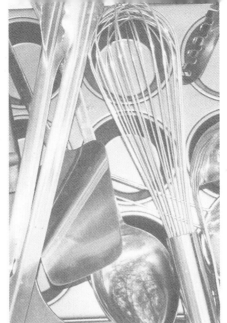

Satisfying Slow Cooker Suppers

Hearty Beef Chili

2 pounds beef stew meat

1 envelope (1 ounce) onion soup mix (from 2-ounce package)

5 teaspoons chili powder

1 teaspoon ground cumin

1 can (15.5 ounces) kidney beans, rinsed and drained

2 cans (10 ounces each) diced tomatoes and mild green chilies, undrained

1 can (15 ounces) tomato sauce

1 can (14.5 ounces) diced tomatoes, undrained

PREP **10 min**   COOK **9 hr**   SERVINGS **10**

1. Place all ingredients in order listed in 3 1/2- to 4-quart slow cooker.

2. Cover and cook on Low heat setting 8 to 9 hours.

3. Stir gently to mix before serving.

1 SERVING Calories 255 (Calories from Fat 100) | Fat 11g (Saturated 4g) | Cholesterol 55mg | Sodium 820mg | Carbohydrate 20g (Dietary Fiber 5g) | Protein 24g %DAILY VALUE Vitamin A 22% | Vitamin C 22% | Calcium 6% | Iron 24% EXCHANGES 1 Starch, 1 Vegetable, 2 1/2 Lean Meat CARBOHYDRATE CHOICES 1

BETTY'S TIP

To create a fun chili fest, set out bowls of your family's favorite toppings so that each member can create their own personalized "bowl of red." Shredded Cheddar cheese, chopped onion, sour cream, guacamole and pickled sliced jalapeño chilies are all tasty options.

Italian Beef Stew

1. Place beef, beef base, carrots, celery, garlic, onion, pepper, cannellini beans, tomatoes and gravy in order listed in 3 1/2- to 4-quart slow cooker.

2. Cover and cook on Low heat setting 10 to 12 hours.

3. Stir in Italian seasoning, sugar and frozen green beans. Increase heat setting to High. Cover and cook about 15 minutes or until green beans are tender.

1 SERVING Calories 340 (Calories from Fat 100) | Fat 11g (Saturated 4g) | Cholesterol 50mg | Sodium 800mg | Carbohydrate 41g (Dietary Fiber 10g) | Protein 29g %DAILY VALUE Vitamin A 100% | Vitamin C 22% | Calcium 16% | Iron 38% EXCHANGES 2 Starch, 2 Vegetable, 2 1/2 Lean Meat CARBOHYDRATE CHOICES 3

1 pound beef stew meat

1 teaspoon beef base

3 large carrots, cut into 1-inch pieces (2 cups)

2 medium stalks celery, cut into 1-inch pieces (1 1/2 cups)

2 cloves garlic, finely chopped

1 medium onion, coarsely chopped (1 1/2 cups)

1/4 teaspoon pepper

1 can (19 ounces) cannellini beans, rinsed and drained

1 can (28 ounces) crushed tomatoes in puree, undrained

1 jar (12 ounces) beef gravy

2 teaspoons Italian seasoning

1 teaspoon sugar

2 cups frozen cut green beans (from 1-pound bag)

BETTY'S TIP

Edible bowls are a fun and delicious way to serve up stew, chili or soup. To make chewy bread bowls, cut off the tops of small, round bread loaves and scoop out the bread, leaving a 1-inch-thick wall. Fill the loaves with the stew, chili or soup, and replace the top of the bread.

Old-Fashioned Beef Stew

PREP **20** min   COOK **10** hr   SERVINGS **5**

1 1/2 pounds beef stew meat, cut into 3/4-inch cubes

4 medium carrots, cut into 1/2-inch slices

3 medium unpeeled potatoes, cut into 1/2-inch cubes

1 large onion, cut into 1-inch pieces

3 cups vegetable juice cocktail

3 tablespoons quick-cooking tapioca

3 teaspoons beef bouillon granules

2 teaspoons Worcestershire sauce

1/4 teaspoon pepper

1. Mix all ingredients in 3 1/2- to 4-quart slow cooker.

2. Cover and cook on Low heat setting 9 to 10 hours.

1 SERVING Calories 390 (Calories from Fat 145) | Fat 16g (Saturated 6g) | Cholesterol 85mg | Sodium 1260mg | Carbohydrate 36g (Dietary Fiber 5g) | Protein 31g   **%DAILY VALUE** Vitamin A 100% | Vitamin C 46% | Calcium 6% | Iron 30%   **EXCHANGES** 2 Starch, 1 Vegetable, 3 Lean Meat, 1 Fat   **CARBOHYDRATE CHOICES** 2 1/2

BETTY'S TIP

You may be tempted to stir this hearty family meal as it cooks, but there's no need. Beef stew meat becomes flavorful and tender after long, moist cooking at a low temperature—which is exactly what a slow cooker does.

Beef Stew with Sun-Dried Tomatoes

PREP **20 min**   COOK **9 hr 15 min**   SERVINGS **6**

1 cup sun-dried tomatoes (not in oil)

1 1/2 pounds beef stew meat

12 new potatoes (1 1/2 pounds), cut in half

1 medium onion, cut into 8 wedges

1 bag (8 ounces) baby-cut carrots (about 30)

2 cups water

1 1/2 teaspoons seasoned salt

1 dried bay leaf

1/4 cup water

2 tablespoons all-purpose flour

1. Rehydrate tomatoes as directed on package; drain and coarsely chop.

2. Mix tomatoes and remaining ingredients except 1/4 cup water and the flour in 3 1/2- to 4-quart slow cooker.

3. Cover and cook on Low heat setting 8 to 9 hours.

4. Mix 1/4 cup water and the flour; gradually stir into beef mixture. Increase heat setting to High. Cover and cook 10 to 15 minutes or until slightly thickened. Remove bay leaf.

1 SERVING Calories 410 (Calories from Fat 155) | Fat 17g (Saturated 6g) | Cholesterol 70mg | Sodium 620mg | Carbohydrate 30g (Dietary Fiber 5g) | Protein 34g   %DAILY VALUE Vitamin A 100% | Vitamin C 16% | Calcium 4% | Iron 34%   EXCHANGES 1 1/2 Starch, 1 Vegetable, 4 Lean Meat, 1 Fat CARBOHYDRATE CHOICES 2

BETTY'S TIP

When buying new potatoes, avoid those that are wrinkled, sprouted or cracked. It's common, however, for new potatoes to have spots where they are missing their feathery skin.

Colombian Beef and Sweet Potato Stew

1 pound beef boneless chuck

1/2 teaspoon salt

1/4 teaspoon pepper

1 1/2 teaspoons olive or vegetable oil

2 dark-orange sweet potatoes, peeled and cut into 1-inch pieces (3 cups)

4 cloves garlic, finely chopped

2 whole cloves

1 dried bay leaf

1 stick cinnamon

1 large onion, cut into eighths

1 can (28 ounces) Italian-style (plum) tomatoes, undrained

8 dried apricots, cut in half

Chopped fresh parsley, if desired

PREP **15 min**   COOK **10 hr 15 min**   SERVINGS **6**

1. Remove excess fat from beef. Cut beef into 1-inch pieces. Sprinkle beef with salt and pepper. Heat oil in 10-inch skillet over medium-high heat. Cook beef in oil about 5 minutes, stirring occasionally, until brown.

2. Mix beef and remaining ingredients except apricots and parsley in 4- to 5-quart slow cooker.

3. Cover and cook on Low heat setting about 8 to 10 hours.

4. Stir in apricots. Cover and cook on Low heat setting about 15 minutes or until apricots are softened. Discard cloves, bay leaf and cinnamon stick. Sprinkle stew with parsley.

1 SERVING Calories 270 (Calories from Fat 90) | Fat 10g (Saturated 3g) | Cholesterol 45mg | Sodium 440mg | Carbohydrate 27g (Dietary Fiber 4g) | Protein 18g   %DAILY VALUE Vitamin A 100% | Vitamin C 28% | Calcium 6% | Iron 18%   EXCHANGES 1 Starch, 1/2 Fruit, 1 Vegetable, 2 Lean Meat CARBOHYDRATE CHOICES 2

BETTY'S TIP

Serve this stick-to-your-ribs stew over cooked couscous in large pasta bowls, and garnish with Italian parsley sprigs.

Mediterranean Pot Roast

PREP **10 min**   COOK **10 hr**   STAND **15 min**   SERVINGS **8 to 10**

1. Spray 12-inch skillet with cooking spray; heat over medium-high heat. Cook beef in skillet about 5 minutes, turning once, until brown. Sprinkle with salt, Italian seasoning and garlic; remove from skillet.

2. Place beef, seasoned side up, in 4- to 5-quart slow cooker. Spread tomatoes and olives over roast. Add broth and onions.

3. Cover and cook on Low heat setting 8 to 10 hours.

4. Remove beef from slow cooker; cover and let stand 15 minutes. Slice beef; serve with beef juice and onions from slow cooker.

3-pound beef boneless chuck roast

1 teaspoon salt

1 tablespoon Italian seasoning

1 large clove garlic, finely chopped

1/3 cup sun-dried tomatoes in oil, drained and chopped

1/2 cup sliced pitted Kalamata or ripe olives

1/2 cup beef broth

1/2 cup frozen small whole onions (from 1-pound bag)

1 SERVING Calories 220 (Calories from Fat 115) | Fat 13g (Saturated 5g) | Cholesterol 60mg | Sodium 470mg | Carbohydrate 5g (Dietary Fiber 1g) | Protein 22g %DAILY VALUE Vitamin A 0% | Vitamin C 4% | Calcium 2% | Iron 16% EXCHANGES 1 Vegetable, 3 Lean Meat, 1/2 Fat CARBOHYDRATE CHOICES 0

BETTY'S TIP

In keeping with the Mediterranean theme, try sprinkling crumbled feta cheese over the slices of beef just before serving. Pita bread triangles make yummy sides.

Beef and Potatoes with Rosemary

1 pound medium red potatoes, cut into fourths

1 cup baby-cut carrots

3-pound beef boneless chuck roast

3 tablespoons Dijon mustard

2 tablespoons chopped fresh or 1 1/2 teaspoons dried rosemary leaves, crumbled

1 teaspoon chopped fresh or 1/2 teaspoon dried thyme leaves

1 teaspoon salt

1/2 teaspoon pepper

1 small onion, finely chopped (1/4 cup)

1 1/2 cups beef broth

1. Arrange potatoes and carrots around outer edge in 4- to 5-quart slow cooker.

2. Trim excess fat from beef. Mix mustard, rosemary, thyme, salt and pepper; spread evenly over beef. Place beef in slow cooker (it will overlap vegetables slightly).

3. Sprinkle onion over beef. Pour broth evenly over beef and vegetables. Cover and cook on Low heat setting 8 to 9 hours.

4. Remove beef and vegetables from slow cooker with slotted spoon. Slice beef. To serve, spoon beef juices from slow cooker over beef and vegetables.

1 SERVING Calories 395 (Calories from Fat 245) | Fat 27g (Saturated 10g) | Cholesterol 140mg | Sodium 960mg | Carbohydrate 18g (Dietary Fiber 3g) | Protein 49g %DAILY VALUE Vitamin A 78% | Vitamin C 10% | Calcium 4% | Iron 36% EXCHANGES 1 Starch, 1 Vegetable, 2 High-Fat Meat CARBOHYDRATE CHOICES 1

BETTY'S TIP

If your family likes gravy, you may want to thicken the beef juices with 2 tablespoons cornstarch mixed with 1/4 cup cold water. Shake the cornstarch mixture in a covered container, then reheat it with the beef juices in a saucepan on the stove until thickened.

Cajun Pot Roast with Maque Choux

PREP 10 min   COOK 10 hr   SERVINGS 6

1. Rub both sides of beef with Cajun seasoning. Place beef in 3 1/2- to 4-quart slow cooker. Top with corn, onion and bell pepper.

2. Mix tomatoes, pepper and pepper sauce. Pour over vegetables in slow cooker.

3. Cover and cook on Low heat setting 8 to 10 hours.

4. Remove beef and vegetables from slow cooker with slotted spoon. Slice beef. To serve, spoon beef juices from slow cooker over beef and vegetables.

1 SERVING Calories 270 (Calories from Fat 80) | Fat 9g (Saturated 3g) | Cholesterol 105mg | Sodium 590mg | Carbohydrate 12g (Dietary Fiber 2g) | Protein 36g   %DAILY VALUE Vitamin A 24% | Vitamin C 4% | Calcium 6% | Iron 32%   EXCHANGES 1 Starch, 4 1/2 Very Lean Meat, 1 Fat   CARBOHYDRATE CHOICES 1

2- to 2 1/2-pound beef boneless chuck roast

1 tablespoon Cajun seasoning

1 package (10 ounces) frozen whole kernel corn

1 medium onion, chopped (1/2 cup)

1/2 cup chopped green bell pepper

1 can (14.5 ounces) diced tomatoes, undrained

1/8 teaspoon pepper

1/2 teaspoon red pepper sauce

BETTY'S TIP

Cajun cuisine is hearty, country-style food influenced by French and Southern cooking. *Maque choux* (pronounced MOCK shoo) means "smothered corn" in Cajun country. The corn is loaded with tomatoes, peppers and onions.

Zesty Italian Beef Tips

2 pounds beef stew meat

1 cup frozen small whole onions (from 1-pound bag)

1 jar (6 ounces) pitted Kalamata or Greek olives, drained

1/3 cup sun-dried tomatoes in oil, drained and chopped

1 jar (28 ounces) marinara sauce

6 cups hot cooked pasta

PREP **10 min** COOK **10 hr** SERVINGS **6**

1. Place beef and onions in 3 1/2- to 4-quart slow cooker. Top with olives and tomatoes. Pour marinara sauce over top.

2. Cover and cook on Low heat setting 8 to 10 hours. Serve over pasta.

1 SERVING Calories 660 (Calories from Fat 245) | Fat 27g (Saturated 8g) | Cholesterol 95mg | Sodium 990mg | Carbohydrate 69g (Dietary Fiber 5g) | Protein 40g %DAILY VALUE Vitamin A 22% | Vitamin C 22% | Calcium 8% | Iron 40% EXCHANGES 4 Starch, 1 Vegetable, 3 1/2 Medium-Fat Meat, 1 Fat CARBOHYDRATE CHOICES 4 1/2

BETTY'S TIP

If some beef pieces are large and some are small, it's hard to get them to cook evenly. So to make sure all the beef tips will be tender at the same time, try to cut the pieces the same size.

Garlic-Braised Beef and Potatoes

PREP **15 min**   COOK **9 hr 15 min**   SERVINGS **8**

1. Trim fat from beef. Place potatoes and garlic in 4- to 5-quart slow cooker. Place beef on potatoes. Sprinkle dry soup mix over beef; pour mushroom soup evenly over top.

2. Cover and cook on Low heat setting 8 to 9 hours.

3. Remove beef and vegetables from slow cooker with slotted spoon. Slice beef. Arrange beef and vegetables on serving platter. Cover and keep warm.

4. Place frozen broccoli in slow cooker with remaining sauce. Increase heat setting to High. Cover and cook about 15 minutes or until broccoli is tender. Serve with beef and potatoes.

3-pound beef boneless bottom round roast

8 small red potatoes (about 1 1/2 pounds), cut in half

8 cloves garlic, peeled

1 envelope garlic-and-herb dry soup mix (from 2.4-ounce package)

1 can (10 3/4 ounces) condensed beefy mushroom soup

2 cups frozen broccoli flowerets (from 1-pound bag)

1 SERVING Calories 335 (Calories from Fat 70) | Fat 8g (Saturated 2g) | Cholesterol 90mg | Sodium 500mg | Carbohydrate 28g (Dietary Fiber 3g) | Protein 38g %DAILY VALUE Vitamin A 10% | Vitamin C 18% | Calcium 4% | Iron 26% EXCHANGES 1 1/2 Starch, 1 Vegetable, 4 1/2 Very Lean Meat, 1 Fat CARBOHYDRATE CHOICES 2

BETTY'S TIP

The garlic cloves you toss in at the start of this recipe become soft and sweet as they slow roast along with the beef and veggies. Fish the cloves out with a slotted spoon at the end of the cooking time—they taste great spread on buttered rolls.

Mexicali Round Steak

PREP **15 min**   COOK **9 hr**   SERVINGS **6**

1 1/2 pounds beef boneless round steak

1 cup frozen whole kernel corn (from 1-pound bag), thawed and drained

1 cup chopped fresh cilantro

1/2 cup beef broth

3 medium stalks celery, thinly sliced (1 1/2 cups)

1 large onion, sliced

1 jar (20 ounces) salsa

1 can (15 ounces) black beans, rinsed and drained

1 cup shredded Monterey Jack cheese with jalapeño peppers (4 ounces), if desired

1. Trim fat from beef. Cut beef into 6 serving pieces. Place beef in 3 1/2- to 6-quart slow cooker.

2. Mix remaining ingredients except cheese; pour over beef.

3. Cover and cook on Low heat setting 8 to 9 hours. Sprinkle cheese over beef mixture.

1 SERVING Calories 250 (Calories from Fat 35) | Fat 4g (Saturated 1g) | Cholesterol 60mg | Sodium 830mg | Carbohydrate 31g (Dietary Fiber 8g) | Protein 31g   %DAILY VALUE Vitamin A 20% | Vitamin C 16% | Calcium 10% | Iron 28%   EXCHANGES 2 Starch, 3 Very Lean Meat   CARBOHYDRATE CHOICES 2

BETTY'S TIP

Give this round steak a flavor twist by using pinto beans instead of the black beans and sprinkling with Cheddar cheese in place of the Monterey Jack cheese.

Beef Steak Chili

PREP **15 min**   COOK **7 hr 15 min**   SERVINGS **8**

1. Mix all ingredients except bell pepper, beans and cheese in 3 1/2- to 4-quart slow cooker.

2. Cover and cook on Low heat setting 6 to 7 hours.

3. Stir in bell pepper and beans. Increase heat setting to High. Cook uncovered about 15 minutes or until slightly thickened. Serve with cheese.

1 SERVING Calories 170 (Calories from Fat 25) | Fat 3g (Saturated 1g) | Cholesterol 30mg | Sodium 660mg | Carbohydrate 24g (Dietary Fiber 6g) | Protein 18g   %DAILY VALUE Vitamin A 16% | Vitamin C 30% | Calcium 6% | Iron 20%   EXCHANGES 1 Starch, 2 Vegetable, 1 Lean Meat   CARBOHYDRATE CHOICES 1 1/2

1 pound beef boneless round steak, cut into 1/2-inch pieces

1 large onion, chopped (1 cup)

2 medium stalks celery, cut into 1/2-inch pieces (1 cup)

2 cans (14 1/2 ounces each) diced tomatoes, undrained

1 can (15 ounces) tomato sauce

3 teaspoons chili powder

2 teaspoons ground cumin

1/4 teaspoon dried oregano leaves

1/4 teaspoon ground cinnamon

1 medium bell pepper, cut into 1-inch pieces (1 cup)

1 can (15 to 16 ounces) kidney beans, rinsed and drained

Shredded Cheddar cheese, if desired

BETTY'S TIP

You also can use a 28-ounce can of whole tomatoes instead of the diced tomatoes. Use a spoon to break up the whole tomatoes in the slow cooker.

Swiss Steak Supper

PREP 15 min   COOK 8 hr   SERVINGS 6

1 1/2 pounds beef
boneless round steak,
cut into 6 serving pieces

1/2 teaspoon peppered
seasoned salt

6 to 8 new potatoes,
cut into fourths

1 1/2 cups baby-cut carrots

1 medium onion, sliced

1 can (14 1/2 ounces) diced
tomatoes with basil, garlic
and oregano, undrained

1 jar (12 ounces) home-style
beef gravy

Chopped fresh parsley,
if desired

1. Spray 12-inch skillet with cooking spray; heat over medium-high heat. Sprinkle beef with seasoned salt. Cook beef in skillet 6 to 8 minutes, turning once, until brown.

2. Layer potatoes, carrots, beef and onion in 4- to 5-quart slow cooker. Mix tomatoes and gravy; spoon over mixture in slow cooker.

3. Cover and cook on Low heat setting 7 to 8 hours. Sprinkle with parsley.

1 SERVING Calories 220 (Calories from Fat 45) | Fat 5g (Saturated 2g) | Cholesterol 60mg | Sodium 680mg | Carbohydrate 20g (Dietary Fiber 3g) | Protein 27g %DAILY VALUE Vitamin A 50% | Vitamin C 15% | Calcium 4% | Iron 20% EXCHANGES 1 Starch, 1 Vegetable, 3 Very Lean Meat CARBOHYDRATE CHOICES 1

BETTY'S TIP

Peppered seasoned salt is one of the newer varieties of seasoned salt available in the supermarket. If you have trouble finding it, use regular seasoned salt and sprinkle the beef with pepper, or you can just use salt and pepper.

Burgundy Stew with Herb Dumplings

1. Mix all ingredients except water, flour and Herb Dumplings in 3 1/2- to 4-quart slow cooker.

2. Cover and cook on Low heat setting 8 to 10 hours.

3. Mix water and flour; gradually stir into beef mixture.

4. Make Herb Dumplings. Drop dough by spoonfuls onto hot beef mixture. Increase heat setting to High. Cover and cook 25 to 35 minutes or until toothpick inserted in center of dumplings comes out clean.

Herb Dumplings

    1 1/2 cups Original Bisquick mix

    1/2 teaspoon dried thyme leaves

    1/4 teaspoon dried sage leaves, crumbled

    1/2 cup milk

Stir together Bisquick mix, thyme and sage in small bowl. Stir in milk just until Bisquick mix is moistened.

1 SERVING Calories 400 (Calories from Fat 90) | Fat 10g (Saturated 3g) | Cholesterol 80mg | Sodium 1370mg | Carbohydrate 35g (Dietary Fiber 4g) | Protein 36g %DAILY VALUE Vitamin A 100% | Vitamin C 14% | Calcium 12% | Iron 28% EXCHANGES 2 Starch, 1 Vegetable, 4 Lean Meat CARBOHYDRATE CHOICES 2

2 pounds beef boneless bottom or top round, tip or chuck steak, cut into 1-inch pieces

4 medium carrots, cut into 1/4-inch slices (2 cups)

2 medium stalks celery, sliced (1 cup)

2 medium onions, sliced

1 can (14 1/2 ounces) diced tomatoes, undrained

1 can (8 ounces) sliced mushrooms, drained

3/4 cup dry red wine or beef broth

1 1/2 teaspoons salt

1 teaspoon dried thyme leaves

1 teaspoon ground mustard

1/4 teaspoon pepper

1/4 cup water

3 tablespoons all-purpose flour

Herb Dumplings (above left)

BETTY'S TIP

If you like, you can skip the dumplings and make Bisquick biscuits instead. Before serving, plop a biscuit on top of each bowl of stew or serve them on the side.

Cheesy Ravioli Casserole

PREP **15 min**   COOK **7 hr**   SERVINGS **12**

1 tablespoon olive or vegetable oil

1 medium onion, chopped (1/2 cup)

1 large clove garlic, finely chopped

1 can (26 ounces) four cheese–flavored spaghetti sauce

1 can (15 ounces) tomato sauce

1 teaspoon Italian seasoning

2 packages (25 ounces each) frozen beef-filled ravioli

2 cups shredded mozzarella cheese (8 ounces)

1/4 cup chopped fresh parsley

1. Heat oil in 10-inch skillet over medium heat. Cook onion and garlic in oil about 4 minutes, stirring occasionally, until onion is tender. Stir in spaghetti sauce, tomato sauce and Italian seasoning.

2. Place 1 cup of the sauce mixture in bottom of 4 1/2- to 6-quart slow cooker. Add 1 package frozen ravioli; top with 1 cup of the cheese. Top with remaining package of ravioli; top with remaining 1 cup cheese. Pour remaining sauce mixture over top.

3. Cover and cook on Low heat setting 5 to 7 hours. Sprinkle with parsley.

1 SERVING Calories 350 (Calories from Fat 125) | Fat 14g (Saturated 6g) | Cholesterol 145mg | Sodium 1510mg | Carbohydrate 39g (Dietary Fiber 3g) | Protein 20g   %DAILY VALUE Vitamin A 58% | Vitamin C 16% | Calcium 28% | Iron 18%   EXCHANGES 2 1/2 Starch, 2 Medium-Fat Meat   CARBOHYDRATE CHOICES 2 1/2

BETTY'S TIP

Virtually everyone loves pasta and cheese, so this ravioli casserole makes a great potluck pick. You may also want to tote along a loaf of crusty French bread to serve on the side.

Chicken Stew with Pepper and Pineapple

PREP **20 min**   COOK **8 hr 15 min**   SERVINGS **4**

1. Mix chicken, carrots, broth, gingerroot, brown sugar, soy sauce, allspice and pepper sauce in 3 1/2- to 4-quart slow cooker.

2. Cover and cook on Low heat setting 7 to 8 hours.

3. Mix cornstarch and reserved pineapple juice; gradually stir into chicken mixture. Stir in pineapple and bell pepper. Increase heat setting to High. Cover and cook about 15 minutes or until slightly thickened and bubbly.

1 pound boneless, skinless chicken breasts, cut into 1 1/2-inch pieces

4 medium carrots, cut into 1-inch pieces

1/2 cup chicken broth

1 tablespoon finely chopped gingerroot

1 tablespoon packed brown sugar

2 tablespoons soy sauce

1/2 teaspoon ground allspice

1/2 teaspoon red pepper sauce

1 tablespoon cornstarch

1 can (8 ounces) pineapple chunks in juice, drained and juice reserved

1 medium red bell pepper, cut into 1-inch pieces (1 cup)

1 SERVING Calories 245 (Calories from Fat 35) | Fat 4g (Saturated 1g) | Cholesterol 60mg | Sodium 670mg | Carbohydrate 25g (Dietary Fiber 3g) | Protein 27g %DAILY VALUE Vitamin A 100% | Vitamin C 50% | Calcium 4% | Iron 10% EXCHANGES 1 Starch, 1 Vegetable, 1/2 Fruit, 3 Very Lean Meat CARBOHYDRATE CHOICES 1 1/2

BETTY'S TIP

If you don't have fresh gingerroot on hand, no problem! Just use 1 teaspoon ground ginger instead.

Lime-Garlic Chicken with Rice

PREP 10 min   COOK 10 hr   SERVINGS 6

1 1/4 pounds bone-in, skinless chicken thighs

1/4 cup fresh lime juice (2 limes)

1 1/2 cups chicken broth

2 cloves garlic, finely chopped

1/2 teaspoon dried thyme leaves

1/4 teaspoon pepper

2 tablespoons butter or margarine

1 cup uncooked instant rice

1. Place chicken in 3- to 4-quart slow cooker. Add remaining ingredients except rice.

2. Cover and cook on Low heat setting 8 to 10 hours. During last 15 minutes of cooking, stir in rice.

3. Remove chicken from slow cooker. Place cooked rice on each serving plate. Top with chicken. Spoon any remaining juices over chicken.

1 SERVING Calories 215 (Calories from Fat 80) | Fat 9g (Saturated 4g) | Cholesterol 50mg | Sodium 320mg | Carbohydrate 17g (Dietary Fiber 0g) | Protein 16g %DAILY VALUE Vitamin A 4% | Vitamin C 2% | Calcium 2% | Iron 10% EXCHANGES 1 Starch, 2 Lean Meat, 1 Fat CARBOHYDRATE CHOICES 1

BETTY'S TIP

For a picture-perfect presentation, garnish individual plates with chopped fresh parsley and fresh lime wedges.

Chunky Chicken Chili

PREP 5 min   COOK 9 hr 15 min   SERVINGS 6

1. Place chicken in 3 1/2- to 4-quart slow cooker. Mix tomatoes, tomato sauce and chili seasoning; pour over chicken.

2. Cover and cook on Low heat setting 7 to 9 hours.

3. Stir to break up chicken. Stir in hominy. Cover and cook on Low heat setting about 15 minutes or until thoroughly heated. Serve chili with sour cream and cilantro.

1 SERVING Calories 390 (Calories from Fat 125) | Fat 14g (Saturated 4g) | Cholesterol 95mg | Sodium 1230mg | Carbohydrate 36g (Dietary Fiber 6g) | Protein 36g   %DAILY VALUE Vitamin A 18% | Vitamin C 22% | Calcium 10% | Iron 26%   EXCHANGES 2 Starch, 1 Vegetable, 4 Lean Meat   CARBOHYDRATE CHOICES 2 1/2

2 pounds boneless, skinless chicken thighs

2 cans (14 1/2 ounces each) diced tomatoes with green chilies, undrained

1 can (15 ounces) tomato sauce

1 envelope (1 1/4 ounces) mild chili seasoning mix

2 cans (15 1/2 ounces each) hominy

Sour cream, if desired

Cilantro, if desired

BETTY'S TIP

To add some kick to this chunky chili, use hot chili seasoning instead of the mild and add a 4.5-ounce can of chopped green chiles with the tomatoes.

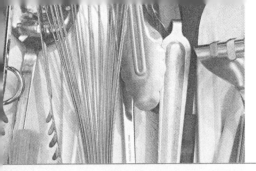

Chicken and Wild Rice Soup

PREP **5 min**   COOK **8 hr 30 min**   SERVINGS **8**

1 pound boneless, skinless chicken thighs, cut into 1-inch pieces

1/2 cup uncooked wild rice

1/4 cup frozen chopped onions (from 12-ounce bag)

2 cans (10 3/4 ounces each) condensed cream of potato soup

1 can (14 ounces) chicken broth with roasted garlic

2 cups frozen sliced carrots (from 1-pound bag)

1 cup half-and-half

1. Place chicken in 3 1/2- to 4-quart slow cooker. Mix wild rice, onions, soup, broth and carrots; pour over chicken.

2. Cover and cook on Low heat setting 7 to 8 hours.

3. Stir in half-and-half. Increase heat setting to High. Cover and cook 15 to 30 minutes or until hot.

1 SERVING Calories 240 (Calories from Fat 90) | Fat 10g (Saturated 4g) | Cholesterol 50mg | Sodium 840mg | Carbohydrate 24g (Dietary Fiber 3g) | Protein 17g   **%DAILY VALUE** Vitamin A 100% | Vitamin C 2% | Calcium 8% | Iron 10%   **EXCHANGES** 1 Starch, 2 Vegetable, 1 1/2 Medium-Fat Meat   **CARBOHYDRATE CHOICES** 1 1/2

BETTY'S TIP

On the slight chance you have leftovers, this soup is a snap to reheat. Just cook over low heat and stir frequently to avoid curdling.

White Chicken Chili

PREP **15 min**   COOK **5 hr 20 min**   SERVINGS **8**

1. Remove excess fat from chicken. Mix onion, garlic, broth, cumin, oregano, salt and pepper sauce in 3 1/2- to 6-quart slow cooker. Add chicken.

2. Cover and cook on Low heat setting 4 to 5 hours.

3. Remove chicken from slow cooker. Use 2 forks to remove bones and shred chicken into pieces. Discard bones; return chicken to slow cooker. Stir in beans, corn, lime juice and cilantro. Cover and cook on Low heat setting 15 to 20 minutes or until beans and corn are hot.

1 SERVING Calories 265 (Calories from Fat 45) | Fat 5g (Saturated 2g) | Cholesterol 30mg | Sodium 540mg | Carbohydrate 39g (Dietary Fiber 8g) | Protein 24g %DAILY VALUE Vitamin A 0% | Vitamin C 6% | Calcium 12% | Iron 30% EXCHANGES 2 1/2 Starch, 2 Very Lean Meat CARBOHYDRATE CHOICES 2 1/2

6 skinless chicken thighs (1 1/2 pounds)

1 large onion, chopped (1 cup)

2 cloves garlic, finely chopped

1 can (14 1/2 ounces) chicken broth

1 teaspoon ground cumin

1 teaspoon dried oregano leaves

1/2 teaspoon salt

1/4 teaspoon red pepper sauce

2 cans (15 to 16 ounces each) great northern beans, rinsed and drained

1 can (15 ounces) white shoepeg corn, drained

3 tablespoons lime juice

2 tablespoons chopped fresh cilantro

BETTY'S TIP

White corn varies from yellow corn in that white corn kernels are smaller and sweeter. If you can't find white shoepeg corn, you can use regular whole kernel corn instead.

Chicken and Vegetables with Dumplings

2 1/2 to 3 pounds boneless, skinless chicken thighs

1 pound small red potatoes (about 2 1/2 inches in diameter)

1 medium onion, coarsely chopped (3/4 cup)

2 cups baby-cut carrots

3 cans (14 ounces each) chicken broth

2 cups Original Bisquick mix

1/2 cup water

2 teaspoons parsley flakes

PREP **10 min**   COOK **10 hr 50 min**   SERVINGS **5**

1.   Place chicken, potatoes, onion and carrots in 6-quart slow cooker. Add broth.

2.   Cover and cook on Low heat setting 9 to 10 hours.

3.   Increase heat setting to High. Mix Bisquick mix, water and parsley in medium bowl. Drop dough by rounded tablespoonfuls onto hot chicken mixture. Cover and cook 45 to 50 minutes or until dumplings are dry in center.

1 SERVING Calories 680 (Calories from Fat 235) | Fat 26g (Saturated 8g) | Cholesterol 140mg | Sodium 1910mg | Carbohydrate 56g (Dietary Fiber 5g) | Protein 59g   %DAILY VALUE Vitamin A 100% | Vitamin C 14% | Calcium 18% | Iron 40%   EXCHANGES 3 1/2 Starch, 1 Vegetable, 6 Lean Meat, 1 Fat CARBOHYDRATE CHOICES 4

BETTY'S TIP

Add a tossed green salad garnished with grapefruit sections and drizzled with poppy seed dressing to this country-style dinner.

Smothered Buttermilk Chicken with Peas

PREP **30 min** COOK **8 hr 15 min** SERVINGS **5**

1. Mix chicken, carrots, onion, water, butter, salt, pepper and bay leaf in 4- to 6–quart slow cooker.

2. Cover and cook on Low heat setting 6 to 8 hours. During last 20 minutes of cooking, stir in gravy mix.

3. Remove bay leaf. Mix buttermilk and flour. Stir flour mixture and peas into chicken mixture. Increase heat setting to High. Cover and cook 10 to 15 minutes or until peas are hot.

4. While chicken mixture is cooking, make biscuits as directed on can. Split biscuits; serve chicken mixture over biscuits.

1 SERVING Calories 470 (Calories from Fat 200) | Fat 22g (Saturated 6g) | Cholesterol 60mg | Sodium 1380mg | Carbohydrate 42g (Dietary Fiber 4g) | Protein 26g %DAILY VALUE Vitamin A 100% | Vitamin C 6% | Calcium 8% | Iron 20% EXCHANGES 2 1/2 Starch, 1 Vegetable, 2 Medium-Fat Meat, 2 Fat CARBOHYDRATE CHOICES 3

1 pound boneless, skinless chicken thighs, cut into 3/4-inch pieces

3 medium carrots, sliced (1 1/2 cups)

1 small onion, chopped (1/3 cup)

1/2 cup water

2 tablespoons butter or margarine, melted

1/4 teaspoon salt

1/4 teaspoon pepper

1 dried bay leaf

1 package (1.2 ounces) roasted chicken gravy mix

1/3 cup buttermilk

2 teaspoons all-purpose flour

1 cup frozen green peas (from 1-pound bag), thawed and drained

1 can (10.2 ounces) refrigerated buttermilk biscuits (5 biscuits)

BETTY'S TIP

If you don't have buttermilk on hand, you can use 3 tablespoons of sour cream or yogurt mixed with 2 tablespoons of milk instead.

Turkey Chili Verde

2 1/2-pound boneless turkey breast half

1 jar (16 ounces) mild green salsa

1 medium onion, chopped (1/2 cup)

1 medium potato, chopped (3/4 cup)

4 cloves garlic, finely chopped

1/2 cup chicken broth

1 teaspoon ground cumin

6 flour tortillas (8 to 10 inches in diameter), warmed

Fresh cilantro leaves, if desired

Sour cream, if desired

PREP **15** min   COOK **10** hr   SERVINGS **6**

1. Place turkey in 3 1/2- to 4-quart slow cooker. Mix salsa, onion, potato, garlic, broth and cumin; pour over turkey.

2. Cover and cook on Low heat setting 8 to 10 hours.

3. Remove turkey from slow cooker. Slice turkey. Serve turkey and sauce in tortillas with cilantro and sour cream.

1 SERVING Calories 375 (Calories from Fat 45) | Fat 5g (Saturated 1g) | Cholesterol 125mg | Sodium 700mg | Carbohydrate 35g (Dietary Fiber 3g) | Protein 50g   %DAILY VALUE Vitamin A 10% | Vitamin C 10% | Calcium 10% | Iron 26%   EXCHANGES 2 Starch, 1 Vegetable, 6 Very Lean Meat   CARBOHYDRATE CHOICES 2

Chicken Chili Verde Substitute boneless, skinless chicken thighs for the turkey breast, cooking until tender enough to be shredded into the sauce.

BETTY'S TIP

To warm tortillas in the oven before serving, wrap in aluminum foil and heat at 325° for about 15 minutes. Or place them on a paper towel and microwave on High for 30 seconds.

Turkey Breast with Wild Rice Stuffing

PREP **15 min**   COOK **9 hr**   SERVINGS **12**

1. Mix all ingredients except turkey.

2. Place turkey in 3 1/2- to 6-quart slow cooker. Place wild rice mixture around edge of cooker.

3. Cover and cook on Low heat setting 8 to 9 hours.

1 SERVING Calories 310 (Calories from Fat 80) | Fat 9g (Saturated 3g) | Cholesterol 85mg | Sodium 70mg | Carbohydrate 21g (Dietary Fiber 2g) | Protein 34g %DAILY VALUE Vitamin A 2% | Vitamin C 2% | Calcium 2% | Iron 8% EXCHANGES 1 1/2 Starch, 4 Very Lean Meat, 1 Fat CARBOHYDRATE CHOICES 1 1/2

4 cups cooked wild rice

1 large onion, finely chopped (3/4 cup)

1/2 cup dried cranberries

1/3 cup slivered almonds

2 medium peeled or unpeeled cooking apples, coarsely chopped (2 cups)

4- to 5-pound boneless whole turkey breast, thawed if frozen

BETTY'S TIP

Cooking apples have a crisp or slightly crisp texture and hold their shape well. Braeburn, Cortland, Empire and Greening are all good cooking apple choices.

Dill-Turkey Chowder

1 pound uncooked turkey breast slices, cut into 1-inch pieces

3/4 teaspoon garlic pepper

1/2 teaspoon salt

6 to 8 new potatoes, cut into 1-inch pieces

1 medium onion, chopped (1/2 cup)

2 medium carrots, sliced (1 cup)

2 teaspoons dried dill weed

2 1/2 cups chicken broth

1 can (15 1/4 ounces) whole kernel corn, drained

1 cup half-and-half

3 tablespoons cornstarch

PREP 15 min   COOK 8 hr 20 min   SERVINGS 6

1. Place turkey in 4- to 5-quart slow cooker; sprinkle with garlic pepper and salt. Stir in remaining ingredients except half-and-half and cornstarch.

2. Cover and cook on Low heat setting 6 to 8 hours.

3. Mix half-and-half and cornstarch; gradually stir into chowder until blended. Increase heat setting to High. Cover and cook about 20 minutes, stirring occasionally, until thickened.

1 SERVING Calories 265 (Calories from Fat 65) | Fat 7g (Saturated 3g) | Cholesterol 55mg | Sodium 840mg | Carbohydrate 33g (Dietary Fiber 3g) | Protein 21g %DAILY VALUE Vitamin A 36% | Vitamin C 12% | Calcium 8% | Iron 14% EXCHANGES 2 Starch, 1 Vegetable, 1 1/2 Very Lean Meat CARBOHYDRATE CHOICES 2

BETTY'S TIP

Using a jar is a quick way to mix the cornstarch with the liquid. Screw the lid on tight, and shake the jar until the mixture is smooth. This is faster than trying to stir until all the cornstarch is dissolved.

Hearty Turkey Dinner

1. Place potatoes and carrots in 3 1/2- to 4-quart slow cooker. Place turkey on vegetables.

2. Mix remaining ingredients; pour over turkey.

3. Cover and cook on Low heat setting 8 to 10 hours.

1 SERVING Calories 570 (Calories from Fat 125) | Fat 14g (Saturated 4g) | Cholesterol 5mg | Sodium 1110mg | Carbohydrate 52g (Dietary Fiber 6g) | Protein 65g %DAILY VALUE Vitamin A 100% | Vitamin C 20% | Calcium 14% | Iron 42% EXCHANGES 3 Starch, 1 Vegetable, 7 Very Lean Meat, 1 Fat CARBOHYDRATE CHOICES 3 1/2

6 small red potatoes (about 2 1/2 inches in diameter), cut into fourths

4 medium carrots, sliced (2 cups)

4 turkey thighs (about 2 pounds), skin removed

1/4 cup all-purpose flour

2 tablespoons onion soup mix (dry)

1 can (10 3/4 ounces) condensed cream of mushroom soup

1/3 cup chicken broth

BETTY'S TIP

If you find you're out of chicken broth, use water instead.

Italian Turkey-Rice Dinner

3 medium carrots, shredded (2 cups)

2 medium stalks celery, sliced (1 cup)

1 small red bell pepper, chopped (1/2 cup)

1/2 teaspoon dried basil leaves

1/3 cup water

4 turkey thighs (8 to 12 ounces each), skin removed

1 teaspoon salt

1/4 teaspoon pepper

1/2 cup uncooked regular long-grain rice

1 teaspoon dried oregano leaves

1/2 cup shredded Italian-style six-cheese blend or mozzarella cheese (2 ounces)

1. Mix carrots, celery, bell pepper, basil and water in 3 1/2- to 4-quart slow cooker. Sprinkle turkey with salt and pepper; place on vegetable mixture.

2. Cover and cook on Low heat setting 6 to 7 hours.

3. Remove turkey from slow cooker. Stir rice and oregano into vegetable mixture; return turkey to slow cooker. Cover and cook on Low heat setting about 1 hour or until rice is tender.

4. Remove turkey from slow cooker. Stir cheese into rice mixture until melted. Serve with turkey.

1 SERVING Calories 370 (Calories from Fat 80) | Fat 9g (Saturated 4g) | Cholesterol 165mg | Sodium 810mg | Carbohydrate 27g (Dietary Fiber 2g) | Protein 47g %DAILY VALUE Vitamin A 100% | Vitamin C 34% | Calcium 16% | Iron 26% EXCHANGES 1 1/2 Starch, 1 Vegetable, 6 Very Lean Meat, 1/2 Fat CARBOHYDRATE CHOICES 2

BETTY'S TIP

Get a jump start by preparing the vegetables for this dinner ahead of time. Cut them as directed and refrigerate them in a plastic storage container or resealable bag until you're ready to make the recipe.

Turkey and Sweet Potatoes

PREP **15 min**   COOK **8 hr**   SERVINGS **6**

1. Layer sweet potatoes and turkey in 4- to 5-quart slow cooker. Mix remaining ingredients except beans until smooth. Pour over mixture in slow cooker.

2. Cover and cook on High heat setting 1 hour. Reduce heat setting to Low. Cover and cook 5 hours. Stir in beans. Cover and cook 1 to 2 hours.

3. Remove turkey and vegetables from slow cooker with slotted spoon. Stir sauce and serve with turkey and vegetables.

1 SERVING Calories 360 (Calories from Fat 80) | Fat 9g (Saturated 3g) | Cholesterol 155mg | Sodium 460mg | Carbohydrate 26g (Dietary Fiber 4g) | Protein 44g   **% DAILY VALUE** Vitamin A 100% | Vitamin C 16% | Calcium 8% | Iron 24%   **EXCHANGES** 1 1/2 Starch, 1 Vegetable, 5 Very Lean Meat, 1 Fat   **CARBOHYDRATE CHOICES** 2

3 medium sweet potatoes, peeled and cut into 2-inch pieces

3 turkey thighs, skin removed (about 1 1/2 pounds)

1 jar (12 ounces) home-style turkey gravy

2 tablespoons all-purpose flour

1 teaspoon parsley flakes

1/2 teaspoon dried rosemary leaves, crumbled

1/8 teaspoon pepper

1 package (10 ounces) frozen cut green beans

BETTY'S TIP

If you're not a fan of sweet potatoes, it's perfectly fine to use regular potatoes instead. There's no need to peel them—just cut the potatoes into 2-inch pieces.

Harvest Sausage and Vegetable Casserole

3 tablespoons zesty Italian dressing

1 tablespoon Dijon mustard

2 medium unpeeled potatoes, cut into 1-inch slices (2 cups)

2 medium onions, sliced

2 medium carrots, cut into 1-inch pieces (1 cup)

2 cups chopped green cabbage

1 ring (1 pound) fully cooked smoked turkey or chicken sausage, cut into 1-inch slices

1 can (14 1/2 ounces) diced tomatoes with green pepper, celery and onion, undrained

PREP **20** min   COOK **8** hr   SERVINGS **4 to 6**

1. Mix dressing and mustard. Arrange potatoes in even layer in 3 1/2- to 4-quart slow cooker; drizzle with one-third of the dressing mixture. Arrange onions on potatoes; drizzle with one-third of the dressing mixture. Top with carrots and cabbage; drizzle with remaining dressing mixture.

2. Arrange sausage on vegetables. Pour tomatoes in even layer over sausage.

3. Cover and cook on Low heat setting 7 to 8 hours or until vegetables are tender.

1 SERVING Calories 335 (Calories from Fat 135) | Fat 15g (Saturated 3g) | Cholesterol 60mg | Sodium 1630mg | Carbohydrate 34g (Dietary Fiber 5g) | Protein 21g   %DAILY VALUE Vitamin A 100% | Vitamin C 32% | Calcium 10% | Iron 14%   EXCHANGES 2 Starch, 1 Vegetable, 2 Medium-Fat Meat CARBOHYDRATE CHOICES 2

BETTY'S TIP
If you use preshredded coleslaw mix from the produce department, you can skip slicing the carrots and chopping the cabbage.

Potato and Ham Chowder

PREP **10 min**   COOK **8 hr**   SERVINGS **5**

1package (5 ounces) scalloped potato mix

1 cup diced fully cooked ham

4 cups chicken broth

2 medium stalks celery, chopped (1 cup)

1 medium onion, chopped (1/2 cup)

1/8 teaspoon pepper

2 cups half-and-half

1/3 cup all-purpose flour

1. Mix Potatoes and Sauce Mix from potato mix, the ham, broth, celery, onion and pepper in 3 1/2- to 4-quart slow cooker.

2. Cover and cook on Low heat setting 7 hours.

3. Mix half-and-half and flour. Gradually stir half-and-half mixture into chowder until blended.

4. Cover and cook on Low heat setting about 1 hour, stirring occasionally, until thickened and vegetables are tender.

1 SERVING Calories 340 (Calories from Fat 145) | Fat 16g (Saturated 9g) | Cholesterol 50mg | Sodium 1840mg | Carbohydrate 35g (Dietary Fiber 2g) | Protein 16g   **%DAILY VALUE** Vitamin A 8% | Vitamin C 2% | Calcium 12% | Iron 10%   **EXCHANGES** 2 Starch, 1 Vegetable, 1 High-Fat Meat, 1 Fat **CARBOHYDRATE CHOICES** 2

BETTY'S TIP

The name *chowder* comes from the French *chaudière*, the caldron fishermen used to prepare fresh seafood stews. Enjoy this heart-warming chowder with warm biscuits or grilled cheese sandwiches on rye bread.

Smoky Ham and Navy Bean Stew

1 cup dried navy beans

5 cups water

1 pound fully cooked ham, cut into 1/2-inch cubes (3 cups)

2 medium stalks celery, sliced (1 cup)

2 medium carrots, sliced (1 cup)

1 small onion, chopped (1/4 cup)

1 cup water

1/4 teaspoon dried thyme leaves

1/4 teaspoon liquid smoke

1/4 cup chopped fresh parsley

PREP **15 min**   COOK **13 hr 30 min**   SERVINGS **4**

1. Heat beans and 5 cups water to boiling in 4-quart sauce-pan; reduce heat. Cover and simmer 1 hour 30 minutes. Drain and discard liquid.

2. Mix beans and remaining ingredients except parsley in 3 1/2- to 4-quart slow cooker.

3. Cover and cook on Low heat setting 10 to 12 hours.

4. Just before serving, stir in parsley.

1 SERVING Calories 355 (Calories from Fat 100) | Fat 11g (Saturated 4g) | Cholesterol 65mg | Sodium 1740mg | Carbohydrate 37g (Dietary Fiber 9g) | Protein 36g   %DAILY VALUE Vitamin A 100% | Vitamin C 10% | Calcium 12% | Iron 28%   EXCHANGES 2 Starch, 1 Vegetable, 4 Very Lean Meat, 1/2 Fat CARBOHYDRATE CHOICES 2 1/2

BETTY'S TIP

Liquid smoke is exactly that: liquid mixed with smoke. Brushed on or stirred into foods, liquid smoke lends a smoky hickory flavor. Look for it in the condiment aisle of your grocery store.

Corn, Ham and Potato Scallop

PREP **10 min**   COOK **9 hr**   SERVINGS **6**

6 cups 1-inch cubes peeled baking potatoes

1 1/2 cups cubed fully cooked ham

1 can (15 1/4 ounces) whole kernel corn, drained

1/4 cup chopped green bell pepper

2 teaspoons instant minced onion

1 can (10 3/4 ounces) condensed Cheddar cheese soup

1/2 cup milk

2 tablespoons all-purpose flour

1. Mix potatoes, ham, corn, bell pepper and onion in 3 1/2- to 4-quart slow cooker.

2. Mix soup, milk and flour in small bowl; beat with wire whisk until smooth. Pour soup mixture over potato mixture; stir gently to mix.

3. Cover and cook on Low heat setting 7 to 9 hours.

1 SERVING Calories 335 (Calories from Fat 70) | Fat 8g (Saturated 3g) | Cholesterol 30mg | Sodium 1130mg | Carbohydrate 51g (Dietary Fiber 4g) | Protein 15g **%DAILY VALUE** Vitamin A 22% | Vitamin C 18% | Calcium 8% | Iron 10% **EXCHANGES** 3 1/2 Starch, 1/2 Lean Meat, 1 Fat **CARBOHYDRATE CHOICES** 3 1/2

Corn, Roast Beef and Potato Scallop Substitute cooked roast beef for the ham.

BETTY'S TIP

Potatoes cook more quickly when cut into small pieces, so cubed potatoes will cook faster than quartered potatoes. The 1-inch chunks of potato in our recipe work well because they won't get too soft during the long cooking time.

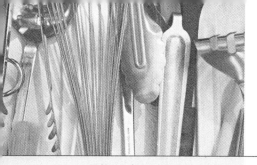

Ravioli with Sausage and Peppers

PREP 5 min   COOK 6 hr   SERVINGS 4

1/2 package (25-ounce size) frozen cheese-filled ravioli

2 cups frozen stir-fry bell peppers and onions (from 1-pound bag)

1 jar (26 ounces) chunky spaghetti sauce

8 ounces fully cooked smoked sausage, sliced

1/4 cup freshly shredded Parmesan cheese (1 ounce)

1. Mix all ingredients except cheese in 3 1/2- to 4-quart slow cooker.

2. Cover and cook on Low heat setting 5 to 6 hours.

3. Sprinkle individual servings with cheese.

1 SERVING Calories 635 (Calories from Fat 305) | Fat 34g (Saturated 12g) | Cholesterol 140mg | Sodium 2500g | Carbohydrate 55g (Dietary Fiber 4g) | Protein 27g %DAILY VALUE Vitamin A 32% | Vitamin C 50% | Calcium 34% | Iron 18% EXCHANGES 3 Starch, 2 Vegetable, 2 High-Fat Meat, 3 Fat CARBOHYDRATE CHOICES 3 1/2

BETTY'S TIP

If you'd prefer to use 2 cups of fresh veggies in this ravioli dish, go right ahead. Slice the sweet bell peppers and cut an onion into wedges.

Jambalaya

PREP **20 min**   COOK **9 hr**   SERVINGS **8**

1. Mix all ingredients except shrimp and rice in 3 1/2- to 6-quart slow cooker.

2. Cover and cook on Low heat setting 7 to 8 hours (or High heat setting 3 to 4 hours).

3. Stir in shrimp. Cover and cook on Low heat setting about 1 hour or until shrimp are pink and firm. Serve jambalaya with rice.

1 SERVING Calories 260 (Calories from Fat 90) | Fat 10g (Saturated 4g) | Cholesterol 80mg | Sodium 730mg | Carbohydrate 30g (Dietary Fiber 2g) | Protein 12g %DAILY VALUE Vitamin A 10% | Vitamin C 24% | Calcium 6% | Iron 16% EXCHANGES 1 1/2 Starch, 1 Vegetable, 1 High-Fat Meat CARBOHYDRATE CHOICES 2

1 large onion, chopped (1 cup)

1 medium green bell pepper, chopped (1 cup)

2 medium stalks celery, chopped (1 cup)

3 cloves garlic, finely chopped

1 can (28 ounces) diced tomatoes, undrained

2 cups chopped fully cooked smoked sausage

1 tablespoon parsley flakes

1/2 teaspoon dried thyme leaves

1/2 teaspoon salt

1/4 teaspoon pepper

1/4 teaspoon red pepper sauce

3/4 pound uncooked peeled deveined medium shrimp, thawed if frozen and tails peeled

4 cups hot cooked rice

BETTY'S TIP

Jambalaya is a classic Creole dish that consists of rice, tomatoes, onions, peppers, seafood and a variety of different meats such as sausage, ham or beef. If you like your food with a bit of a kick, use andouille sausage and diced tomatoes with green chilies.

Curried Pork and Veggie Stew

PREP **20 min**   COOK **10 hr**   SERVINGS **6**

3 tablespoons all-purpose flour

2 tablespoons curry powder

1/2 teaspoon salt

1 pound pork boneless center-cut loin, cut into 1-inch pieces

1 tablespoon olive or vegetable oil

1 medium onion, chopped (1/2 cup)

1 pound small red potatoes, cut into fourths (3 cups)

1 can (14 1/2 ounces) whole tomatoes, undrained

1/2 cup apple juice

2 1/2 cups cauliflowerets

1. Mix flour, 1 tablespoon curry powder and salt in resealable plastic food-storage bag. Add pork; toss to coat. Heat oil in 10-inch skillet over medium-high heat. Cook pork in oil, stirring occasionally, until brown.

2. Place onion and potatoes in 3 1/2- to 4-quart slow cooker. Top with pork and tomatoes. Mix apple juice and remaining 1 tablespoon curry powder; pour mixture over pork.

3. Cover and cook on Low heat setting 8 to 9 hours.

4. Stir in cauliflowerets. Cover and cook on Low heat setting about 1 hour or until cauliflower is tender.

1 SERVING Calories 360 (Calories from Fat 110) | Fat 12g (Saturated 4g) | Cholesterol 70mg | Sodium 420mg | Carbohydrate 38g (Dietary Fiber 5g) | Protein 30g   %DAILY VALUE Vitamin A 6% | Vitamin C 46% | Calcium 6% | Iron 20%   EXCHANGES 2 Starch, 2 Vegetable, 3 Lean Meat   CARBOHYDRATE CHOICES 2 1/2

BETTY'S TIP

Play up the Indian-inspired flavor of this stew by serving it over basmati rice with yogurt, mango chutney and cilantro or in pita folds or Indian naan bread.

Porketta with Two Potatoes

PREP **15 min**   COOK **10 hr**   SERVINGS **6**

1. Place potatoes in 3 1/2- to 4-quart slow cooker. Mix fennel seed, oregano, paprika, garlic powder, salt and pepper. Rub herb mixture into pork. Place pork on potatoes. Pour broth over pork and potatoes.

2. Cover and cook on Low heat setting 8 to 10 hours.

3. Remove pork from slow cooker; place on serving platter. Slice pork. Serve pork with potatoes.

1 SERVING Calories 340 (Calories from Fat 110) | Fat 12g (Saturated 4g) | Cholesterol 95mg | Sodium 430mg | Carbohydrate 21g (Dietary Fiber 3g) | Protein 36g   **%DAILY VALUE** Vitamin A 100% | Vitamin C 14% | Calcium 2% | Iron 12%   **EXCHANGES** 1/1 2 Starch, 4 Lean Meat   **CARBOHYDRATE CHOICES** 1 1/2

2 medium dark–orange sweet potatoes, peeled and cut into 1/2-inch cubes (about 2 1/2 cups)

2 medium Yukon gold potatoes, cut into 1/2-inch cubes (about 2 1/2 cups)

2 teaspoons fennel seed, crushed

1 teaspoon dried oregano leaves

1 teaspoon paprika

1/2 teaspoon garlic powder

1/2 teaspoon salt

1/4 teaspoon pepper

2-pound pork boneless loin roast

1 cup chicken broth

BETTY'S TIP

Some pork roasts come wrapped in netting. If this is the case with yours, carefully remove the netting before seasoning the roast and retie it with twine after you're done seasoning.

Southwestern Pork Stew

1 medium onion, chopped (1/2 cup)

3 large cloves garlic, finely chopped

2 pounds pork boneless top loin, trimmed of fat and cut into 1 1/2-inch pieces

1/4 cup cornmeal

2 teaspoons ground cumin

1/2 teaspoon dried oregano leaves

1/2 teaspoon salt

1 can (15 to 16 ounces) chili beans in sauce, undrained

1 can (14 1/2 ounces) diced tomatoes and mild chilies, undrained

1 cup chicken broth

2 cups frozen whole kernel corn (from 1-pound bag), thawed and drained

PREP **20 min**   COOK **10 hr 30 min**   SERVINGS **8**

1. Place onion and garlic in 3 1/2- to 4-quart slow cooker. Top with pork. Mix cornmeal, cumin, oregano and salt; sprinkle over pork and mix well. Add beans, tomatoes and broth; mix well.

2. Cover and cook on Low heat setting 8 to 10 hours.

3. Stir in corn. Cover and cook on Low heat setting about 30 minutes or until corn is tender.

1 SERVING Calories 290 (Calories from Fat 90) | Fat 10g (Saturated 3g) | Cholesterol 70mg | Sodium 770mg | Carbohydrate 23g (Dietary Fiber 4g) | Protein 31g   %DAILY VALUE Vitamin A 8% | Vitamin C 16% | Calcium 4% | Iron 14%   EXCHANGES 1 1/2 Starch, 4 Very Lean Meat, 1 Fat   CARBOHYDRATE CHOICES 1 1/2

BETTY'S TIP

When you're in a hurry, use 1 tablespoon ready-to-use minced garlic. You'll find it in jars in the produce department of the supermarket.

Pork Chop Supper

PREP **15 min**   COOK **7 hr 15 min**   SERVINGS **6**

1. Spray 10-inch nonstick skillet with cooking spray; heat over medium-high heat. Cook pork in skillet, turning once, until brown.

2. Place potatoes in 3 1/2- to 6-quart slow cooker. Mix soup, mushrooms, wine, thyme, garlic powder, Worcestershire sauce and flour; spoon half of soup mixture over potatoes. Place pork on potatoes; cover with remaining soup mixture.

3. Cover and cook on Low heat setting 6 to 7 hours.

4. Remove pork from slow cooker; keep warm. Stir pimientos and peas into slow cooker. Cover and cook on Low heat setting about 15 minutes or until peas are tender. Serve vegetable mixture with pork.

6 pork loin or rib chops, 1/2 inch thick

1 1/2 pounds medium new potatoes, cut into eighths (about 6 potatoes)

1 can (10 3/4 ounces) condensed cream of mushroom soup

1 can (4 ounces) mushroom pieces and stems, drained

2 tablespoons dry white wine

1/4 teaspoon dried thyme leaves

1/2 teaspoon garlic powder

1/2 teaspoon Worcestershire sauce

3 tablespoons all-purpose flour

1 tablespoon diced pimientos

1 package (10 ounces) frozen green peas, rinsed and drained

1 SERVING Calories 320 (Calories from Fat 100) | Fat 11g (Saturated 4g) | Cholesterol 65mg | Sodium 520mg | Carbohydrate 33g (Dietary Fiber 6g) | Protein 28g %DAILY VALUE Vitamin A 6% | Vitamin C 16% | Calcium 6% | Iron 20% EXCHANGES 2 Starch, 3 Lean Meat CARBOHYDRATE CHOICES 2

BETTY'S TIP

Virtually any cream soup will work in this recipe. Try golden cream of mushroom, cream of chicken or cream of celery instead of the cream of mushroom.

Pork Chops with Spiced Fruit Stuffing

1 cup diced dried fruit and raisin mixture

1 cup chicken broth

1/2 cup apple juice

3 tablespoons butter or margarine

1/4 teaspoon ground cinnamon

1/8 teaspoon ground nutmeg

1 package (6 ounces) herb stuffing mix

4 pork boneless loin chops, about 1/2 inch thick (about 1 pound)

1/8 teaspoon salt

1/8 teaspoon pepper

PREP **10** min   COOK **6** hr   SERVINGS **4**

1. Mix dried fruit, broth, 1/4 cup apple juice, the butter, cinnamon and nutmeg in 3-quart saucepan. Heat to boiling. Stir in stuffing mix; remove saucepan from heat.

2. Arrange pork in 3 1/2- to 4-quart slow cooker. Pour remaining 1/4 cup apple juice over pork. Sprinkle with salt and pepper. Top with stuffing mixture.

3. Cover and cook on Low heat setting 5 to 6 hours.

4. Remove stuffing from slow cooker; place in serving bowl. Stir gently. Serve pork with stuffing.

1 SERVING Calories 505 (Calories from Fat 160) | Fat 18g (Saturated 4g) | Cholesterol 65mg | Sodium 1170mg | Carbohydrate 55g (Dietary Fiber 4g) | Protein 28g   %DAILY VALUE Vitamin A 14% | Vitamin C 0% | Calcium 6% | Iron 18%   EXCHANGES 3 Starch, 1 Fruit, 2 1/2 Lean Meat, 1 1/2 Fat CARBOHYDRATE CHOICES 3 1/2

BETTY'S TIP

One cup of your favorite chopped dried fruit, such as apples or apricots, can be used in place of the dried fruit and raisin mixture.

Pork Chops with Apple-Cherry Stuffing

PREP **15 min**   COOK **8 hr**   SERVINGS **6**

1 package (6 ounces) herb stuffing mix

2 medium stalks celery, chopped (1 cup)

1 medium tart cooking apple, peeled and chopped

1 medium onion, chopped (1/2 cup)

1 cup dried cherries

1/4 cup butter or margarine, melted

1 cup chicken broth

6 pork boneless loin chops, about 1/2 inch thick

1. Spray inside of 4- to 5-quart slow cooker with cooking spray. Mix all ingredients except pork. Place half of the stuffing mixture in slow cooker; top with pork. Spoon remaining stuffing over pork.

2. Cover and cook on Low heat setting 6 to 8 hours.

> 1 SERVING Calories 365 (Calories from Fat 155) | Fat 17g (Saturated 4g) | Cholesterol 65mg | Sodium 500mg | Carbohydrate 35g (Dietary Fiber 8g) | Protein 26g %DAILY VALUE Vitamin A 12% | Vitamin C 20% | Calcium 4% | Iron 10% EXCHANGES 1 1/2 Starch, 1 Fruit, 3 Lean Meat, 1/2 Fat CARBOHYDRATE CHOICES 2

Pork Chops with Apple-Cranberry Stuffing Substitute dried cranberries for the cooking apple.

BETTY'S TIP

Steamed green beans and baked sweet potatoes are tasty accompaniments for the pork chops.

Brown Sugar–Glazed Pork with Sweet Potatoes

PREP **10 min**   COOK **10 hr**   SERVINGS **6**

1 1/2 pounds sweet potatoes, peeled and cut into 1/2-inch slices

2 1/2-pound pork boneless shoulder roast (tied or in netting)

2 tablespoons packed brown sugar

1/4 teaspoon ground red pepper (cayenne)

1/4 teaspoon salt

1/8 teaspoon pepper

1 clove garlic, finely chopped

1. Place sweet potatoes in 3 1/2- to 4-quart slow cooker. Place pork on sweet potatoes. Mix remaining ingredients; sprinkle over pork.

2. Cover and cook on Low heat setting 8 to 10 hours.

3. Remove pork from slow cooker; place on cutting board. Remove strings or netting from pork. Slice pork, or pull pork into serving pieces using 2 forks. Serve with sweet potatoes, spooning juices over pork.

1 SERVING Calories 445 (Calories from Fat 205) | Fat 23g (Saturated 8g) | Cholesterol 120mg | Sodium 180mg | Carbohydrate 18g (Dietary Fiber 2g) | Protein 41g   %DAILY VALUE Vitamin A 100% | Vitamin C 12% | Calcium 2% | Iron 10%   EXCHANGES 1 Starch, 5 1/2 Lean Meat, 1 1/2 Fat   CARBOHYDRATE CHOICES 1

BETTY'S TIP

When a pork shoulder is boned, the butcher uses kitchen string or an elastic net to shape the meat into a tidy roast. If you leave the string or netting on while the roast cooks, you'll wind up with neat slices at serving time.

Honey-Barbecue-Glazed Pork Roast with Carrots and Corn

PREP **15 min**   COOK **10 hr 20 min**   SERVINGS **6**

1. Remove fat from pork. Place pork in 3 1/2- to 4-quart slow cooker. Arrange carrots around and on top of pork. Mix 1/2 cup barbecue sauce, the honey, vinegar and seasoned salt in small bowl; pour over pork and carrots.

2. Cover and cook on Low heat setting 8 to 10 hours.

3. Remove pork and vegetables from slow cooker; place on serving platter. Cover to keep warm. Mix 2/3 cup barbecue sauce and the flour; gradually stir into juices in slow cooker. Increase heat setting to High. Cover and cook about 15 minutes, stirring occasionally, until thickened.

4. Stir corn into mixture in slow cooker. Cover and cook on High heat setting 5 minutes. Serve sauce over pork and vegetables.

3-pound pork boneless shoulder roast

1 bag (1 pound) baby-cut carrots

1/2 cup barbecue sauce

1/4 cup honey

3 tablespoons balsamic vinegar

1 teaspoon seasoned salt

2/3 cup barbecue sauce

1/4 cup all-purpose flour

1 cup frozen whole kernel corn (from 1-pound bag)

1 SERVING Calories 635 (Calories from Fat 250) | Fat 27g (Saturated 10g) | Cholesterol 145mg | Sodium 890mg | Carbohydrate 46g (Dietary Fiber 3g) | Protein 51g   %DAILY VALUE Vitamin A 100% | Vitamin C 8% | Calcium 4% | Iron 16%   EXCHANGES 3 Starch, 5 1/2 Medium-Fat Meat   CARBOHYDRATE CHOICES 3

BETTY'S TIP

The flavor of the sauce for this roast depends on purchased barbecue sauce, so use your family's favorite brand.

Easy Pork Chili

PREP **10 min**   COOK **10 hr 5 min**   SERVINGS **6**

1 pound pork boneless shoulder, cut into 1-inch pieces

1 medium onion, chopped (1/2 cup)

1 jar (16 ounces) salsa

1 can (15 ounces) chunky tomato sauce with onions, celery and green bell peppers

1 teaspoon Mexican seasoning

1 can (4.5 ounces) chopped green chiles, drained

1 can (15 ounces) black beans, rinsed and drained

1. Mix all ingredients except beans in 3 1/2- to 4-quart slow cooker.

2. Cover and cook on Low heat setting 8 to 10 hours.

3. Stir in beans. Cover and cook about 5 minutes or until hot.

1 SERVING Calories 275 (Calories from Fat 90) | Fat 10g (Saturated 3g) | Cholesterol 50mg | Sodium 960mg | Carbohydrate 30g (Dietary Fiber 8g) | Protein 24g   %DAILY VALUE Vitamin A 12% | Vitamin C 32% | Calcium 10% | Iron 20%   EXCHANGES 2 Starch, 2 1/2 Very Lean Meat, 1 Fat   CARBOHYDRATE CHOICES 2

Easy Steak Chili Substitute beef round steak for the pork.

BETTY'S TIP

If you like your chili with a little less heat, use mild salsa and omit the Mexican seasoning. If you'd like to kick the spice up a notch, use medium-spicy salsa and 1 teaspoon Mexican seasoning.

Easy Bean and Kielbasa Soup

PREP **25 min**   COOK **11 hr**   SERVINGS **8**

1. Heat bean soup mix and broth to boiling in 4-quart saucepan; reduce heat. Cover and simmer 1 hour.

2. Pour bean mixture into 5- to 6-quart slow cooker. Stir in remaining ingredients.

3. Cover and cook on Low heat setting 8 to 10 hours.

1 **SERVING** Calories 310 (Calories from Fat 165) | Fat 17g (Saturated 6g) | Cholesterol 30mg | Sodium 1330mg | Carbohydrate 27g (Dietary Fiber 7g) | Protein 17g   %**DAILY VALUE** Vitamin A 54% | Vitamin C 12% | Calcium 10% | Iron 20%   **EXCHANGES** 1 Starch, 2 Vegetable, 1 1/2 High-Fat Meat, 1 Fat **CARBOHYDRATE CHOICES** 2

Easy Bean Soup Omit the kielbasa.

1/2 package (20-ounce size) 15- or 16-dried bean soup mix, sorted and rinsed

5 cans (14 ounces each) chicken broth

1 package (16 ounces) kielbasa sausage, cut lengthwise in half, then sliced

1 can (14 1/2 ounces) diced tomatoes, undrained

4 medium carrots, chopped (2 cups)

3 medium stalks celery, chopped (1 1/2 cups)

1 large onion, chopped (1 cup)

2 tablespoons tomato paste

1 teaspoon dried thyme leaves

1/2 teaspoon salt

1/2 teaspoon pepper

BETTY'S TIP

To add a touch of color and flavor, stir 1/4 cup of chopped fresh parsley into the soup just before serving.

Moroccan Lamb and Rice

1 pound boneless lamb, cut into 1-inch pieces, or 1 pound lamb stew meat

1 small apple, shredded

1 package (6.9 ounces) rice and vermicelli mix with chicken seasonings

1 1/2 cups chicken broth

1 teaspoon curry powder

1/4 cup raisins

1/4 cup slivered almonds

PREP **10** min   COOK **9** hr   SERVINGS **4**

1. Mix lamb, apple, seasoning packet from rice mix, broth and curry powder in 3 1/2- to 4-quart slow cooker.

2. Cover and cook on Low heat setting 7 to 9 hours. During last 25 minutes of cooking, stir in rice and raisins. Increase heat setting to High. Cover and cook 20 minutes or until rice is tender.

3. Sprinkle almonds over individual servings.

1 SERVING Calories 305 (Calories from Fat 100) | Fat 11g (Saturated 3g) | Cholesterol 65mg | Sodium 630mg | Carbohydrate 26g (Dietary Fiber 2g) | Protein 25g   %DAILY VALUE Vitamin A 0% | Vitamin C 0% | Calcium 4% | Iron 14%   EXCHANGES 1 Starch, 1/2 Fruit, 3 Lean Meat, 1 1/2 Fat CARBOHYDRATE CHOICES 2

BETTY'S TIP

Use the largest holes on a kitchen grater to shred the apple for this stew. Large holes produce less juice and the bigger shreds mean the job is done faster.

Cioppino

1. Mix all ingredients except fish, shrimp, clams, crabmeat and parsley in 5- to 6-quart slow cooker.

2. Cover and cook on High heat setting 3 to 4 hours.

3. Stir in fish, shrimp, clams and crabmeat. Reduce heat setting to Low. Cover and cook 30 to 45 minutes or until fish flakes easily with fork. Remove bay leaf. Stir in parsley.

1 SERVING Calories 200 (Calories from Fat 35) | Fat 4g (Saturated 1g) | Cholesterol 125mg | Sodium 600mg | Carbohydrate 15g (Dietary Fiber 3g) | Protein 29g   %DAILY VALUE Vitamin A 24% | Vitamin C 30% | Calcium 12% | Iron 52%   EXCHANGES 1/2 Starch, 2 Vegetable, 3 Very Lean Meat   CARBOHYDRATE CHOICES 1

2 large onions, chopped (2 cups)

2 medium stalks celery, finely chopped (1 cup)

5 cloves garlic, finely chopped

1 can (28 ounces) diced tomatoes, undrained

1 bottle (8 ounces) clam juice

1 can (6 ounces) tomato paste

1/2 cup dry white wine or water

1 tablespoon red wine vinegar

1 tablespoon olive oil

2 1/2 teaspoons Italian seasoning

1/4 teaspoon sugar

1/4 teaspoon crushed red pepper

1 dried bay leaf

1 pound firm-fleshed white fish, cut into 1-inch pieces

3/4 pound uncooked peeled deveined medium shrimp, thawed if frozen and tails peeled

1 can (6 1/2 ounces) chopped clams with juice, undrained

1 can (6 ounces) crabmeat, drained, cartilage removed and flaked

1/4 cup chopped fresh parsley

BETTY'S TIP

Serve this tasty fish stew over rice along with plenty of hot bread or rolls and a glass of white wine to complete the meal.

Spicy Black Bean Barbecue Chili

2 cups dried black beans (1 pound), sorted and rinsed

10 cups water

1 tablespoon olive or vegetable oil

1 large onion, chopped (1 cup)

6 cloves garlic, finely chopped

4 cups water

1 can (14 1/2 ounces) diced tomatoes with green chilies, undrained

1 cup hickory barbecue sauce

1 chipotle chili in adobo sauce, finely chopped, plus 1 teaspoon adobo sauce (from 11-ounce can)

2 cups frozen veggie crumbles

1 medium green or red bell pepper, chopped (1 cup)

1/4 cup chopped fresh cilantro

PREP 15 min   STAND 1 hr   COOK 12 hr 30 min   SERVINGS 6

1. Heat beans and 10 cups water to boiling in 4-quart Dutch oven; reduce heat. Simmer uncovered 10 minutes; remove from heat. Cover and let stand 1 hour.

2. Heat oil in 10-inch skillet over medium-high heat. Cook onion and garlic in oil about 8 minutes, stirring occasionally, until onion is tender and light golden brown.

3. Drain beans. Place beans in 3 1/2- to 4-quart slow cooker. Add 4 cups water and onion mixture.

4. Cover and cook on Low heat setting 10 to 12 hours. Stir in tomatoes, barbecue sauce, chili, adobo sauce and frozen veggie crumbles. Increase heat setting to High. Cover and cook 30 minutes. Serve chili sprinkled with bell pepper and cilantro.

1 SERVING Calories 350 (Calories from Fat 35) | Fat 4g (Saturated 1g) | Cholesterol 0mg | Sodium 840mg | Carbohydrate 66g (Dietary Fiber 11g) | Protein 22g %DAILY VALUE Vitamin A 10% | Vitamin C 30% | Calcium 16% | Iron 34% EXCHANGES 3 Starch, 3 Vegetable, 1 Very Lean Meat CARBOHYDRATE CHOICES 4 1/2

BETTY'S TIP

Heat things up by using 2 chipotle chilies and 2 teaspoons adobo sauce in this barbecue chili.

French Onion Soup

PREP **15 min**   COOK **5 hr 35 min**   SERVINGS **8**

3 large onions, sliced

3 tablespoons butter
or margarine, melted

4 cans (14 ounces each)
beef broth

3 tablespoons all-purpose
flour

1 tablespoon
Worcestershire sauce

1 teaspoon sugar

1/4 teaspoon pepper

Cheesy Broiled French
Bread (below left)

1. Mix onions and butter in 5- to 6-quart slow cooker. Cover and cook on High heat setting 4 to 5 hours or until onions begin to brown slightly around edges.

2. Mix 1/4 cup of the broth, the flour, Worcestershire sauce, sugar and pepper in small bowl. Stir flour mixture and remaining broth into onions. Cover and cook on High heat setting 30 to 35 minutes or until hot.

3. Make Cheesy Broiled French Bread. Place 1 slice bread on each bowl of soup.

Cheesy Broiled French Bread

8 slices French bread, 1 inch thick

3/4 cup shredded mozzarella cheese (3 ounces)

2 tablespoons grated or shredded Parmesan cheese

Set oven control to broil. Place bread slices on ungreased cookie sheet. Sprinkle with cheeses. Broil with tops 5 to 6 inches from heat 1 to 2 minutes or until cheeses are melted.

1 SERVING Calories 295 (Calories from Fat 80) | Fat 9g (Saturated 5g) | Cholesterol 20mg | Sodium 1410mg | Carbohydrate 40g (Dietary Fiber 3g) | Protein 13g %DAILY VALUE Vitamin A 6% | Vitamin C 2% | Calcium 18% | Iron 14% EXCHANGES 2 1/2 Starch, 1 Vegetable, 1 1/2 Fat CARBOHYDRATE CHOICES 2 1/2

BETTY'S TIP

Top this soup with large crouton cubes instead of making the cheesy bread, and simply sprinkle soup with shredded Parmesan or mozzarella cheese before serving.

Ratatouille Bean Stew

PREP 10 min   COOK 12 hr   SERVINGS 5

1 cup dried garbanzo beans

1 medium onion, chopped (1/2 cup)

2 cloves garlic, finely chopped

1 can (14 ounces) chicken broth

1 jar (4 1/2 ounces) sliced mushrooms, drained

1/4 teaspoon salt

1 large zucchini, sliced

1 medium red or green bell pepper, cut into pieces

1 teaspoon Italian seasoning

1 can (14.5 ounces) diced tomatoes with Italian-style herbs, undrained

1. Soak and drain beans as directed on package.

2. Mix beans, onion, garlic, broth, mushrooms and salt in 3 1/2- to 4-quart slow cooker.

3. Cover and cook on Low heat setting 10 to 12 hours. During last 35 minutes of cooking, stir in zucchini, bell pepper, Italian seasoning and tomatoes. Increase heat setting to High. Cover and cook 30 to 35 minutes or until vegetables are tender.

1 SERVING Calories 220 (Calories from Fat 25) | Fat 3g (Saturated 0g) | Cholesterol 0mg | Sodium 85mg | Carbohydrate 35g (Dietary Fiber 9g) | Protein 11g   %DAILY VALUE Vitamin A 40% | Vitamin C 52% | Calcium 8% | Iron 20%   EXCHANGES 2 Starch, 1 Vegetable, 1/2 Very Lean Meat, 1/2 Fat   CARBOHYDRATE CHOICES 2

BETTY'S TIP

It's easy to make this recipe vegetarian; simply use vegetable broth in place of the chicken broth.

Pizzas with Pizzazz

Pepperoni Pizza-Hamburger Pie

1 pound lean ground beef

1/3 cup dry bread crumbs

1 1/2 teaspoons chopped fresh or 1/2 teaspoon dried oregano leaves

1/4 teaspoon salt

1 egg

1/2 cup sliced mushrooms

1/2 cup chopped green bell pepper

1/3 cup chopped pepperoni (2 ounces)

1/4 cup sliced ripe olives

1 cup spaghetti sauce

1 cup shredded mozzarella cheese (4 ounces)

PREP 20 min   BAKE 30 min   STAND 5 min   SERVINGS 6

1. Heat oven to 400°. Mix beef, bread crumbs, oregano, salt and egg. Press mixture evenly against bottom and side of ungreased pie plate, 9×1 1/4 inches.

2. Sprinkle mushrooms, bell pepper, pepperoni and olives into beef-lined plate. Pour spaghetti sauce over toppings.

3. Bake uncovered about 25 minutes or until beef is no longer pink in center and juice is clear; carefully drain. Sprinkle with cheese. Bake about 5 minutes longer or until cheese is light brown. Let stand 5 minutes before cutting.

1 SERVING Calories 335 (Calories from Fat 190) | Fat 21g (Saturated 8g) | Cholesterol 95mg | Sodium 740mg | Carbohydrate 14g (Dietary Fiber 1g) | Protein 24g %DAILY VALUE Vitamin A 8% | Vitamin C 14% | Calcium 18% | Iron 14% EXCHANGES 3 Vegetable, 3 Medium-Fat Meat, 1 Fat CARBOHYDRATE CHOICES 1

BETTY'S TIP

Kids can get a little picky about their pizza toppings. If they don't happen to be fans of mushrooms or green peppers, you can leave them out if you like. You can always toss in a little extra ground beef or pepperoni to make up the difference.

Salsa Pizza with Cheese Crust

PREP 15 min   COOK 10 min   BAKE 28 min   SERVINGS 8

1 pound lean ground beef

1 1/4 cups thick-and-chunky salsa

2 cups Original Bisquick mix

1/4 cup mild salsa-flavored or jalapeño-flavored process cheese sauce

1/4 cup hot water

8 medium green onions, sliced (1/2 cup)

1 cup shredded Colby-Monterey Jack cheese (4 ounces)

1. Heat oven to 375°. Spray large cookie sheet with cooking spray. Cook beef in 10-inch skillet over medium heat 8 to 10 minutes, stirring occasionally, until brown; drain. Stir in salsa; remove from heat.

2. Stir Bisquick mix, cheese sauce and water in medium bowl until soft dough forms; beat vigorously 20 strokes. Place dough on surface dusted with Bisquick mix; gently roll in Bisquick mix to coat. Shape into ball; knead about 5 times or until smooth. Roll dough into 14-inch circle; place on cookie sheet. Spread beef mixture over dough to within 2 inches of edge. Sprinkle with onions. Fold edge of dough over beef mixture. Sprinkle cheese over beef mixture.

3. Bake 25 to 28 minutes or until crust is golden brown and cheese is melted.

1 SERVING Calories 315 (Calories from Fat 160) | Fat 18g (Saturated 8g) | Cholesterol 50mg | Sodium 750mg | Carbohydrate 22g (Dietary Fiber 1g) | Protein 17g %DAILY VALUE Vitamin A 12% | Vitamin C 6% | Calcium 16% | Iron 14% EXCHANGES 1 Starch, 1 Vegetable, 2 High-Fat Meat CARBOHYDRATE CHOICES 1 1/2

Salsa Pork Pizza with Cheese Crust Substitute 1 pound of bulk pork sausage for the ground beef.

BETTY'S TIP

Garnish this Mexican-style pizza with chopped tomato, shredded lettuce and sliced ripe olives. A dollop of guacamole or sour cream makes a tasty topping.

Taco Pizza

PREP 20 min   BAKE 12 min   SERVINGS 4

1 round focaccia bread
or 1 package (14 ounces)
ready-to-serve original
Italian pizza crust (12 inches
in diameter)

3/4 pound extra-lean
ground beef

2 tablespoons taco
seasoning mix (from
1 1/4-ounce envelope)

1 can (10 ounces) diced
tomatoes and green
chilies, drained

1/2 cup shredded
reduced-fat Cheddar
cheese (2 ounces)

Shredded lettuce,
if desired

Reduced-fat sour cream,
if desired

Chopped tomatoes,
if desired

1. Heat oven to 425°. Place bread on 12-inch pizza pan or cookie sheet.

2. Cook beef in 10-inch nonstick skillet over medium heat 8 to 10 minutes, stirring occasionally, until brown; drain. Stir in taco seasoning mix; stir in half the amount of water as directed on package. Reduce heat to low. Simmer uncovered 5 minutes.

3. Spoon beef mixture over bread. Top with tomatoes. Sprinkle with cheese. Bake about 12 minutes or until tomatoes are hot and cheese is melted. Serve topped with lettuce, sour cream and tomatoes.

1 SERVING Calories 585 (Calories from Fat 180) | Fat 20g (Saturated 5g) | Cholesterol 50mg | Sodium 1600mg | Carbohydrate 73g (Dietary Fiber 4g) | Protein 32g %DAILY VALUE Vitamin A 18% | Vitamin C 10% | Calcium 16% | Iron 36% EXCHANGES 5 Starch, 2 Lean Meat, 2 Fat CARBOHYDRATE CHOICES 5

BETTY'S TIP

A pizza crust by any other name . . . .When you're looking for ready-to-serve pizza crusts, keep in mind they have many names, including "Italian flatbread" and "Italian bread shell."

Cheeseburger Pizza

PREP **20 min**   BAKE **28 min**   STAND **5 min**   SERVINGS **8**

1 pound lean ground beef

1/2 cup process cheese sauce

2 cups Original Bisquick mix

1/4 cup process cheese sauce

1/4 cup hot water

1/4 cup shredded Colby-Monterey Jack cheese (1 ounce)

1 roma (plum) tomato, chopped (1/3 cup)

1. Heat oven to 375°. Spray large cookie sheet with cooking spray. Cook beef in 10-inch skillet over medium-high heat 5 to 7 minutes, stirring occasionally, until brown; drain. Stir in 1/2 cup cheese sauce until cheese is melted.

2. Stir Bisquick mix, 1/4 cup cheese sauce and the hot water until soft dough forms; beat vigorously 20 strokes. Place dough on surface dusted with Bisquick mix; gently roll in Bisquick mix to coat. Shape into ball; knead about 5 times or until smooth. Roll dough into 14-inch circle; place on cookie sheet. Spoon beef mixture over dough to within 2 inches of edge. Fold edge of dough over beef mixture.

3. Bake 25 to 28 minutes or until crust is golden brown. Sprinkle with cheese and tomato. Let stand 5 minutes before cutting.

1 SERVING Calories 455 (Calories from Fat 250) | Fat 28g (Saturated 13g) | Cholesterol 75mg | Sodium 990mg | Carbohydrate 29g (Dietary Fiber 1g) | Protein 22g   %DAILY VALUE Vitamin A 12% | Vitamin C 2% | Calcium 18% | Iron 16%   EXCHANGES 2 Starch, 2 High-Fat Meat, 2 Fat   CARBOHYDRATE CHOICES 2

Turkey Burger Pizza Substitute 1 pound ground turkey for the ground beef.

BETTY'S TIP

Cheeseburger lovers will want to top this pizza with all their favorite fixin's—chopped onion, pickle relish, chopped tomato, ketchup and mustard.

Sloppy Joe Pizza

1 pound lean ground beef

3 tablespoons taco seasoning mix (from 1 1/4-ounce envelope)

1 package (14 ounces) ready-to-serve original Italian pizza crust or other 12-inch ready-to-serve pizza crust

1/3 cup purchased black bean dip

1 cup shredded Monterey Jack cheese with jalapeño peppers (4 ounces)

Salsa and guacamole, if desired

PREP **10 min**　BAKE **10 min**　SERVINGS **6**

1. Heat oven to 425°. Cook beef in 10-inch nonstick skillet over medium heat 8 to 10 minutes, stirring occasionally, until brown; drain. Stir in taco seasoning mix.

2. Place pizza crust on ungreased cookie sheet. Spread evenly with bean dip. Spoon beef over bean layer. Sprinkle with cheese.

3. Bake 8 to 10 minutes or until cheese is melted. Serve with salsa and guacamole.

1 SERVING Calories 515 (Calories from Fat 190) | Fat 21g (Saturated 9g) | Cholesterol 65mg | Sodium 660mg | Carbohydrate 55g (Dietary Fiber 3g) | Protein 27g %DAILY VALUE Vitamin A 16% | Vitamin C 0% | Calcium 18% | Iron 26% EXCHANGES 3 1/2 Starch, 2 1/2 High-Fat Meat CARBOHYDRATE CHOICES 3 1/2

BETTY'S TIP

Using purchased black bean dip makes this easy recipe even easier. You may find a variety of flavors, so feel free to experiment to find your family's favorite.

Easy Philly Cheesesteak Pizza

PREP **10 min**   BAKE **10 min**   SERVINGS **6**

1 can (13.8 ounces) refrigerated pizza crust dough

2 cups frozen stir-fry bell peppers and onions (from 1-pound bag)

2 tablespoons Dijon-mayonnaise blend

8 ounces thinly sliced cooked deli roast beef

2 cups shredded process American cheese (8 ounces)

1. Heat oven to 425°. Spray 12-inch pizza pan with cooking spray. Press pizza crust dough in pan. Bake 8 minutes.

2. While crust is baking, spray 10-inch nonstick skillet with cooking spray; heat over medium-high heat. Cook frozen bell pepper mixture in skillet 4 to 5 minutes, stirring frequently, until crisp-tender.

3. Spread Dijon-mayonnaise blend over partially baked crust. Top with roast beef, bell pepper mixture and cheese. Bake 8 to 10 minutes or until crust is golden brown.

1 SERVING Calories 370 (Calories from Fat 160) | Fat 18g (Saturated 9g) | Cholesterol 50mg | Sodium 830mg | Carbohydrate 28g (Dietary Fiber 2g) | Protein 24g   %DAILY VALUE Vitamin A 12% | Vitamin C 20% | Calcium 20% | Iron 16%   EXCHANGES 2 Starch, 2 1/2 Medium-Fat Meat, 1/2 Fat CARBOHYDRATE CHOICES 2

BETTY'S TIP

Here's a quick take on the cheesesteak sandwich made famous in Philadelphia in the 1930s. Turning it into a hearty pizza means it can serve the whole family super-fast.

Thai Chicken Pizzas

6 flour tortillas (8 to 10 inches in diameter)

1/2 cup peanut butter

1/4 cup soy sauce

2 tablespoons seasoned rice vinegar

2 teaspoons sugar

2 cups shredded mozzarella cheese (8 ounces)

2 cups chopped cooked chicken breast

1 bag (1 pound) frozen stir-fry vegetables, thawed and drained

PREP 5 min   BAKE 20 min   SERVINGS 6

1. Heat oven to 400°. Place tortillas on ungreased cookie sheet. Bake about 5 minutes or until crisp.

2. Mix peanut butter, soy sauce, vinegar and sugar; spread over tortillas. Top each with 1/4 cup of the cheese. Spread chicken and vegetables evenly over tortillas. Sprinkle with remaining 1/2 cup cheese.

3. Bake 10 to 15 minutes or until pizzas are hot and cheese is melted.

1 SERVING Calories 490 (Calories from Fat 215) | Fat 24g (Saturated 10g) | Cholesterol 60mg | Sodium 1330mg | Carbohydrate 37g (Dietary Fiber 5g) | Protein 36g   %DAILY VALUE Vitamin A 20% | Vitamin C 22% | Calcium 36% | Iron 18%   EXCHANGES 2 Starch, 1 Vegetable, 4 Lean Meat, 2 Fat CARBOHYDRATE CHOICES 2 1/2

BETTY'S TIP

Peanut sauce, found in the Asian foods section of your grocery store, can be used in place of the peanut butter, soy sauce, vinegar and sugar. Use slightly less than 1 cup.

Chicken, Artichoke and Red Onion Pizza

PREP **5 min**   BAKE **10 min**   SERVINGS **4**

1. Heat oven to 400°. Melt butter in 8-inch skillet over medium heat. Cook onion in butter 3 to 5 minutes, stirring occasionally, until crisp-tender.

2. Place pizza crust on ungreased cookie sheet. Spread onion over pizza crust. Top with chicken, artichoke hearts, bell peppers and cheese.

3. Bake 8 to 10 minutes or until cheese is melted.

1 SERVING Calories 560 (Calories from Fat 170) | Fat 19g (Saturated 10g) | Cholesterol 65mg | Sodium 1015mg | Carbohydrate 68g (Dietary Fiber 7g) | Protein 29g %DAILY VALUE Vitamin A 20% | Vitamin C 18% | Calcium 28% | Iron 26% EXCHANGES 4 Starch, 1 Vegetable, 2 High-Fat Meat, 1/2 Fat CARBOHYDRATE CHOICES 4 1/2

2 teaspoons butter or margarine

1 large red onion, sliced (2 cups)

1 package (14 ounces) ready-to-serve original Italian pizza crust or other 12-inch ready-to-serve pizza crust

1 cup cubed cooked chicken or turkey

1 jar (6 to 7 ounces) marinated artichoke hearts, drained and sliced

3 tablespoons sliced drained roasted red bell peppers (from 7-ounce jar)

1 cup shredded sharp Cheddar cheese (4 ounces)

BETTY'S TIP

Artichoke hearts add a distinctive flavor to this easy pizza. Serve the pizza for a light supper, or cut it into small squares for a great appetizer. If you don't have roasted red bell peppers, use jarred pimientos.

Chicken Pizza Mexicana

2 cups shredded taco-seasoned cheese (8 ounces)

1 package (14 ounces) ready-to-serve original Italian pizza crust or other 12-inch ready-to-serve pizza crust

1 1/2 cups chopped cooked chicken

2 roma (plum) tomatoes, thinly sliced

1 small jalapeño chili, seeded and finely chopped

PREP **10 min**   GRILL **10 min**   SERVINGS **4**

1. Heat coals or gas grill for direct heat. Sprinkle cheese evenly over pizza crust. Top with remaining ingredients.

2. Cover and grill pizza 4 to 6 inches from medium heat 8 to 10 minutes or until crust is crisp and cheese is melted. (If crust browns too quickly, place a piece of aluminum foil between crust and grill.)

1 SERVING Calories 640 (Calories from Fat 245) | Fat 27g (Saturated 14g) | Cholesterol 105mg | Sodium 890mg | Carbohydrate 59g (Dietary Fiber 3g) | Protein 39g %DAILY VALUE Vitamin A 16% | Vitamin C 10% | Calcium 32% | Iron 26% EXCHANGES 4 Starch, 4 Lean Meat, 2 Fat CARBOHYDRATE CHOICES 4

BETTY'S TIP

For individual pizzas, use two 6-inch Italian pizza crusts and just divide the ingredients equally between them. The grilling time should be about the same.

Double-Cheese, Spinach and Chicken Pizza

PREP **5 min**   BAKE **10 min**   SERVINGS **6**

1. Heat oven to 425°. Place pizza crust on ungreased 12-inch pizza pan.

2. Top with Havarti cheese, spinach, chicken, bell peppers, garlic salt and Cheddar cheese.

3. Bake 8 to 10 minutes or until crust is golden brown.

1 SERVING Calories 450 (Calories from Fat 160) | Fat 18g (Saturated 9g) | Cholesterol 60mg | Sodium 750mg | Carbohydrate 51g (Dietary Fiber 2g) | Protein 23g   **%DAILY VALUE** Vitamin A 36% | Vitamin C 12% | Calcium 22% | Iron 22%   **EXCHANGES** 3 Starch, 1 Vegetable, 2 Medium-Fat Meat, 1 Fat   **CARBOHYDRATE CHOICES** 3 1/2

1 package (14 ounces) ready-to-serve original Italian pizza crust or other 12-inch ready-to-serve pizza crust

1 cup shredded Havarti cheese (4 ounces)

2 cups washed fresh baby spinach leaves (from 10-ounce bag)

1 cup diced cooked chicken

1/4 cup chopped drained roasted red bell peppers (from 7-ounce jar)

1/2 teaspoon garlic salt

1 cup shredded Cheddar cheese (4 ounces)

BETTY'S TIP

To make shredding cheese a breeze, shred it right from the refrigerator or put it in the freezer for 30 minutes.

Hawaiian Pizza

1 package (14 ounces) ready-to-serve original Italian pizza crust or other 12-inch ready-to-serve pizza crust

1 can (8 ounces) tomato sauce

2 cups cubed cooked chicken

1 can (8 ounces) pineapple tidbits, well drained

1 cup shredded mozzarella cheese (4 ounces)

1. Heat oven to 400°. Place pizza crust on ungreased cookie sheet.

2. Spread tomato sauce over pizza crust. Top with chicken and pineapple. Sprinkle with cheese.

3. Bake 8 to 10 minutes or until pizza is hot and cheese is melted.

1 SERVING Calories 375 (Calories from Fat 80) | Fat 9g (Saturated 4g) | Cholesterol 50mg | Sodium 830mg | Carbohydrate 47g (Dietary Fiber 3g) | Protein 26g %DAILY VALUE Vitamin A 8% | Vitamin C 6% | Calcium 20% | Iron 18% EXCHANGES 3 Starch, 2 1/2 Lean Meat   CARBOHYDRATE CHOICES 3

BETTY'S TIP

Crushed pineapple, very well drained, can be substituted for the pineapple tidbits.

Turkey Gyros Pizzas

PREP **10 min**   BAKE **10 min**   SERVINGS **4**

1. Heat oven to 400°. Place pita breads on ungreased cookie sheet.

2. Mix sour cream and mint; spread evenly over pitas. Sprinkle each pita with 1/4 cup of the mozzarella cheese. Top with turkey, cucumber, tomato and feta cheese. Sprinkle with remaining 1/2 cup mozzarella cheese.

3. Bake about 10 minutes or until pizzas are hot and cheese is melted.

1 SERVING Calories 475 (Calories from Fat 205) | Fat 23g (Saturated 14g) | Cholesterol 100mg | Sodium 1500mg | Carbohydrate 35g (Dietary Fiber 1g) | Protein 33g   %DAILY VALUE Vitamin A 16% | Vitamin C 4% | Calcium 58% | Iron 12%   EXCHANGES 2 Starch, 1 Vegetable, 3 Lean Meat, 3 Fat CARBOHYDRATE CHOICES 2

4 pita breads (6 inches in diameter)

1/2 cup sour cream

1 1/2 teaspoons chopped fresh or 1/2 teaspoon dried mint leaves

1 1/2 cups shredded mozzarella cheese (6 ounces)

1/2 pound sliced cooked deli turkey breast, cut into strips

1/2 cup chopped cucumber

1 small tomato, chopped (1/2 cup)

1 cup crumbled feta cheese (4 ounces)

BETTY'S TIP

Look to your deli to jump-start your dinner. Cooked turkey, chicken or roast beef—or whatever you have on hand—works great in this recipe.

Deep-Dish Turkey Pizza

1 1/3 cups Original
Bisquick mix

1/3 cup Italian dressing

1 can (15 ounces) cannellini
beans, drained, rinsed and
mashed

1 1/2 cups diced cooked
turkey or chicken

1 package (10 ounces)
frozen chopped spinach,
thawed and squeezed to
drain

1 cup (4 ounces) shredded
mozzarella cheese

3 eggs, slightly beaten

1 1/4 cups milk

1/3 cup slivered almonds

PREP **20 min**   BAKE **1 hr 7 min**   SERVINGS **6**

1. Heat oven to 375°F. Mix Bisquick mix, dressing and beans. Spread in bottom and 2 inches up side of spring-form pan, 9 × 3 inches. Bake 10 to 12 minutes or until set.

2. Layer with turkey, spinach and cheese. Mix eggs and milk; pour over cheese. Sprinkle evenly with almonds.

3. Bake 50 to 55 minutes or until golden brown and knife inserted near center comes out clean. Let stand 10 minutes. Loosen edge from side of pan; remove side of pan.

1 SERVING Calories 460 (Calories from Fat 210) | Fat 23g (Saturated 6g) |
Cholesterol 150mg | Sodium 710mg | Carbohydrate 38g (Dietary Fiber 6g) |
Protein 30g   %DAILY VALUE Vitamin A 60% | Vitamin C 4% | Calcium 40% |
Iron 25%   EXCHANGES 3 Lean Meat, 2.5 Fat   CARBOHYDRATE CHOICES 2

BETTY'S TIP

A potato masher makes quick work of smashing the cannelloni beans.

Double-Cheese Pepperoni Pizza

PREP 20 min   STAND 8 min   BAKE 17 min   SERVINGS 8

1. Stir Bisquick mix, water and oil until soft dough forms; beat vigorously 20 strokes. Let stand 8 minutes.

2. Move oven rack to lowest position. Heat oven to 450°. Spray 12-inch pizza pan with cooking spray. Press dough on bottom and 1 inch over side of pizza pan. Place string cheese along edge of dough. Fold 1 inch edge of dough over and around cheese; press to seal. Bake 7 minutes.

3. Spread tomato paste over crust. Top with onion, bell pepper, mushrooms, pepperoni and olives. Sprinkle with mozzarella cheese. Bake 8 to 10 minutes or until crust is golden brown and cheese is melted.

1 SERVING Calories 360 (Calories from Fat 170) | Fat 19g (Saturated 7g) | Cholesterol 25mg | Sodium 1150mg | Carbohydrate 32g (Dietary Fiber 2g) | Protein 15g %DAILY VALUE Vitamin A 10% | Vitamin C 8% | Calcium 34% | Iron 12% EXCHANGES 2 Starch, 1 1/2 High-Fat Meat, 1 Fat CARBOHYDRATE CHOICES 2

3 cups Original Bisquick mix

2/3 cup very hot water

2 tablespoons vegetable oil

4 smoked string cheese pieces (from 4-ounce package), cut lengthwise in half

1/4 cup Italian-style tomato paste

1 small onion, cut lengthwise in half, then cut crosswise into thin slices

1/2 medium bell pepper, thinly sliced

1 can (4 ounces) mushroom pieces and stems, drained

1/2 package (3 1/4-ounce size) sliced pepperoni

1 can (2 1/4 ounces) sliced ripe olives, drained, if desired

2 cups shredded mozzarella cheese (8 ounces)

BETTY'S TIP

Short on time? Omit the string cheese, and press the dough just on the bottom of the pizza pan, not over the side.

Breakfast Pizza

1/3 cup mayonnaise
or salad dressing

1/3 cup sour cream

1 1/2 teaspoons dried
fines herbes

1/2 pound bulk pork
sausage

1 can (3.8 ounces)
refrigerated pizza crust
dough

4 eggs

1/2 cup milk

1/4 teaspoon salt

1/8 teaspoon pepper

1 medium zucchini,
cut lengthwise in half
and sliced

1 medium onion, chopped
(1/2 cup)

1 cup shredded Swiss
cheese (4 ounces)

PREP 25 min   COOK 20 min   BAKE 20 min   SERVINGS 4

1. Heat oven to 425°. Spray cookie sheet with cooking spray. Mix mayonnaise, sour cream and fines herbes; set aside. Cook sausage in 10-inch skillet over medium heat 8 to 10 minutes, stirring occasionally, until no longer pink. Drain and remove sausage, reserving 1 tablespoon drippings in skillet; set aside.

2. Pat crust dough into 10 × 12-inch circle on cookie sheet, building up edge slightly. Bake about 8 minutes or until light brown. Beat eggs, milk, salt and pepper with wire whisk.

3. Heat reserved drippings in skillet over medium heat until hot. Cook zucchini and onion in drippings, stirring frequently, until tender. Pour egg mixture into skillet. As mixture begins to set at bottom and side, gently lift cooked portions with spatula so that thin, uncooked portion can flow to bottom. Avoid constant stirring. Cook 3 to 4 minutes or until eggs are set throughout but still moist; remove from heat.

4. Spread mayonnaise mixture over crust. Top with sausage and egg mixture. Sprinkle with cheese. Bake about 10 minutes or until cheese is melted and crust edge is light brown.

1 SERVING Calories 720 (Calories from Fat 390) | Fat 43g (Saturated Fat 15g) | Cholesterol 285mg | Sodium 1460mg | Carbohydrate 54g (Dietary Fiber 2g) | Protein 30g %DAILY VALUE Vitamin A 25% | Vitamin C 6% | Calcium 40% | Iron 25% EXCHANGES 2.5 High-Fat Meat, 4 Fat CARBOHYDRATE CHOICES 3.5

BETTY'S TIP

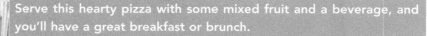

Serve this hearty pizza with some mixed fruit and a beverage, and you'll have a great breakfast or brunch.

Pizza Alfredo

PREP **10 min**   COOK **10 min**   BROIL **2 min**   SERVINGS **6**

1/2 pound bulk Italian sausage

1 large onion, chopped (1 cup)

1 package (8 ounces) sliced mushrooms (3 cups)

1 container (10 ounces) refrigerated Alfredo sauce

1 loaf French bread (12 inches long), cut horizontally in half

1 cup shredded mozzarella cheese (4 ounces)

1. Cook sausage, onion and mushrooms in 10-inch skillet over medium heat 8 to 10 minutes, stirring occasionally, until sausage is no longer pink; drain. Stir in Alfredo sauce.

2. Place bread halves, cut sides up, on ungreased cookie sheet. Spread with sausage mixture. Sprinkle with cheese.

3. Set oven control to broil. Broil with tops 5 inches from heat 1 to 2 minutes or until pizzas are hot and cheese begins to brown.

1 SERVING Calories 430 (Calories from Fat 245) | Fat 27g (Saturated 15g) | Cholesterol 80mg | Sodium 790mg | Carbohydrate 27g (Dietary Fiber 2g) | Protein 19g   %DAILY VALUE Vitamin A 14% | Vitamin C 2% | Calcium 30% | Iron 12%   EXCHANGES 1 1/2 Starch, 1 Vegetable, 2 High-Fat Meat, 2 Fat   CARBOHYDRATE CHOICES 2

BETTY'S TIP

If someone in your family doesn't like mushrooms, simply leave the mushrooms off one of the halves of French bread. Ta-dah! Instant family pleaser!

Sausage Pizza Pie

1 pound bulk pork sausage

1 can (8 ounces) pizza sauce

1/2 teaspoon dried oregano leaves

1 3/4 cups all-purpose flour

1/2 cup process cheese spread (room temperature)

1/4 cup water

Green and red bell pepper rings

1 cup shredded mozzarella cheese (4 ounces)

PREP 15 min   COOK 10 min   BAKE 25 min   SERVINGS 8 to 10

1. Heat oven to 375°. Spray large cookie sheet with cooking spray. Cook sausage in 10-inch skillet over medium heat 8 to 10 minutes, stirring frequently, until no longer pink; drain. Stir in pizza sauce and oregano; set aside.

2. Mix flour, cheese spread and water until soft dough forms. Shape into ball. Roll into 14-inch circle on lightly floured surface. Place dough on cookie sheet. Spread sausage mixture over dough to within 3 inches of edge. Fold dough over edge of mixture. Top sausage with bell pepper rings; sprinkle with cheese.

3. Bake 23 to 25 minutes or until crust is light golden brown and cheese is melted.

1 SERVING Calories 230 (Calories from Fat 110) | Fat 12g (Saturated 5g) | Cholesterol 30mg | Sodium 530mg | Carbohydrate 20g (Dietary Fiber 1g) | Protein 11g %DAILY VALUE Vitamin A 6% | Vitamin C 10% | Calcium 12% | Iron 8% EXCHANGES 1 Starch, 1 Vegetable, 1 High-Fat Meat, 1/2 Fat CARBOHYDRATE CHOICES 1

BETTY'S TIP

If you think you can take the heat, try using hot pork sausage and process cheese with jalapeños.

Classic Pizza

PREP **10 min**   COOK **10 min**   BAKE **18 min**   SERVINGS **8**

1 pound bulk Italian sausage

1 medium onion, chopped (1/2 cup)

1 can (10 ounces) refrigerated pizza crust dough

1/2 cup pizza sauce

1 cup shredded mozzarella cheese (4 ounces)

1/2 cup shredded provolone cheese (2 ounces)

1/4 cup chopped fresh basil leaves

1/2 cup chopped prosciutto

1. Heat oven to 425°. Cook sausage and onion in 10-inch skillet over medium heat 8 to 10 minutes, stirring occasionally, until sausage is no longer pink; drain.

2. Spray cookie sheet with cooking spray. Press pizza crust dough into 12-inch circle on cookie sheet. Press dough from center to edge so edge is slightly thicker than center.

3. Spread pizza sauce over dough to within 1/2 inch of edge. Mix cheeses; sprinkle over sauce. Spoon sausage mixture over cheeses. Sprinkle with basil and prosciutto.

4. Bake about 18 minutes or until crust is golden brown and cheeses are melted and lightly browned.

1 SERVING Calories 295 (Calories from Fat 155) | Fat 17g (Saturated 7g) | Cholesterol 50mg | Sodium 850mg | Carbohydrate 18g (Dietary Fiber 1g) | Protein 18g   %DAILY VALUE Vitamin A 4% | Vitamin C 4% | Calcium 16% | Iron 10%   EXCHANGES 1 Starch, 2 High-Fat Meat   CARBOHYDRATE CHOICES 1

BETTY'S TIP

These days, it's highly likely your local deli stocks prosciutto, but if you're having a tough time tracking down this Italian-seasoned, salt-cured ham, use about 4 ounces of fully cooked smoked ham instead.

Shrimp-Pesto Pizzas

1/4 cup finely chopped sun-dried tomatoes (not in oil)

4 rounds focaccia bread or 2 packages (10 ounces each) ready-to-serve Italian pizza crusts (6 inches in diameter)

1/4 cup basil pesto

3/4 pound cooked peeled deveined medium shrimp, thawed if frozen and tails peeled

1/2 cup shredded reduced-fat mozzarella cheese (2 ounces)

Chopped fresh basil leaves, if desired

PREP 10 min   STAND 3 min   BAKE 12 min   SERVINGS 4

1. Heat oven to 425°. Pour boiling water over sun-dried tomatoes. Let stand 3 minutes; drain.

2. Place breads on cookie sheet. Spread pesto over breads. Top with shrimp and tomatoes. Sprinkle with cheese.

3. Bake about 12 minutes or until cheese is melted and shrimp are thoroughly heated. Sprinkle with basil.

1 SERVING Calories 315 (Calories from Fat 115) | Fat 13g (Saturated 4g) | Cholesterol 175mg | Sodium 700mg | Carbohydrate 23g (Dietary Fiber 2g) | Protein 27g   %DAILY VALUE Vitamin A 12% | Vitamin C 2% | Calcium 22% | Iron 24%   EXCHANGES 1 1/2 Starch, 3 Lean Meat, 1 Fat   CARBOHYDRATE CHOICES 1 1/2

BETTY'S TIP

Instead of chopping the basil, you may want to chiffonade it instead. Those thin strips of fresh basil you see in restaurants are a lot easier to make than you might think: Roll up a basil leaf so you have a tiny tube, then slice it into thin strips.

Pizza Margherita

PREP **10 min**   BAKE **20 min**   SERVINGS **8**

1. Heat oven to 425°. Spray cookie sheet with cooking spray. Press crust dough into 12-inch circle on cookie sheet. Press dough from center to edge so edge is slighter thicker than center.

2. Sprinkle 1 cup cheese over dough to within 1/2 inch of edge. Arrange tomatoes on cheese. Sprinkle salt, pepper and 2 tablespoons basil over tomatoes and cheese. Sprinkle with remaining 1 cup cheese. Drizzle with oil.

3. Bake about 20 minutes or until the crust is golden brown and cheese is melted. Sprinkle with remaining 2 tablespoons basil. Cut into wedges.

1 can (10 ounces) refrigerated pizza crust dough

2 cups shredded mozzarella cheese (8 ounces)

2 roma (plum) tomatoes, sliced

1/4 teaspoon salt

1/8 teaspoon pepper

1/4 cup chopped fresh basil leaves

1 tablespoon olive or vegetable oil

1 SERVING Calories 235 (Calories from Fat 70) | Fat 8g (Saturated 4g) | Cholesterol 15mg | Sodium 380mg | Carbohydrate 30g (Dietary Fiber 1g) | Protein 11g   %DAILY VALUE Vitamin A 4% | Vitamin C 2% | Calcium 20% | Iron 8%   EXCHANGES 1 1/2 Starch, 1 Vegetable, 1 High-Fat Meat CARBOHYDRATE CHOICES 2

BETTY'S TIP

This Italian classic mozzarella and tomato pizza also makes a finger-licking good appetizer. For bite-size portions, cut the pizza into small squares instead of wedges.

Sun-Dried Tomato and Herb Pizza

1 package (14 ounces) ready-to-serve original Italian pizza crust or other 12-inch ready-to-serve pizza crust

1/4 cup soft cream cheese with chives and onions

1/2 cup sun-dried tomatoes in oil, drained and sliced

2 tablespoons chopped fresh or 2 teaspoons dried oregano leaves

2 tablespoons chopped fresh or 2 teaspoons dried basil leaves

1 cup shredded mozzarella cheese (4 ounces)

1/4 cup shredded Cheddar cheese (1 ounce)

PREP **10 min**   BAKE **10 min**   SERVINGS **6**

1. Heat oven to 425°. Place pizza crust on ungreased cookie sheet. Spread with cream cheese. Top with tomatoes, oregano and basil. Sprinkle with cheeses.

2. Bake 8 to 10 minutes or until cheese is melted. Cut into wedges.

1 SERVING Calories 305 (Calories from Fat 90) | Fat 10g (Saturated 5g) | Cholesterol 25mg | Sodium 510mg | Carbohydrate 43g (Dietary Fiber 2g) | Protein 13g   **%DAILY VALUE** Vitamin A 8% | Vitamin C 8% | Calcium 18% | Iron 18%   **EXCHANGES** 2 Starch, 3 Vegetable, 2 Fat   **CARBOHYDRATE CHOICES** 3

Sun-Dried Tomato, Herb and Mushroom Pizza Add 1/2 cup thinly sliced mushrooms to the pizza when topping with the tomatoes and use 1 1/4 cups shredded provolone cheese (5 ounces) instead of the mozzarella and Cheddar cheeses.

BETTY'S TIP

A salad of romaine lettuce, sunflower nuts and crumbled feta cheese drizzled with champagne vinaigrette makes a delicious side dish to this flavorful pizza.

Deluxe Stuffed-Crust Pizza

PREP **25 min**   BAKE **17 min**   SERVINGS **6**

1. Heat oven to 400°. Sprinkle cornmeal over large cookie sheet. Pat or roll dough into 13-inch circle on cookie sheet. Arrange string cheese sticks in circle around edge of dough. Carefully roll edge of dough up over cheese; seal well.

2. Spread tomato paste evenly over dough. Top with onion, bell pepper, mushrooms, pepperoni and olives. Sprinkle with cheese.

3. Bake 15 to 17 minutes or until crust is golden brown and cheese is melted.

1 SERVING Calories 395 (Calories from Fat 110) | Fat 12g (Saturated 7g) | Cholesterol 35mg | Sodium 1140mg | Carbohydrate 46g (Dietary Fiber 4g) | Protein 30g   **%DAILY VALUE** Vitamin A 12% | Vitamin C 18% | Calcium 44% | Iron 18%   **EXCHANGES** 3 Starch, 3 Lean Meat   **CARBOHYDRATE CHOICES** 3

Yellow cornmeal

1 loaf (1 pound) frozen whole wheat bread dough, thawed

4 sticks string cheese (4 ounces), cut lengthwise in half

1/4 cup Italian-style tomato paste

1 small onion, cut lengthwise in half, then thinly sliced

1 medium bell pepper, thinly sliced

1 can (4 ounces) mushroom pieces and stems, drained

1 ounce sliced veggie pepperoni (from 5.5-ounce package), coarsely chopped (1/4 cup)

12 pitted Kalamata or Greek olives, coarsely chopped (1/3 cup)

2 cups shredded mozzarella cheese (8 ounces)

BETTY'S TIP

If veggie pepperoni is hard to find, omit the "meat" from the recipe or substitute 2 thawed vegetable burgers, cut into 1/4-inch pieces, or 1/2 cup thawed meatless crumbles.

Greek Pita Pizzas

4 pita breads (6 inches in diameter)

1/2 cup roasted garlic–flavored or regular hummus

1 cup crumbled feta cheese (4 ounces)

1 small onion, sliced

2 cups shredded spinach

1 large tomato, seeded and chopped (1 cup)

1/4 cup sliced ripe or Kalamata olives

PREP **10 min**   BAKE **10 min**   SERVINGS **4**

1. Heat oven to 400°. Place pita breads in ungreased jelly roll pan, 15 1/2 × 10 1/2 × 1 inch.

2. Spread hummus on each pita bread. Sprinkle with cheese.

3. Bake 8 to 10 minutes or until cheese is melted. Top each pizza with onion, spinach, tomato and olives.

1 SERVING Calories 335 (Calories from Fat 115) | Fat 13g (Saturated 6g) | Cholesterol 35mg | Sodium 930mg | Carbohydrate 44g (Dietary Fiber 5g) | Protein 15g   %DAILY VALUE Vitamin A 20% | Vitamin C 12% | Calcium 28% | Iron 20%   EXCHANGES 2 Starch, 3 Vegetable, 2 Fat   CARBOHYDRATE CHOICES 3

Greek Pita Pizzas with Chicken Sprinkle 1 or 2 tablespoons of chopped cooked chicken over the hummus for each pita.

BETTY'S TIP

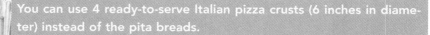

You can use 4 ready-to-serve Italian pizza crusts (6 inches in diameter) instead of the pita breads.

Santa Fe Pizza

PREP **20 min**   BAKE **28 min**   SERVINGS **8**

1. Heat oven to 375°. Spray large cookie sheet with cooking spray.

2. Stir Bisquick mix, cheese sauce and hot water until soft dough forms; beat vigorously 20 strokes. Place dough on surface dusted with Bisquick mix; gently roll in Bisquick mix to coat. Shape into ball; knead about 5 times or until smooth. Roll dough into 14-inch circle; place on cookie sheet.

3. Mix beans and salsa; spread over crust to within 2 inches of edge. Sprinkle with onions. Fold edge over bean mixture. Sprinkle with cheese.

4. Bake 25 to 28 minutes or until crust is golden brown and cheese is melted. Garnish with lettuce and tomato.

2 cups Original Bisquick mix

1/4 cup mild salsa-flavored or jalapeño-flavored process cheese sauce

1/4 cup hot water

1 can (16 ounces) refried beans

1/2 cup thick-and-chunky salsa

4 medium green onions, sliced (1/4 cup)

1 cup shredded Colby-Monterey Jack cheese (4 ounces)

1 cup shredded lettuce

1 medium tomato, chopped (3/4 cup)

1 SERVING Calories 260 (Calories from Fat 100) | Fat 11g (Saturated 5g) | Cholesterol 25mg | Sodium 790mg | Carbohydrate 30g (Dietary Fiber 4g) | Protein 10g   %DAILY VALUE Vitamin A 10% | Vitamin C 8% | Calcium 20% | Iron 12%   EXCHANGES 2 Starch, 1 High-Fat Meat   CARBOHYDRATE CHOICES 2

BETTY'S TIP

If you're stopping at the grocery store, swing by the salad bar and pick up sliced green onions and chopped tomato to save prep time.

Four-Cheese Pesto Pizza

6 whole wheat or white pita breads (6 inches in diameter)

1 package (8 ounces) reduced-fat cream cheese (Neufchâtel) or regular cream cheese, softened

2 tablespoons milk

6 tablespoons basil pesto

1 can (2 1/4 ounces) sliced ripe olives, drained

1/2 cup shredded part-skim mozzarella cheese (3 ounces)

1/2 cup shredded Fontina or provolone cheese (3 ounces)

2 tablespoons grated Parmesan cheese

2 tablespoons chopped fresh parsley

PREP **10 min**   BAKE **12 min**   SERVINGS **6**

1. Heat oven to 425°. Place pita breads on ungreased large cookie sheet.

2. Mix cream cheese and milk until smooth. Spread on pita breads to within 1/4 inch of edge. Gently spread pesto over cream cheese. Top with olives. Sprinkle with cheeses and parsley.

3. Bake 7 to 12 minutes or until thoroughly heated and cheese is melted.

1 SERVING Calories 410 (Calories from Fat 215) | Fat 24g (Saturated 10g) | Cholesterol 45mg | Sodium 900mg | Carbohydrate 35g (Dietary Fiber 5g) | Protein 19g   %DAILY VALUE Vitamin A 20% | Vitamin C 2% | Calcium 36% | Iron 16%   EXCHANGES 2 Starch, 1 Vegetable, 1 1/2 High-Fat Meat, 2 Fat CARBOHYDRATE CHOICES 2

BETTY'S TIP

Pesto used to be available only in restaurants, or it had to be made from scratch. Today, there are a variety of pestos available on supermarket shelves. Try experimenting with different flavors to find your favorite in this recipe.

Main-Dish Salads

Fiesta Taco Salad

1 pound lean ground beef

1/2 cup taco sauce

6 cups bite-size pieces lettuce

1 medium green bell pepper, cut into strips

2 medium tomatoes, cut into wedges

1/2 cup pitted ripe olives, drained

1 cup corn chips

1 cup shredded Cheddar cheese (4 ounces)

1/2 cup Thousand Island dressing, if desired

PREP **15 min**   COOK **10 min**   SERVINGS **6**

1. Cook beef in 10-inch skillet over medium heat 8 to 10 minutes, stirring occasionally, until brown; drain. Stir in taco sauce; heat through.

2. Toss lettuce, bell pepper, tomatoes, olives and corn chips in large bowl. Spoon hot beef mixture over lettuce mixture; toss. Sprinkle with cheese. Serve immediately with dressing.

1 SERVING Calories 285 (Calories from Fat 180) | Fat 20g (Saturated 9g) | Cholesterol 60mg | Sodium 340mg | Carbohydrate 9g (Dietary Fiber 3g) | Protein 20g   %DAILY VALUE Vitamin A 12% | Vitamin C 26% | Calcium 14% | Iron 14%   EXCHANGES 2 Vegetable, 2 Medium-Fat Meat, 2 Fat   CARBOHYDRATE CHOICES 1/2

Vegetarian Fiesta Taco Salad Use 2 cans (15 ounces each) black beans, rinsed and drained, instead of the ground beef. Add the beans with the taco sauce and the ingredients in step 2.

BETTY'S TIP

For an extra-special presentation, try serving this taco salad in a tortilla bowl. To make, simply brush both sides of a tortilla with melted butter. Place each tortilla in an ovenproof bowl, making pleats as needed to fit. Bake the tortillas in bowls in 400° oven for 10 to 15 minutes or until crisp and golden brown. Cool tortillas in bowls.

Steak Caesar Salad

1. Make Caesar Dressing. Sprinkle beef with pepper. Heat coals or gas grill for direct heat.

2. Cover and grill beef 4 to 5 inches from medium heat 15 to 18 minutes for medium doneness, turning once. Cut beef across grain into thin slices.

3. Toss romaine, croutons, 1/2 cup Parmesan cheese and the dressing. Top with beef slices. Serve with additional shredded Parmesan cheese.

Caesar Dressing

> 1/4 cup olive or vegetable oil
>
> 1/4 cup fat-free cholesterol-free egg product
>
> 1 tablespoon lemon juice
>
> 1 teaspoon Dijon mustard
>
> 1 teaspoon anchovy paste
>
> 1 large clove garlic, finely chopped

Shake all ingredients in tightly covered container.

Caesar Dressing
(below left)

1-pound beef boneless top sirloin steak, about 1 inch thick

1 tablespoon freshly ground pepper

1 bunch romaine, torn into bite-size pieces

1 cup garlic-flavored croutons

1/2 cup freshly shredded Parmesan cheese

Shredded Parmesan cheese, if desired

1 SERVING Calories 430 (Calories from Fat 70) | Fat 8g (Saturated 10g) | Cholesterol 75mg | Sodium 390mg | Carbohydrate 11g (Dietary Fiber 2g) | Protein 31g %DAILY VALUE Vitamin A 26% | Vitamin C 40% | Calcium 20% | Iron 26% EXCHANGES 2 Vegetable, 4 Medium-Fat Meat, 2 Fat CARBOHYDRATE CHOICES 1

BETTY'S TIP

Crunched for time? Pick up a bottle of your favorite Caesar dressing instead of making it from scratch. Or toss in pieces of leftover cooked chicken instead of grilling steak.

Fajita Salad

PREP 15 min   COOK 6 min   SERVINGS 4

3/4 pound lean beef
boneless sirloin steak

1 tablespoon vegetable oil

2 medium bell peppers,
cut into strips

1 small onion, thinly sliced

4 cups bite-size pieces
salad greens

1/3 cup Italian dressing

1/4 cup plain yogurt

1. Cut beef with grain into 2-inch strips; cut strips across grain into 1/8-inch slices. Heat oil in 10-inch nonstick skillet over medium-high heat. Cook beef in oil about 3 minutes, stirring occasionally, until brown. Remove beef from skillet.

2. Cook bell peppers and onion in skillet about 3 minutes, stirring occasionally, until bell peppers are crisp-tender. Stir in beef.

3. Place salad greens on serving platter. Top with beef mixture. Mix dressing and yogurt; drizzle over salad.

1 SERVING Calories 230 (Calories from Fat 125) | Fat 14g (Saturated 3g) | Cholesterol 45mg | Sodium 230mg | Carbohydrate 12g (Dietary Fiber 3g) | Protein 17g %DAILY VALUE Vitamin A 8% | Vitamin C 68% | Calcium 4% | Iron 12% EXCHANGES 2 Vegetable, 2 Medium-Fat Meat, 1/2 Fat CARBOHYDRATE CHOICES 1

BETTY'S TIP

Check out the meat case of your local grocery store for the many precut meats now available. In addition to being a timesaving convenience, these precut meats often come in small, one-time-use portions.

Deli Beef and Bean Tossed Salad

PREP 10 min   SERVINGS 6

1 bag (10 ounces) salad mix (about 8 cups)

1 pint (2 cups) deli three-bean salad or 1 can (15 to 17 ounces) three-bean salad, chilled

1/4 pound deli cooked lean beef, cut into julienne strips (3/4 cup)

1 cup shredded reduced-fat Cheddar or Swiss cheese (4 ounces)

12 cherry tomatoes, cut in half

Place all ingredients in large bowl; toss lightly to mix.

1 SERVING Calories 100 (Calories from Fat 20) | Fat 2g (Saturated 1g) | Cholesterol 15mg | Sodium 590mg | Carbohydrate 13g (Dietary Fiber 3g) | Protein 10g   **%DAILY VALUE** Vitamin A 6% | Vitamin C 12% | Calcium 10% | Iron 8%   **EXCHANGES** 1/2 Starch, 1 Vegetable, 1 Very Lean Meat   **CARBOHYDRATE CHOICES** 1

Deli Ham and Bean Tossed Salad Substitute 1/4 pound deli cooked ham, cut into julienne strips (3/4 cup) for the beef.

BETTY'S TIP

For a colorful presentation, select a salad mix that contains lettuce, shredded carrot and shredded red cabbage.

Roast Beef
and Tomato Salad

Sherry Vinaigrette
(below right)

1 head Boston lettuce

1 bunch arugula, torn into
bite-size pieces

1/2 pound thinly sliced
cooked roast beef

1 small red onion, thinly
sliced and separated into
rings

1 medium tomato,
thinly sliced

1 cup crumbled
Gorgonzola or blue
cheese (4 ounces)

1. Make Sherry Vinaigrette.

2. Place Boston lettuce leaves on serving platter. Sprinkle
    arugula over lettuce. Fold roast beef slices. Place roast
    beef, onion and tomato on greens. Sprinkle with cheese.
    Serve with vinaigrette.

Sherry Vinaigrette

1/4 cup olive or vegetable oil

4 teaspoons dry sherry or red wine vinegar

1 teaspoon Dijon mustard

1/8 teaspoon salt

Dash of pepper

1 small shallot, finely chopped

Shake all ingredients in tightly covered container.

1 SERVING Calories 350 (Calories from Fat 225) | Fat 25g (Saturated 8g) |
Cholesterol 70mg | Sodium 550mg | Carbohydrate 6g (Dietary Fiber 2g) |
Protein 25g   %DAILY VALUE Vitamin A 20% | Vitamin C 18% | Calcium 18% |
Iron 12%   EXCHANGES 1 Vegetable, 3 Medium-Fat Meat, 2 Fat   CARBOHYDRATE
CHOICES 1/2

BETTY'S TIP

All this salad needs is some chewy European bread or slices of warm
focaccia to complete the meal. A glass of red wine would also be a
delicious accompaniment.

Caribbean Chicken Salad

PREP **15 min**   COOK **12 min**   SERVINGS **4**

1. Place chicken in heavy-duty resealable plastic food-storage bag. Sprinkle seasoning blend over chicken; seal bag and shake until chicken is evenly coated.

2. Heat oil in 10-inch nonstick skillet over medium-high heat. Cook chicken in oil 10 to 12 minutes, stirring frequently, until no longer pink in center. Remove chicken from skillet; drain on paper towels.

3. Toss salad greens, mango, onion and bell pepper in large bowl; divide among 4 plates. Top with chicken. Drizzle with vinaigrette.

1 pound boneless, skinless chicken breasts, cut into 1/2-inch strips

2 tablespoons blackened seasoning blend

1 tablespoon vegetable oil

1 bag (5 ounces) mixed baby salad greens (4 cups)

1 medium mango, peeled, pitted and diced (1 cup)

1/2 medium red onion, sliced (3/4 cup)

1 small red bell pepper, chopped (1/2 cup)

2/3 cup raspberry or other fruit-flavored vinaigrette

1 SERVING Calories 240 (Calories from Fat 55) | Fat 6g (Saturated 1g) | Cholesterol 70mg | Sodium 550mg | Carbohydrate 22g (Dietary Fiber 3g) | Protein 27g **%DAILY VALUE** Vitamin A 56% | Vitamin C 94% | Calcium 4% | Iron 8% **EXCHANGES** 1/2 Fruit, 3 Vegetable, 3 Very Lean Meat, 1 Fat **CARBOHYDRATE CHOICES** 1 1/2

BETTY'S TIP

Need help cutting a mango? Score the skin lengthwise into fourths with a knife, and peel like a banana. Cut the peeled mango lengthwise close to both sides of the seed, then dice.

Chicken and Strawberry Spinach Salad

Strawberry Dressing
(below right)

4 boneless, skinless
chicken breast halves
(1 1/4 pounds)

8 cups bite-size pieces
spinach

1 cup strawberries,
hulled and cut in half

1/4 cup crumbled
Gorgonzola cheese
(1 ounce)

1/4 cup chopped walnuts

PREP **10 min**   COOK **20 min**   SERVINGS **4**

1. Make Strawberry Dressing. Remove fat from chicken. Spray 8- or 10-inch skillet with cooking spray; heat over medium-high heat. Cook chicken in skillet 15 to 20 minutes, turning once, until juice of chicken is no longer pink when centers of thickest pieces are cut. Remove chicken to cutting board. Add dressing to skillet; stir to loosen any pan drippings.

2. Slice chicken. Arrange spinach on serving plates. Top with chicken, strawberries and cheese. Drizzle with dressing. Sprinkle with walnuts.

Strawberry Dressing

3 tablespoons apple juice

2 tablespoons strawberry spreadable fruit

2 tablespoons balsamic vinegar

Mix all ingredients until blended.

1 SERVING Calories 295 (Calories from Fat 110) | Fat 12g (Saturated 3g) | Cholesterol 80mg | Sodium 230mg | Carbohydrate 14g (Dietary Fiber 4g) | Protein 32g %DAILY VALUE Vitamin A 100% | Vitamin C 66% | Calcium 12% | Iron 16% EXCHANGES 1/2 Fruit, 1 Vegetable, 4 Lean Meat CARBOHYDRATE CHOICES 1

BETTY'S TIP

One of the best things you can do for yourself and your family is to eat more fruits and vegetables. Enjoy this vitamin-rich salad with steamed whole green and yellow beans and warm breadsticks.

Southwestern Chicken BLT Salad

PREP **20 min**   SERVINGS **6**

1. Make Salsa Bacon Dressing.

2. Mix remaining ingredients in large bowl. Add Salsa Bacon Dressing; toss until coated.

Salsa Bacon Dressing

1/2 cup thick-and-chunky salsa

1/2 cup refrigerated bacon-flavored dip

1 tablespoon chopped fresh parsley

Mix all ingredients in small bowl.

1 SERVING Calories 195 (Calories from Fat 80) | Fat 9g (Saturated 4g) |
Cholesterol 60mg | Sodium 410mg | Carbohydrate 7g (Dietary Fiber 2g) |
Protein 22g %DAILY VALUE Vitamin A 40% | Vitamin C 30% | Calcium 6% |
Iron 10% EXCHANGES 1 Vegetable, 3 Lean Meat CARBOHYDRATE CHOICES 1/2

Salsa Bacon Dressing
(below left)

1 bag (10 ounces) romaine
and leaf lettuce mix

2 packages (6 ounces each)
refrigerated cooked
Southwest-flavor chicken
breast strips

4 roma (plum) tomatoes,
coarsely chopped

1/2 cup chopped cooked
bacon

1/2 cup croutons

BETTY'S TIP

The bacon dip in the salad dressing blends nicely with the cooked
bacon in the salad, but if you can't find it, refrigerated ranch dip
works great, too.

Greek Chicken Salad

Mint Vinaigrette
(below right)

6 cups bite-size pieces
assorted salad greens

2 cups cut-up cooked
chicken

1/8 cup crumbled feta
cheese

1 medium tomato, cut into
wedges

1/2 medium cucumber, cut
lengthwise in half, seeded
and cut into 1/4-inch slices

1 small green bell pepper,
coarsely chopped (1/2 cup)

4 medium green onions,
sliced (1/4 cup)

12 Kalamata or large
pitted ripe olives

1.   Make Mint Vinaigrette.

2.   Toss vinaigrette and remaining ingredients in large
      glass or plastic bowl.

Mint Vinaigrette

3 tablespoons lemon juice

1 1/2 teaspoons chopped fresh or 1/2 teaspoon dried mint
leaves

1/2 teaspoon salt

1/8 teaspoon pepper

1 small clove garlic, finely chopped

Shake all ingredients in tightly covered container.

1 SERVING Calories 195 (Calories from Fat 70) | Fat 8g (Saturated 2g) |
Cholesterol 65mg | Sodium 550mg | Carbohydrate 8g (Dietary Fiber 3g) |
Protein 23g   %DAILY VALUE Vitamin A 60% | Vitamin C 70% | Calcium 10% |
Iron 14%   EXCHANGES 1 1/2 Vegetable, 3 Lean Meat   CARBOHYDRATE CHOICES 1/2

BETTY'S TIP

Try adding cut-up grilled chicken to this salad for a delicious char-
broiled flavor. Or to save time, purchase cut-up grilled chicken from
the refrigerated foods section of your supermarket.

Quick Garden Chicken Salad

PREP **10 min**   COOK **15 min**   SERVINGS **6**

1. Cook pasta as directed on package; drain. Rinse with cold water; drain.

2. Mix pasta and remaining ingredients in large bowl. Serve immediately.

1 SERVING Calories 395 (Calories from Fat 45) | Fat 5g (Saturated 1g) | Cholesterol 40mg | Sodium 220mg | Carbohydrate 64g (Dietary Fiber 4g) | Protein 24g   %DAILY VALUE Vitamin A 12% | Vitamin C 90% | Calcium 4% | Iron 20%   EXCHANGES 4 Starch, 1 Vegetable, 1 1/2 Very Lean Meat CARBOHYDRATE CHOICES 4

1 package (16 ounces) fusilli (corkscrew) pasta

2 cups cubed cooked chicken

1 small cucumber, chopped (1 cup)

1 medium yellow or red bell pepper, chopped (1 cup)

1 large tomato, chopped (1 cup)

3/4 cup spicy eight-vegetable juice

1/4 cup lemon juice

1/2 teaspoon freshly ground pepper

1/4 teaspoon salt

1 clove garlic, finely chopped

BETTY'S TIP

Using fresh lemon juice will add a zip to this salad that purchased lemon juice can't beat! Keep in mind that it takes one lemon to get about 2 to 3 tablespoons of juice. To get the most juice out of a lemon, roll it back and forth on the counter several times with firm pressure.

Chicken and Berries Salad

Fruity Yogurt Dressing
(below right)

4 cups bite-size pieces
mixed salad greens
(iceberg, Bibb, romaine
or spinach)

2 cups cut-up cooked
chicken

1 cup raspberries

1/2 cup sliced strawberries

1/4 cup thinly sliced leek

1/4 cup sliced almonds,
toasted

Freshly ground pepper

PREP **15 min**   SERVINGS **4**

1.   Make Fruity Yogurt Dressing.

2.   Toss salad greens, chicken, berries and leek in large bowl.
Sprinkle with almonds. Serve with dressing. Sprinkle
with pepper.

Fruity Yogurt Dressing

1 cup plain fat-free yogurt

1/4 cup raspberries

1/4 cup sliced strawberries

1 tablespoon raspberry or red wine vinegar

2 teaspoons sugar

Place all ingredients in blender or food processor. Cover
and blend on high speed about 15 seconds or process
until smooth.

1 SERVING Calories 265 (Calories from Fat 100) | Fat 11g (Saturated 2g) |
Cholesterol 65mg | Sodium 140mg | Carbohydrate 16g (Dietary Fiber 5g) |
Protein 26g   %DAILY VALUE Vitamin A 36% | Vitamin C 60% | Calcium 18% |
Iron 12%   EXCHANGES 1/2 Fruit, 1 1/2 Vegetable, 3 1/2 Lean Meat
CARBOHYDRATE CHOICES 1

BETTY'S TIP

If raspberries or strawberries aren't in season, use frozen unsweetened loose-pack raspberries or strawberries for the salad and dressing instead.

Chicken-Pasta Salad with Pesto

PREP **10 min**   COOK **15 min**   SERVINGS **4**

1. Cook pasta as directed on package; drain. Rinse with cold water; drain.

2. Mix pasta, chicken, tomatoes, bell pepper, zucchini and onion in large bowl. Stir in pesto.

1 SERVING Calories 405 (Calories from Fat 155) | Fat 17g (Saturated 4g) | Cholesterol 50mg | Sodium 250mg | Carbohydrate 40g (Dietary Fiber 3g) | Protein 23g   %DAILY VALUE Vitamin A 12% | Vitamin C 62% | Calcium 10% | Iron 18%   EXCHANGES 2 1/2 Starch, 1 Vegetable, 2 Medium-Fat Meat, 1/2 Fat CARBOHYDRATE CHOICES 2 1/2

6 ounces uncooked multicolored farfalle (bow-tie) pasta (about 2 1/4 cups)

1 1/2 cups cut-up cooked chicken

1/4 cup sun-dried tomatoes in oil, drained and chopped

1 medium bell pepper, cut into strips

1 small zucchini, thinly sliced

1/2 small red onion, sliced

1/3 cup basil pesto

BETTY'S TIP

Pasta is pretty interchangeable, as long as you stay with similar sizes. Try using radiatore, malfalda or rotelle pasta instead of the farfalle in this recipe.

Main-Dish Salads   273

Turkey Tabbouleh Salad

3/4 cup uncooked cracked wheat or bulgur

1 1/2 cups chopped fresh parsley

1 cup cut-up cooked turkey breast

1 can (8 3/4 ounces) garbanzo beans, rinsed and drained

2 tablespoons chopped fresh mint leaves

3 medium tomatoes, chopped (2 1/4 cups)

4 medium green onions, chopped (1/4 cup)

1/4 cup olive or vegetable oil

1/4 cup lemon juice

1 teaspoon salt

1/4 teaspoon pepper

PREP 10 min   STAND 30 min   CHILL 1 hr   SERVINGS 4

1. Cover cracked wheat with cold water. Let stand 30 minutes. Drain, pressing out as much water as possible.

2. Place cracked wheat, parsley, turkey, beans, mint, tomatoes and onions in large glass or plastic bowl. Mix remaining ingredients. Pour over wheat mixture; toss.

3. Cover and refrigerate at least 1 hour to blend flavors.

1 SERVING Calories 345 (Calories from Fat 155) | Fat 17g (Saturated 2g) | Cholesterol 25mg | Sodium 720mg | Carbohydrate 38g (Dietary Fiber 9g) | Protein 19g %DAILY VALUE Vitamin A 18% | Vitamin C 90% | Calcium 8% | Iron 24% EXCHANGES 2 1/2 Starch, 1 Very Lean Meat, 3 Fat CARBOHYDRATE CHOICES 2 1/2

BETTY'S TIP

If you'd prefer to serve this Middle Eastern salad as a side dish, just leave out the turkey. The flavors pair especially well with a grilled fish or chicken main dish.

Southwestern Turkey Salad

3/4 pound ground turkey breast

1/4 teaspoon garlic powder

2 tablespoons all-purpose flour

1 can (15 ounces) chili beans, undrained

1 tablespoon ground cumin

1 1/2 teaspoons chili powder

1/2 teaspoon onion salt

1/8 teaspoon pepper

6 cups bite-size pieces iceberg lettuce

1 medium onion, chopped (1/2 cup)

1 medium green bell pepper, chopped (1 cup)

2 medium tomatoes, chopped (1 1/2 cups)

1/2 cup shredded reduced-fat Cheddar cheese (4 ounces)

2/3 cup salsa

1/3 cup reduced-calorie Catalina dressing

1 cup fat-free sour cream

1. Cook turkey in 10-inch nonstick skillet over medium heat, stirring occasionally, until no longer pink. (If turkey sticks to skillet, add up to 2 tablespoons water.) Stir in garlic powder, flour, beans, cumin, chili powder, onion salt and pepper. Cook about 5 minutes or until thickened and bubbly.

2. Divide lettuce among 4 plates. Top with turkey mixture, onion, bell pepper, tomatoes and cheese. Mix salsa and dressing; serve with salad. Top salad with sour cream.

1 SERVING Calories 405 (Calories from Fat 110) | Fat 12g (Saturated 3g) | Cholesterol 65mg | Sodium 1850mg | Carbohydrate 44g (Dietary Fiber 8g) | Protein 38g   %DAILY VALUE Vitamin A 42% | Vitamin C 100% | Calcium 42% | Iron 24%   EXCHANGES 2 Starch, 3 Vegetable, 4 1/2 Very Lean Meat, 1/2 Fat CARBOHYDRATE CHOICES 3

BETTY'S TIP

This turkey salad also makes a great filling for hard or soft tacos, or you can serve it over tortilla chips.

Turkey and Fruit Tossed Salad

1 bag (10 ounces) salad mix (about 8 cups)

2 1/2 cups cubed cooked turkey or chicken

1 package (6 ounces) diced dried fruits and raisins (about 1 1/4 cups)

1 medium stalk celery, sliced (1/2 cup)

1/2 cup fat-free sweet-spicy French dressing

PREP **10 min**   SERVINGS **6**

Place salad mix, turkey, dried fruits and celery in large bowl. Pour dressing over mixture; toss lightly to coat.

1 SERVING Calories 210 (Calories from Fat 35) | Fat 4g (Saturated 1g) | Cholesterol 50mg | Sodium 280mg | Carbohydrate 26g (Dietary Fiber 3g) | Protein 18g   %DAILY VALUE Vitamin A 36% | Vitamin C 36% | Calcium 20% | Iron 10%   EXCHANGES 1 Fruit, 2 Vegetable, 2 Very Lean Meat, 1/2 Fat CARBOHYDRATE CHOICES 2

BETTY'S TIP

Although any assortment of greens will taste great in this salad, the slightly bitter tang of an Italian-style mix with romaine and radicchio is especially nice with the chicken, dried fruit and subtly sweet French dressing.

Turkey Salad with Fruit

PREP **20 min**   CHILL **2 hr**   SERVINGS **6**

1. Mix turkey, grapes, orange segments, water chestnuts, celery and onions in large bowl.

2. Mix yogurt and soy sauce. Pour over turkey mixture; toss. Cover and refrigerate about 2 hours or until chilled. Serve on salad greens.

1 SERVING Calories 220 (Calories from Fat 45) | Fat 5g (Saturated 2g) | Cholesterol 55mg | Sodium 430mg | Carbohydrate 23g (Dietary Fiber 1g) | Protein 22g   %DAILY VALUE Vitamin A 6% | Vitamin C 26% | Calcium 8% | Iron 10%   EXCHANGES 1 Fruit, 1 Vegetable, 2 1/2 Lean Meat   CARBOHYDRATE CHOICES 1 1/2

Grilled Chicken Salad with Fruit Substitute 3 cups chopped grilled chicken breast in place of the turkey.

3 cups cut-up cooked turkey or chicken

3/4 cup seedless red grapes

1 can (11 ounces) mandarin orange segments, drained

1 can (8 ounces) sliced water chestnuts, drained

2 medium stalks celery, thinly sliced (1 cup)

2 medium green onions, thinly sliced (2 tablespoons)

1 container (6 ounces) peach, orange or lemon low-fat yogurt (2/3 cup)

2 tablespoons soy sauce

Mixed salad greens

BETTY'S TIP

When fruit is at its peak, serve this salad over wedges of fresh pineapple or in honeydew melon halves instead of on top of the greens.

Turkey and Dried Cherry Salad

2 cups uncooked gemelli (twist) pasta (8 ounces)

1 1/2 cups cubed cooked turkey

1/2 cup dried cherries

1/4 cup slivered almonds, toasted

1 medium stalk celery, thinly sliced (1/2 cup)

3 or 4 medium green onions, chopped (about 1/4 cup)

3/4 cup refrigerated poppy seed dressing

PREP **20 min**   COOK **10 min**   SERVINGS **4**

1. Cook and drain pasta as directed on package.

2. Mix pasta and remaining ingredients except dressing in large bowl. Pour dressing over mixture; toss until coated. Serve immediately, or cover and refrigerate until serving.

1 SERVING Calories 650 (Calories from Fat 270) | Fat 30g (Saturated 5g) | Cholesterol 45mg | Sodium 60mg | Carbohydrate 70g (Dietary Fiber 4g) | Protein 24g   %DAILY VALUE Vitamin A 4% | Vitamin C 14% | Calcium 6% | Iron 20%   EXCHANGES 4 Starch, 1/2 Fruit, 2 Medium-Fat Meat, 3 Fat   CARBOHYDRATE CHOICES 4 1/2

BETTY'S TIP

Toasting almonds is easy. Just place them in an ungreased shallow pan and bake at 350° for 6 to 10 minutes, stirring occasionally, until golden brown.

Ten-Minute
Ham Salad

PREP **10 min**   SERVINGS **6**

6 cups bite-size pieces
salad greens

2 cups cubed fully cooked
smoked ham

1/3 cup Italian dressing

2 tablespoons sesame
seed, toasted

1 medium cucumber,
thinly sliced

1 medium tomato,
cut into thin wedges

2 green onions, thinly
sliced (2 tablespoons)

1/2 cup shredded
Monterey Jack cheese
(2 ounces)

Toss all ingredients except cheese in large bowl. Toss
with cheese.

1 SERVING Calories 205 (Calories from Fat 125) | Fat 14g (Saturated 4g) |
Cholesterol 35mg | Sodium 860mg | Carbohydrate 5g (Dietary Fiber 3g) |
Protein 15g **%DAILY VALUE** Vitamin A 40% | Vitamin C 26% | Calcium 12% |
Iron 10% **EXCHANGES** 1 Vegetable, 2 Lean Meat, 1 1/2 Fat **CARBOHYDRATE
CHOICES** 0

BETTY'S TIP

To toast sesame seed, cook in ungreased heavy skillet over medium
heat about 2 minutes, stirring frequently until browning begins,
then stirring constantly until golden brown.

Ranch Ham and Pasta Salad

4 unpeeled small new potatoes, cubed (2 cups)

2 cups uncooked radiatore (nugget) pasta (6 ounces)

2 cups broccoli flowerets

1 cup diced fully cooked ham

1/4 cup chopped drained roasted red bell peppers (from 7-ounce jar)

2 medium green onions, chopped (2 tablespoons)

1/3 cup mayonnaise or salad dressing

1/3 cup ranch dressing

1/8 teaspoon freshly ground pepper

PREP 20 min   COOK 25 min   CHILL 1 hr   SERVINGS 6

1. Place potatoes in 4-quart Dutch oven; add enough water just to cover potatoes. Cover and heat to boiling; boil 4 minutes. Remove potatoes from water with slotted spoon.

2. Add pasta to boiling water in Dutch oven; cook and drain as directed on package, adding broccoli for last 2 minutes of cooking. Cool potatoes, pasta and broccoli slightly. Refrigerate about 1 hour or until completely chilled.

3. Mix potatoes, pasta, broccoli, ham, bell peppers and onions in large glass or plastic bowl. Mix mayonnaise, ranch dressing and pepper; gently stir into potato mixture. Serve immediately, or cover and refrigerate up to 2 hours before serving.

1 SERVING Calories 385 (Calories from Fat 190) | Fat 21g (Saturated 4g) | Cholesterol 350mg | Sodium 880mg | Carbohydrate 36g (Dietary Fiber 3g) | Protein 16g %DAILY VALUE Vitamin A 16% | Vitamin C 38% | Calcium 4% | Iron 14% EXCHANGES 2 Starch, 1 Vegetable, 1 1/2 Medium-Fat Meat, 2 Fat CARBOHYDRATE CHOICES 2 1/2

BETTY'S TIP

To serve this salad at an outdoor gathering, place the salad bowl in a shallow bowl filled with crushed ice.

Italian Ham and Pasta Salad

PREP **30 min**   CHILL **6 hr**   SERVINGS **12**

2 packages (10 ounces each) frozen chopped broccoli

7 cups uncooked farfalle (bow-tie) pasta (14 ounces)

Italian Dressing (below left)

2 pounds fully cooked ham, cut into julienne strips

1 medium green bell pepper, chopped (1 cup)

1 small onion, finely chopped (1/4 cup)

1. Cook broccoli and pasta as directed on packages; drain. Rinse pasta with cold water; drain.

2. Make Italian Dressing. Add broccoli, pasta and remaining ingredients to dressing in large bowl; toss.

3. Cover and refrigerate at least 6 hours or until chilled.

Italian Dressing

1/2 cup grated Parmesan cheese

1/4 cup chopped fresh parsley

1/2 cup olive or vegetable oil

1/4 cup lemon juice

1/4 cup white vinegar

2 tablespoons chopped fresh or 2 teaspoons dried basil leaves

2 teaspoons dry mustard

1 1/2 teaspoons chopped fresh or 3/4 teaspoon dried oregano leaves

1 1/2 teaspoons chopped fresh or 3/4 teaspoon dried marjoram leaves

1/4 teaspoon pepper

2 medium cloves garlic, finely chopped

Mix all ingredients in large glass or plastic bowl.

1 SERVING Calories 420 (Calories from Fat 160) | Fat 18g (Saturated 4g) | Cholesterol 45mg | Sodium 1210mg | Carbohydrate 41g (Dietary Fiber 3g) | Protein 26g   **%DAILY VALUE** Vitamin A 10% | Vitamin C 38% | Calcium 8% | Iron 18%   **EXCHANGES** 2 1/2 Starch, 2 Medium-Fat Meat, 1 Fat   **CARBOHYDRATE CHOICES** 3

Italian Chicken and Pasta Salad Substitute cubes of cooked chicken breast for the ham.

BETTY'S TIP

In a hurry? Use 1 cup of your favorite bottled Italian dressing instead of making it from scratch.

Ham and Slaw Salad

PREP 15 min   SERVINGS 4

1 pint (2 cups) deli coleslaw (creamy style)

2 cans (8 ounces each) tropical fruit salad, chilled and drained

1/2 cup golden raisins

Lettuce leaves, if desired

1 1/2 cups cubed fully cooked fat-free ham

1. If coleslaw is very wet, drain off excess liquid. Mix coleslaw, fruit salad and raisins in large bowl.

2. Line salad plates with lettuce leaves. Spoon coleslaw mixture over lettuce. Make indentation in center of each mound of coleslaw mixture; fill with ham.

1 SERVING Calories 275 (Calories from Fat 115) | Fat 13g (Saturated 2g) | Cholesterol 25mg | Sodium 750mg | Carbohydrate 34g (Dietary Fiber 3g) | Protein 8g %DAILY VALUE Vitamin A 18% | Vitamin C 12% | Calcium 4% | Iron 8% EXCHANGES 1 Starch, 1 Fruit, 1 Very Lean Meat, 2 Fat CARBOHYDRATE CHOICES 2

BETTY'S TIP

This is a great salad to serve when the weather is hot and you don't want to heat up your kitchen. Pair it with slices of crusty French bread and tall glasses of lemonade or iced tea.

Asian Pork Salad

PREP 10 min   COOK 5 min   SERVINGS 4

1. Mix soy sauce, chili puree and oil. Mix pork and 1 tablespoon of the soy sauce mixture; reserve remaining soy sauce mixture.

2. Spray 10-inch nonstick skillet with cooking spray; heat over medium-high heat. Cook pork in skillet, stirring occasionally, until no longer pink.

3. Place pork in large bowl. Add remaining soy sauce mixture and remaining ingredients; toss.

1 SERVING Calories 240 (Calories from Fat 35) | Fat 4g (Saturated 1g) | Cholesterol 35mg | Sodium 950mg | Carbohydrate 35g (Dietary Fiber 9g) | Protein 24g %DAILY VALUE Vitamin A 2% | Vitamin C 32% | Calcium 10% | Iron 22% EXCHANGES 2 Starch, 1 Vegetable, 2 Very Lean Meat CARBOHYDRATE CHOICES 2

2 tablespoons soy sauce

1 tablespoon chili puree with garlic

1 teaspoon sesame or vegetable oil

1/2 pound pork tenderloin, cut into 1 1/2 × 1/2-inch strips

3 cups coleslaw mix (8 ounces)

1 small red bell pepper, cut into 1/2-inch strips

1 can (15 ounces) black beans, rinsed and drained

BETTY'S TIP

Look for packaged chopped coleslaw mix in the produce department of your supermarket. If it's unavailable, you can use 3 cups of shredded cabbage.

Antipasto Vegetable Salad

1/2 cup red wine vinegar

1/8 cup olive or
vegetable oil

2 tablespoons lemon juice

1 pound broccoli, separated
into flowerets (6 cups)

2 large bulbs fennel,
cut into 1-inch pieces

4 ounces mozzarella
cheese, cut into 1/2-inch
cubes

1 stick (2 1/2 ounces)
pepperoni, cut into
1/2-inch cubes

2 jars (6 ounces each)
marinated artichoke
hearts, drained

1 jar (12 ounces) marinated
mushrooms, drained

6 ounces whole Kalamata
olives, pitted and cut in half

Freshly ground pepper

PREP 25 min   CHILL 2 hr   SERVINGS 6

1.   Mix vinegar, oil and lemon juice in large glass or plastic
      bowl. Add remaining ingredients, except pepper; toss.

2.   Cover and refrigerate about 2 hours or until chilled.
      Toss before serving. Sprinkle with pepper.

1 SERVING Calories 365 (Calories from Fat 155) | Fat 17g (Saturated 5g) |
Cholesterol 20mg | Sodium 1000mg | Carbohydrate 21g (Dietary Fiber 8g) |
Protein 14g   %DAILY VALUE Vitamin A 28% | Vitamin C 100% | Calcium 24% |
Iron 16%   EXCHANGES 4 Vegetable, 1 High-Fat Meat, 1 1/2 Fat   CARBOHYDRATE
CHOICES 1 1/2

BETTY'S TIP

Look for prewashed and cut-up broccoli flowerets at the salad bar or
in plastic bags in the produce section of the supermarket.

Italian Tortellini Salad

PREP **20 min**   COOK **5 min**   SERVINGS **4**

1. Cook tortellini as directed on package; drain. Rinse with cold water; drain.

2. Mix marinara sauce and dressing in large bowl. Add tortellini and remaining ingredients; toss to mix.

1 SERVING Calories 365 (Calories from Fat 215) | Fat 24g (Saturated 7g) | Cholesterol 75mg | Sodium 920mg | Carbohydrate 26g (Dietary Fiber 3g) | Protein 12g   %DAILY VALUE Vitamin A 100% | Vitamin C 100% | Calcium 8% | Iron 10%   EXCHANGES 1 Starch, 2 Vegetable, 1 High-Fat Meat, 3 1/2 Fat   CARBOHYDRATE CHOICES 2

1 package (9 ounces) refrigerated cheese-filled tortellini

3/4 cup garlic-and-onion-flavored marinara sauce (from 28-ounce jar)

1/4 cup Italian dressing

1 cup broccoli flowerets

1/2 cup matchstick-cut carrots (from 10-ounce bag)

1 medium red or green bell pepper, chopped (1 cup)

1 package (3.5 ounces) sliced pepperoni, cut in half

BETTY'S TIP

For a heartier salad, add one can of kidney or other beans, rinsed and drained, and cubes of mozzarella or mild Cheddar cheese.

Spinach-Shrimp Salad with Hot Bacon Dressing

4 slices bacon, cut into 1-inch pieces

1/4 cup white vinegar

1 tablespoon sugar

1/4 teaspoon ground mustard

4 cups lightly packed bite-size pieces spinach leaves

1 cup sliced mushrooms (3 ounces)

1 cup crumbled feta cheese (4 ounces)

1/2 pound cooked peeled deveined medium shrimp, thawed if frozen and tails peeled

PREP **10** min   COOK **10** min   SERVINGS **4**

1. Cook bacon in 10-inch skillet over medium-high heat, stirring occasionally, until crisp. Stir in vinegar, sugar and mustard; continue stirring until sugar is dissolved.

2. Toss spinach, mushrooms, cheese and shrimp in large bowl. Drizzle hot bacon dressing over spinach mixture; toss. Serve immediately.

1 SERVING Calories 210 (Calories from Fat 100) | Fat 11g (Saturated 6g) | Cholesterol 140mg | Sodium 570mg | Carbohydrate 7g (Dietary Fiber 1g) | Protein 20g   %DAILY VALUE Vitamin A 62% | Vitamin C 16% | Calcium 18% | Iron 16%   EXCHANGES 1 Vegetable, 2 1/2 Medium-Fat Meat   CARBOHYDRATE CHOICES 1/2

BETTY'S TIP

Instead of plain feta, try using crumbled feta flavored with sun-dried tomatoes or basil-and-tomato in this easy-to-fix salad recipe.

Caribbean Shrimp Salad

PREP **20 min**   SERVINGS **4**

1. Make Honey-Lime Dressing.

2. Mix remaining ingredients in large bowl. Add dressing; toss until coated.

Honey-Lime Dressing

3 tablespoons honey

1 teaspoon grated lime peel

2 tablespoons lime juice

1 tablespoon vegetable oil

1 to 2 teaspoons finely chopped jalapeño chili

1/4 teaspoon salt

Mix all ingredients.

Honey-Lime Dressing
(below left)

1 bag (5 ounces) spring greens salad blend

1 pound cooked peeled deveined medium shrimp, thawed if frozen and tails peeled

1 small red onion, thinly sliced

1 can (15 1/4 ounces) pineapple shapes, drained

1 cup snow (Chinese) pea pods, strings removed

1 SERVING Calories 285 (Calories from Fat 45) | Fat 5g (Saturated 1g) | Cholesterol 220mg | Sodium 410mg | Carbohydrate 34g (Dietary Fiber 2g) | Protein 26g   %DAILY VALUE Vitamin A 30% | Vitamin C 48% | Calcium 8% | Iron 26%   EXCHANGES 1 Starch, 1 Vegetable, 3 Very Lean Meat   CARBOHYDRATE CHOICES 2

BETTY'S TIP

Pineapple shapes are a relatively new product and can be found with the canned fruit. The little shapes included in the can are stars, circles and half-moons. If you'd prefer, you can substitute pineapple tidbits instead.

Three-Bean and Tuna Salad

PREP **20 min**   SERVINGS **4**

Lemon Vinaigrette
(below right)

1 can (15 to 16 ounces)
cannellini beans, rinsed
and drained

1 can (15 to 16 ounces)
kidney beans, rinsed and
drained

1 can (15 to 16 ounces)
cut green beans, rinsed
and drained

1 large bell pepper,
chopped (1 1/2 cups)

1 medium onion, chopped
(1/2 cup)

1/4 cup chopped fresh
parsley

Lettuce leaves

1 can (6 ounces) tuna
in water, drained

Lemon wedges, if desired

1. Make Lemon Vinaigrette.

2. Mix beans, bell pepper, onion and parsley in large bowl.
    Pour vinaigrette over bean mixture; toss.

3. Line salad plates with lettuce leaves. Spoon bean mixture
    over lettuce. Top with tuna. Serve with lemon wedges.

Lemon Vinaigrette

   1/4 cup olive or vegetable oil

   2 tablespoons lemon juice

   1/4 teaspoon red pepper sauce

Shake all ingredients in tightly covered container.

1 SERVING Calories 365 (Calories from Fat 135) | Fat 15g (Saturated 3g) |
Cholesterol 10mg | Sodium 790mg | Carbohydrate 45g (Dietary Fiber 12g) |
Protein 25g   %DAILY VALUE Vitamin A 10% | Vitamin C 88% | Calcium 10% |
Iron 32%   EXCHANGES 2 1/2 Starch, 2 Vegetable, 2 Lean Meat   CARBOHYDRATE
CHOICES 3

Three-Bean and Caper Salad Omit the tuna and add
1/4 cup drained capers.

BETTY'S TIP

For a super shortcut, use 1/3 cup Italian dressing in place of the
Lemon Vinaigrette.

Italian Tuna Toss

PREP **15 min**   SERVINGS **6 to 8**

1 bag (10 ounces) salad mix (about 8 cups)

1 bag (16 ounces) fresh cauliflowerets

1 medium cucumber, sliced (1 1/2 cups)

2 cans (6 ounces each) tuna in water, drained

1 jar (2 ounces) sliced pimientos, drained (1/4 cup)

1/3 cup Italian dressing

1/4 cup bacon-flavor bits or chips

Toss all ingredients except dressing and bacon bits in large bowl. Add dressing and bacon bits; toss.

1 SERVING Calories 175 (Calories from Fat 65) | Fat 7g (Saturated 1g) | Cholesterol 20mg | Sodium 400mg | Carbohydrate 9g (Dietary Fiber 4g) | Protein 19g %DAILY VALUE Vitamin A 36% | Vitamin C 88% | Calcium 6% | Iron 12% EXCHANGES 2 Vegetable, 2 Very Lean Meat, 1 Fat CARBOHYDRATE CHOICES 1/2

Italian Salami Toss Substitute 1/4 pound diced salami (about 3/4 cup) for the tuna.

BETTY'S TIP

You can also separate a small head of cauliflower into flowerets instead of using the bag of flowerets. One small head will yield about 3 cups. Instead of the bag of greens, you can use a small bunch of curly endive or romaine, torn into bite-size pieces.

Summer Salmon Salad

Toasted Sesame Dressing
(below right)

1 small zucchini, thinly
sliced

1 small yellow summer
squash, thinly sliced
(1 1/2 cups)

4 roma (plum) tomatoes,
thinly sliced

1 small onion, sliced and
separated into rings

1 cup sliced mushrooms
(3 ounces)

Lettuce leaves

1 can (14 3/4 ounces)
salmon, chilled, drained
and flaked

1. Make Toasted Sesame Dressing.

2. Toss zucchini, summer squash, tomatoes, onion and
mushrooms.

3. Line salad plates with lettuce leaves. Spoon vegetable
mixture onto lettuce leaves. Place salmon on center of
vegetable mixture. Spoon dressing over salads.

Toasted Sesame Dressing

1 tablespoon sesame seed

1/8 cup white wine vinegar

1 tablespoon sugar

2 tablespoons olive or vegetable oil

1 teaspoon ground mustard

1/2 teaspoon salt

1 large clove garlic, finely chopped

To toast sesame seed, cook in ungreased heavy skillet
over medium heat about 2 minutes, stirring frequently
until browning begins, then stirring constantly until
golden brown; cool. Shake sesame seed and remaining
ingredients in tightly covered container.

1 SERVING Calories 270 (Calories from Fat 135) | Fat 15g (Saturated 3g) |
Cholesterol 60mg | Sodium 880mg | Carbohydrate 11g (Dietary Fiber 2g) |
Protein 23g   %DAILY VALUE Vitamin A 16% | Vitamin C 32% | Calcium 24% |
Iron 10%   EXCHANGES 2 Vegetable, 3 Lean Meat, 1 Fat   CARBOHYDRATE CHOICES 1

Summer Salmon-Pasta Salad Add 2 cups cooked farfalle
(bow-tie) pasta and double the dressing. Toss with the vegetable mixture and salmon before spooning onto lettuce.

BETTY'S TIP

If you have sesame seed oil in your pantry, use it in place of the olive
oil and omit the sesame seed.

Chopped Vegetable and Crabmeat Salad

PREP **20 min**   SERVINGS **4**

1.   Make Lime Dressing.
2.   Place remaining ingredients except peanuts and cilantro in large bowl. Pour dressing over salad; toss. Top with peanuts and cilantro.

Lime Dressing

   1/3 cup frozen (thawed) limeade concentrate

   1/4 cup vegetable oil

   1 tablespoon rice or white vinegar

   1 teaspoon grated gingerroot

   1/4 teaspoon salt

Shake all ingredients in tightly covered container.

1 SERVING Calories 430 (Calories from Fat 215) | Fat 24g (Saturated 4g) | Cholesterol 75mg | Sodium 590mg | Carbohydrate 37g (Dietary Fiber 9g) | Protein 25g   %DAILY VALUE Vitamin A 38% | Vitamin C 100% | Calcium 14% | Iron 12%   EXCHANGES 2 Fruit, 1 Vegetable, 3 High-Fat Meat   CARBOHYDRATE CHOICES 2 1/2

Lime Dressing (below left)

2 cups chopped escarole

2 cans (6 ounces each) crabmeat, drained and flaked, or 2 cups chopped cooked turkey or chicken

1 small jicama, peeled and chopped (1 cup)

1 large papaya, peeled, seeded and chopped (1 cup)

1 medium yellow or red bell pepper, chopped (1 cup)

1/2 cup dry-roasted peanuts

1/4 cup chopped fresh cilantro

BETTY'S TIP

To get a head start on dinner, chop the papaya and bell pepper, wrap separately and refrigerate. You can also make the dressing a day ahead and refrigerate it.

Caesar Salad with Lobster

1 bag (10 ounces) salad mix (about 8 cups)

1 can (11 ounces) mandarin orange segments, chilled and drained

1 package (8 ounces) refrigerated imitation lobster chunks

1 small unpeeled cucumber, cut into 1/4-inch slices

1/3 cup fat-free Caesar or ranch dressing

Sliced almonds, if desired

PREP **10 min**   SERVINGS **4**

Place all ingredients except almonds in large bowl; toss lightly to coat. Sprinkle with almonds.

1 SERVING Calories 120 (Calories from Fat 10) | Fat 1g (Saturated 0g) | Cholesterol 40mg | Sodium 480mg | Carbohydrate 17g (Dietary Fiber 2g) | Protein 13g %DAILY VALUE Vitamin A 4% | Vitamin C 18% | Calcium 6% | Iron 6%   EXCHANGES 1/2 Fruit, 2 Vegetable, 1 Very Lean Meat   CARBOHYDRATE CHOICES 1

Caesar Salad with Crabmeat Substitute imitation crabmeat chunks in place of the lobster chunks.

BETTY'S TIP

For an extra-special touch, use the tines of a fork to create stripes down the side of an unwaxed cucumber before you cut it into slices.

Couscous-Vegetable Salad

PREP **15 min**   COOK **5 min**   SERVINGS **6**

1. Make couscous as directed on package.

2. While couscous is cooking, heat oil in 10-inch nonstick skillet over medium-high heat. Cook zucchini, yellow squash, bell pepper and onion in oil about 5 minutes, stirring frequently, until vegetables are crisp-tender.

3. Toss couscous, vegetable mixture, pesto and vinegar in large bowl. Serve warm or cool.

1 SERVING Calories 330 (Calories from Fat 180) | Fat 20g (Saturated 4g) | Cholesterol 5mg | Sodium 300mg | Carbohydrate 30g (Dietary Fiber 4g) | Protein 8g   %DAILY VALUE Vitamin A 42% | Vitamin C 100% | Calcium 14% | Iron 8%   EXCHANGES 1 1/2 Starch, 2 Vegetable, 3 1/2 Fat   CARBOHYDRATE CHOICES 2

1 cup uncooked couscous

1 tablespoon olive or vegetable oil

1 medium zucchini, cut into 1/4-inch slices (2 cups)

1 medium yellow summer squash, cut into 1/4-inch slices (1 1/2 cups)

1 large red bell pepper, cut into 1-inch pieces

1/2 medium red onion, cut into 8 wedges

1 container (7 ounces) refrigerated basil pesto with sun-dried tomatoes or regular basil pesto

2 tablespoons balsamic vinegar

BETTY'S TIP

If you don't have balsamic vinegar on hand, use the same amount of cider vinegar instead.

Tuscan Panzanella Salad

1 bag (10 ounces) romaine and leaf lettuce mix

1 can (19 ounces) cannellini beans, rinsed and drained

2 cups large croutons

1 cup sweet grape tomatoes

1/2 cup thinly sliced red onion

1/3 cup Kalamata olives, cut in half

1/3 cup balsamic vinaigrette

PREP **15 min**   SERVINGS **6**

Mix all ingredients except vinaigrette in large bowl. Add vinaigrette; toss until coated.

1 SERVING Calories 250 (Calories from Fat 80) | Fat 9g (Saturated 1g) | Cholesterol 5mg | Sodium 360mg | Carbohydrate 36g (Dietary Fiber 8g) | Protein 12g **%DAILY VALUE** Vitamin A 26% | Vitamin C 30% | Calcium 14% | Iron 26% **EXCHANGES** 2 Starch, 1 Vegetable, 1/2 High-Fat Meat, 1/2 Fat **CARBOHYDRATE CHOICES** 2 1/2

BETTY'S TIP

Sweet grape tomatoes are small and very sweet. If they're not available, you can use cherry tomatoes instead and just cut them in half. Or try yellow pear tomatoes if they are available at your market.

Spring Vegetable Paella

PREP **15 min**   COOK **15 min**   SERVINGS **6**

1. Heat 1 inch water to boiling in 2-quart saucepan. Add asparagus and broccoli. Heat to boiling; boil about 4 minutes or until crisp-tender; drain.

2. Heat oil in 10-inch skillet over medium-high heat. Cook asparagus, broccoli, bell pepper, zucchini, onion, salt and saffron in oil about 5 minutes, stirring occasionally, until onion is crisp-tender.

3. Stir in remaining ingredients. Serve on platter or individual serving plates lined with lettuce.

1 SERVING Calories 425 (Calories from Fat 65) | Fat 7g (Saturated 1g) | Cholesterol 0mg | Sodium 560mg | Carbohydrate 86g (Dietary Fiber 19g) | Protein 22g %DAILY VALUE Vitamin A 60% | Vitamin C 100% | Calcium 14% | Iron 36% EXCHANGES 5 Starch, 2 Vegetable CARBOHYDRATE CHOICES 6

Spring Vegetable and Chicken Paella Omit 1 can of garbanzo beans. Add 1 1/2 cups chopped cooked chicken or turkey with remaining ingredients in step 3. Continue as directed.

1 pound asparagus, cut into 2-inch pieces

3 cups broccoli flowerets

2 teaspoons olive or vegetable oil

1 medium red bell pepper, chopped (1 cup)

2 small zucchini, chopped (1 1/4 cups)

1 medium onion, chopped (1/2 cup)

3/4 teaspoon salt

1/2 teaspoon saffron threads

4 cups cooked brown or white rice, cold

2 large tomatoes, seeded and chopped (2 cups)

2 cans (15 to 16 ounces each) garbanzo beans, rinsed and drained

1 package (10 ounces) frozen green peas, thawed and drained

BETTY'S TIP

Saffron, the dried stigmas of crocus, is a fragrant spice that gives food a pretty yellow color. Because it is expensive, you may prefer to use 1/4 teaspoon ground turmeric as an affordable substitute.

Greek Pasta Salad

1 1/4 cups uncooked orzo
or rosamarina pasta
(8 ounces)

2 cups thinly sliced
cucumber (about 2 small)

1 medium red onion,
chopped (1/2 cup)

1/2 cup Italian dressing

1 medium tomato,
chopped (3/4 cup)

1 can (15 to 16 ounces)
garbanzo beans, rinsed
and drained

1 can (2 1/4 ounces) sliced
ripe olives, drained

1/2 cup crumbled feta
cheese (2 ounces)

PREP 15 min   COOK 10 min   CHILL 1 hr   SERVINGS 5

1. Cook pasta as directed on package; drain. Rinse with cold water; drain.

2. Mix pasta and remaining ingredients except cheese in large glass or plastic bowl. Cover and refrigerate at least 1 hour to blend flavors but no longer than 24 hours.

3. To serve, top salad with cheese.

1 SERVING Calories 445 (Calories from Fat 155) | Fat 17g (Saturated 3g) |
Cholesterol 15mg | Sodium 580mg | Carbohydrate 66g (Dietary Fiber 9g) |
Protein 16g   %DAILY VALUE Vitamin A 8% | Vitamin C 14% | Calcium 14% |
Iron 28%   EXCHANGES 4 Starch, 1 Vegetable, 2 Fat   CARBOHYDRATE CHOICES 6

BETTY'S TIP

Feta cheese is bursting with sharp, tangy, salty flavor. This crumbly cheese is traditionally made from goat's or sheep's milk, but due to its popularity is often made with cow's milk. Crumbled blue cheese, in place of the feta, is also good on this salad.

One-Dish Grilling

Cheddar Burgers and Veggies

1 1/2 pounds lean ground beef

1 1/2 cups shredded Cheddar cheese (6 ounces)

1 1/2 tablespoons Worcestershire sauce

3 medium green onions, chopped (3 tablespoons)

2 teaspoons peppered seasoned salt

3 medium Yukon gold potatoes, thinly sliced

2 cups baby-cut carrots

18 cherry tomatoes, cut in half, if desired

6 medium green onions, sliced (1/3 cup)

1. Heat coals or gas grill for direct heat. Cut six 18×12-inch sheets of heavy-duty aluminum foil. Spray with cooking spray.

2. Mix beef, cheese, Worcestershire sauce, chopped onions and 1 1/2 teaspoons of the peppered seasoned salt. Shape mixture into 6 patties, about 1 inch thick.

3. Place potatoes on one side of each foil sheet. Top with beef patty, carrots, tomatoes and sliced onions; sprinkle with remaining 1/2 teaspoon peppered seasoned salt. Fold foil over patties and vegetables so edges meet. Seal edges, making tight 1/2-inch fold; fold again. Allow space on sides for circulation and expansion.

4. Cover and grill packets 4 to 6 inches from medium heat 17 to 20 minutes or until potatoes are tender. Place packets on plates. Cut large X across top of each packet; fold back foil.

1 SERVING Calories 430 (Calories from Fat 235) | Fat 26g (Saturated 12g) | Cholesterol 95mg | Sodium 470mg | Carbohydrate 20g (Dietary Fiber 4g) | Protein 30g   %DAILY VALUE Vitamin A 100% | Vitamin C 14% | Calcium 20% | Iron 22%   EXCHANGES 1 Starch, 1 Vegetable, 3 1/2 Medium-Fat Meat, 2 Fat CARBOHYDRATE CHOICES 1

BETTY'S TIP

If you don't have peppered seasoned salt, use 1 teaspoon seasoned salt or 1/2 teaspoon salt for each teaspoon of peppered seasoned salt.

Skewered Steak Dinner

1. Mix beef and dressing in shallow glass or plastic dish. Cover and refrigerate, stirring occasionally, at least 30 minutes but no longer than 24 hours.

2. Heat 1 inch water to boiling in 1 1/2-quart saucepan. Add potatoes. Boil about 15 minutes or until almost tender; drain. Cool slightly.

3. Heat coals or gas grill for direct heat. Remove beef from marinade; reserve marinade. Thread beef, potatoes, onion, mushrooms, bell peppers and squash alternately on each of six 15-inch metal skewers, leaving about 1/4-inch space between each piece. Brush kabobs generously with marinade.

4. Cover and grill kabobs 4 to 6 inches from medium heat 12 to 15 minutes for medium beef doneness, turning frequently and brushing with marinade. Discard any remaining marinade.

1 1/2 pounds beef boneless sirloin, cut into strips

1/2 cup fat-free Italian dressing

6 new potatoes (1/2 pound)

1 medium onion, cut into 6 wedges

6 small whole mushrooms

6 mini red bell peppers

6 mini pattypan squash

1 Serving. Calories 185 (Calories from Fat 35) | Fat 4g (Saturated 1g) | Cholesterol 60mg | Sodium 230mg | Carbohydrate 13g (Dietary Fiber 2g) | Protein 24g   %DAILY VALUE Vitamin A 18% | Vitamin C 32% | Calcium 2% | Iron 16%   EXCHANGES 1/2 starch, 1 Vegetable, 3 Very Lean Meat, 1/2 Fat CARBOHYDRATE CHOICES 1

BETTY'S TIP

The new mini red bell peppers and pattypan squash are fun and easy to use for kabobs. If they are unavailable, use 1 medium bell pepper and 1 medium yellow summer squash, each cut into 1-inch pieces.

Beef and Corn Kabobs

1/3 cup vegetable oil

1/4 cup red wine vinegar

1 tablespoon chopped fresh or 1 teaspoon dried thyme leaves

1/2 teaspoon ground red pepper (cayenne)

1 clove garlic, finely chopped

1 1/2 pounds beef boneless top round steak, cut into 1-inch cubes

4 small ears corn, husks removed

2 green or red bell peppers, cut into 1 1/2-inch pieces

PREP 20 min   MARINATE 4 hr   GRILL 20 min   SERVINGS 6

1. Mix oil, vinegar, thyme, red pepper and garlic in medium nonmetal bowl or resealable plastic food-storage bag. Add beef; stir to coat with marinade. Cover dish or seal bag and refrigerate, stirring beef occasionally, at least 4 hours but no longer than 24 hours.

2. Heat coals or gas grill for direct heat. Cut each ear of corn into 3 pieces. Remove beef from marinade; reserve marinade. Thread beef, corn and bell peppers alternately on each of six 10- to 12-inch metal skewers, leaving about 1/4-inch space between each piece. Brush kabobs with marinade.

3. Cover and grill kabobs 4 to 5 inches from medium heat 15 to 20 minutes for medium beef doneness, turning frequently and brushing with marinade. Discard any remaining marinade.

1 SERVING Calories 280 (Calories from Fat 115) | Fat 13g (Saturated 3g) | Cholesterol 60mg | Sodium 55mg | Carbohydrate 18g (Dietary Fiber 2g) | Protein 25g   %DAILY VALUE Vitamin A 6% | Vitamin C 30% | Calcium 0% | Iron 14%   EXCHANGES 1 Starch, 1 Vegetable, 2 1/2 Medium-Fat Meat   CARBOHYDRATE CHOICES 1

BETTY'S TIP

It's important to marinate food in a nonmetal dish. Acid-based marinades, such as those with lemon juice and vinegar, can react with some metals and gives foods an off-flavor.

Italian Chicken Packets

PREP **10 min**   GRILL **22 min**   SERVINGS **4**

4 boneless, skinless
chicken breast halves
(about 1 1/4 pounds)

1 medium yellow bell
pepper, cut into 4 wedges

4 roma (plum) tomatoes,
cut in half

1 small red onion, cut into
8 wedges

1/2 cup Italian vinaigrette
dressing

1. Heat coals or gas grill for direct heat. Cut four 18 × 12-inch sheets of heavy-duty aluminum foil. Place 1 chicken breast half, 1 bell pepper wedge, 2 tomato halves and 2 onion wedges on one side of each foil sheet. Top each with 2 tablespoons dressing.

2. Fold foil over chicken and vegetables so edges meet. Seal edges, making tight 1/2-inch fold; fold again. Allow space on sides for circulation and expansion.

3. Cover and grill packets 4 to 5 inches from medium heat 18 to 22 minutes or until juice of chicken is no longer pink when centers are cut. Place packets on plates. Cut large X across top of each packet; fold back foil.

1 SERVING Calories 250 (Calories from Fat 110) | Fat 12g (Saturated 2g) | Cholesterol 75mg | Sodium 250mg | Carbohydrate 8g (Dietary Fiber 1g) | Protein 28g %DAILY VALUE Vitamin A 10% | Vitamin C 54% | Calcium 4% | Iron 8% EXCHANGES 2 Vegetable, 3 1/2 Lean Meat CARBOHYDRATE CHOICES 1/2

BETTY'S TIP

If you have time, marinate the chicken in Italian dressing for 1 to 2 hours before grilling.

Spicy Southwest Chicken Kabobs

1 tablespoon garlic pepper

2 tablespoons olive or vegetable oil

4 small ears corn, husks removed

1 1/2 pounds boneless, skinless chicken breasts, cut into 1-inch cubes

2 medium yellow or red bell peppers, cut into 1 1/2-inch pieces

3/4 cup ranch dressing

1 canned chipotle chili in adobo sauce, chopped

PREP **10 min**   GRILL **20 min**   SERVINGS **6**

1. Heat coals or gas grill for direct heat. Mix garlic pepper and oil. Cut each ear of corn into 3 pieces. Thread chicken, corn and bell peppers alternately on each of six 10- to 12-inch metal skewers, leaving 1/4-inch space between each piece. Brush kabobs with oil mixture.

2. Cover and grill kabobs 4 to 5 inches from medium heat 15 to 20 minutes, turning 2 or 3 times, until chicken is no longer pink in center.

3. Mix dressing and chili. Serve with kabobs.

1 SERVING Calories 390 (Calories from Fat 205) | Fat 23g (Saturated 3g) | Cholesterol 80mg | Sodium 430mg | Carbohydrate 19g (Dietary Fiber 2g) | Protein 28g   %DAILY VALUE Vitamin A 6% | Vitamin C 64% | Calcium 6% | Iron 8%   EXCHANGES 1 Starch, 1 Vegetable, 3 Lean Meat, 2 1/2 Fat CARBOHYDRATE CHOICES 1

BETTY'S TIP

For quick and easy grilling, cut the chicken and vegetables the night before. Store in plastic food-storage bags in the refrigerator.

Paella on the Grill

PREP **20 min**   MARINATE **1 hr**   GRILL **25 min**   SERVINGS **6**

Saffron Marinade (below)

1 pound boneless, skinless chicken breasts, cut into 1-inch pieces

1 pound uncooked medium shrimp in shells, thawed if frozen

1/2 pound chorizo sausage, cut into 1-inch pieces

8 roma (plum) tomatoes, cut into fourths

1 can (about 14 ounces) artichoke hearts, drained and cut in half

1 cup pitted Kalamata or Greek olives

Hot cooked rice, if desired

1. Make Saffron Marinade. Place remaining ingredients except rice in glass or plastic dish or resealable plastic food-storage bag. Pour marinade over mixture; stir to coat. Cover dish or seal bag and refrigerate 1 hour.

2. Heat coals or gas grill for direct heat. Remove chicken mixture from marinade; reserve marinade. Place chicken mixture in grill basket (grill "wok").

3. Cover and grill chicken mixture 4 inches from medium heat 20 to 25 minutes, stirring and brushing with marinade occasionally, until chicken is no longer pink in center. Discard any remaining marinade. Serve chicken mixture with rice.

Saffron Marinade

   1 cup chicken broth

   1/2 cup sherry wine vinegar

   1/2 teaspoon salt

   1/4 teaspoon curry powder

   1/4 teaspoon crushed saffron threads or ground turmeric

   2 cloves garlic, finely chopped

Mix all ingredients.

1 SERVING Calories 365 (Calories from Fat 180) | Fat 20g (Saturated 7g) | Cholesterol 150mg | Sodium 1280mg | Carbohydrate 14g (Dietary Fiber 5g) | Protein 37g %DAILY VALUE Vitamin A 26% | Vitamin C 18% | Calcium 8% | Iron 24% EXCHANGES 3 Vegetable, 4 1/2 Lean Meat, 1 Fat CARBOHYDRATE CHOICES 1

BETTY'S TIP

Chorizo sausage is a highly seasoned, coarsely ground pork sausage. If it is not available, use any smoked sausage.

Lemon Chicken with Fennel and Onions

6 bone-in chicken breast halves (about 3 pounds)

1/3 cup olive or vegetable oil

1 teaspoon grated lemon peel

1/4 cup lemon juice

2 tablespoons chopped fresh or 2 teaspoons dried oregano leaves

1/2 teaspoon salt

2 medium bulbs fennel, cut into 1/2-inch slices

1 medium red onion, cut into 1/2-inch slices

PREP **20 min**   MARINATE **15 min**   GRILL **20 min**   SERVINGS **6**

1. Place chicken in shallow glass or plastic dish. Mix oil, lemon peel, lemon juice, oregano and salt; pour over chicken. Cover and let stand 15 minutes.

2. Heat coals or gas grill for direct heat. Remove chicken from marinade. Brush fennel and onion with marinade. Cover and grill chicken (skin sides down), fennel and onion 4 to 5 inches from medium heat 15 to 20 minutes, turning once and brushing frequently with marinade, until juice of chicken is no longer pink when centers of thickest pieces are cut. Discard any remaining marinade.

1 SERVING Calories 265 (Calories from Fat 135) | Fat 15g (Saturated 3g) | Cholesterol 75mg | Sodium 210mg | Carbohydrate 8g (Dietary Fiber 3g) | Protein 28g   %DAILY VALUE Vitamin A 4% | Vitamin C 10% | Calcium 6% | Iron 8%   EXCHANGES 1 Vegetable, 4 Lean Meat, 1 Fat   CARBOHYDRATE CHOICES 1/2

BETTY'S TIP

For an easy summer meal, serve this lemony chicken with fresh tomato slices and angel hair pasta.

Caribbean Chicken Kabobs

1. Brush grill rack with vegetable oil. Heat coals or gas grill for direct heat.

2. Brush chicken with 2 tablespoons of the oil. Place chicken and seasoning blend in resealable plastic food-storage bag. Shake bag to coat chicken with seasoning. Thread chicken, pineapple, bell pepper and onion alternately on each of eight 12-inch metal skewers, leaving 1/4-inch space between each piece. Brush kabobs with remaining 2 tablespoons oil.

3. Cover and grill kabobs 4 to 5 inches from medium heat 15 to 20 minutes, turning once, until chicken is no longer pink in center.

1 3/4 pounds boneless, skinless chicken breasts, cut into 1 1/2-inch pieces

1/4 cup vegetable oil

3 tablespoons Key West–style coarsely ground seasoning blend

1 small pineapple, peeled and cut into 1-inch cubes

1 medium red bell pepper, cut into 1-inch pieces

1 small red onion, cut into 1-inch pieces

1 SERVING Calories 210 (Calories from Fat 90) | Fat 10g (Saturated 2g) | Cholesterol 60mg | Sodium 350mg | Carbohydrate 8g (Dietary Fiber 1g) | Protein 22g   %DAILY VALUE Vitamin A 18% | Vitamin C 30% | Calcium 2% | Iron 6%   EXCHANGES 1/2 Fruit, 3 Lean Meat, 1/2 Fat   CARBOHYDRATE CHOICES 1/2

BETTY'S TIP

For a right-out-of-a-restaurant presentation, place romaine leaves on a large serving platter and arrange kabobs on top.

Mediterranean Chicken Packets

1 package (4 ounces) crumbled basil-and-tomato feta cheese (1 cup)

2 tablespoons grated lemon peel

1 teaspoon dried oregano leaves

4 boneless, skinless chicken breast halves (about 1 1/4 pounds)

4 roma (plum) tomatoes, each cut into 3 slices

1 small red onion, finely chopped (1 cup)

20 pitted Kalamata olives

1. Heat coals or gas grill for direct heat. Cut four 18 × 12-inch sheets of heavy-duty aluminum foil. Mix cheese, lemon peel and oregano. Place 1 chicken breast half, 3 tomato slices, 1/4 cup onion and 5 olives on one side of each foil sheet. Top each with one-fourth of the cheese mixture.

2. Fold foil over chicken and vegetables so edges meet. Seal edges, making tight 1/2-inch fold; fold again. Allow space on sides for circulation and expansion.

3. Cover and grill packets 4 to 5 inches from medium heat 20 to 25 minutes or until juice of chicken is no longer pink when centers of thickest pieces are cut. Place packets on plates. Cut large X across top of each packet; fold back foil.

1 SERVING Calories 250 (Calories from Fat 110) | Fat 12g (Saturated 6g) | Cholesterol 100mg | Sodium 560mg | Carbohydrate 7g (Dietary Fiber 2g) | Protein 31g %DAILY VALUE Vitamin A 12% | Vitamin C 8% | Calcium 18% | Iron 10% EXCHANGES 1 Vegetable, 4 Lean Meat CARBOHYDRATE CHOICES 1/2

BETTY'S TIP

You can use a package of crumbled plain feta cheese instead of the flavored feta.

Pesto Chicken Packets

PREP **15 min**   GRILL **25 min**   SERVINGS **4**

4 boneless, skinless chicken breast halves (about 1 1/4 pounds)

8 roma (plum) tomatoes, cut into 1/2 inch slices

4 small zucchini, cut into 1/2-inch slices

1/2 cup basil pesto

1. Heat coals or gas grill for direct heat. Cut four 18 × 12-inch sheets of heavy-duty aluminum foil. Place 1 chicken breast half, 2 sliced tomatoes and 1 sliced zucchini on one side of each foil sheet. Top each 2 tablespoons pesto.

2. Fold foil over chicken and vegetables so edges meet. Seal edges, making tight 1/2-inch fold; fold again. Allow space on sides for circulation and expansion.

3. Cover and grill packets 4 to 5 inches from medium heat 20 to 25 minutes or until juice of chicken is no longer pink when centers of thickest pieces are cut. Place packets on plates. Cut large X across top of each packet; fold back foil.

1 SERVING Calories 330 (Calories from Fat 180) | Fat 20g (Saturated 4g) | Cholesterol 75mg | Sodium 350mg | Carbohydrate 10g (Dietary Fiber 3g) | Protein 31g %DAILY VALUE Vitamin A 36% | Vitamin C 26% | Calcium 16% | Iron 14% EXCHANGES 2 Vegetable, 4 Very Lean Meat, 3 Fat CARBOHYDRATE CHOICES 1/2

BETTY'S TIP

Instead of using foil packets, try the new heavy-duty foil bags made especially for grilling.

Tex-Mex Chicken Enchilada Packets

1 cup diced cooked chicken

2 cups shredded Mexican cheese blend (8 ounces)

1 can (4.5 ounces) chopped green chiles

2 tablespoons finely chopped onion

1 container (8 ounces) sour cream

8 corn tortillas (6 inches in diameter)

Cooking spray

1 can (10 ounces) enchilada sauce

PREP **20 min**   GRILL **12 min**   SERVINGS **4**

1. Mix chicken, 1 1/2 cups of the cheese, the green chiles, onion and sour cream in medium bowl. Set aside.

2. If using charcoal grill, place drip pan directly under grilling area, and arrange coals around edge of firebox. Heat coals or gas grill for indirect heat. Spray both sides of each tortilla with cooking spray. Stack tortillas on microwavable plate; cover with microwavable paper towel. Microwave on High 30 seconds.

3. Cut four 18 × 12-inch sheets of heavy-duty aluminum foil. Spray with cooking spray. Spread 1/3 cup chicken mixture down center of each warm tortilla; roll up. Place 2 enchiladas, seam sides down, on one side of each foil sheet; drizzle each with about 1/4 cup enchilada sauce. Fold foil over enchiladas so edges meet. Seal edges, making tight 1/2-inch fold; fold again. Allow space on sides for circulation and expansion.

4. Place packets, seam sides up, over drip pan or over unheated side of gas grill and 4 to 6 inches from medium heat. Cover and grill packets 10 to 12 minutes or until enchiladas are hot. Carefully open packets to allow steam to escape. Place enchiladas on serving plates. Top with remaining 1/2 cup cheese.

1 SERVING Calories 600 (Calories from Fat 350) | Fat 39g (Saturated 21g) | Cholesterol 110mg | Sodium 920mg | Carbohydrate 33g (Dietary Fiber 4g) | Protein 28g   %DAILY VALUE Vitamin A 30% | Vitamin C 10% | Calcium 60% | Iron 10%   EXCHANGES 2 Starch, 3 High-Fat Meat, 3 Fat   CARBOHYDRATE CHOICES 2

BETTY'S TIP

These enchilada packets are great for a casual backyard get-together. Serve with tortilla chips and salsa on the side, and wash it all down with a pitcher of margaritas or sangria.

Pizza Chicken Kabobs

PREP **20 min**   GRILL **11 min**   SERVINGS **6**

1 1/2 pounds chicken
breast tenders (not breaded)

1 medium red bell pepper,
cut into 1-inch pieces

1 package (8 ounces)
whole mushrooms

1/3 cup Italian dressing

2 teaspoons pizza seasoning

1/4 cup grated Parmesan
cheese

1/2 cup pizza sauce
(from 14-ounce jar)

1. Heat coals or gas grill for direct heat. Thread chicken, bell pepper and mushrooms alternately on each of six 11-inch metal skewers, leaving 1/2-inch space between each piece. Brush kabobs with dressing; sprinkle with pizza seasoning.

2. Cover and grill kabobs 4 to 6 inches from medium heat 9 to 11 minutes, turning once, until chicken is no longer pink in center. Immediately sprinkle with cheese.

3. While kabobs are grilling, heat pizza sauce in small saucepan over low heat. Serve kabobs with warm sauce.

1 SERVING Calories 245 (Calories from Fat 100) | Fat 11g (Saturated 2g) | Cholesterol 75mg | Sodium 400mg | Carbohydrate 7g (Dietary Fiber 1g) | Protein 29g   %DAILY VALUE Vitamin A 28% | Vitamin C 36% | Calcium 10% | Iron 8%   EXCHANGES 1/2 Starch, 4 Lean Meat   CARBOHYDRATE CHOICES 1/2

BETTY'S TIP

Pizza seasoning can be found in the spice aisle of the supermarket.
If it's not available, use 1 teaspoon Italian seasoning instead.

Smoked Sausage and Cheddar Potato Packets

3/4 cup process Cheddar cheese sauce (from 16-ounce jar)

1/2 cup shredded Cheddar cheese (2 ounces)

2 cups frozen stir-fry bell peppers and onions (from 1-pound bag)

2 cups refrigerated diced potatoes with onions (from 20-ounce bag)

1 pound fully cooked smoked sausage, cut into 1 1/2-inch pieces

PREP **10 min**   GRILL **25 min**   SERVINGS **4**

1. Heat coals or gas grill for direct heat. Cut four 18×12-inch sheets of heavy-duty aluminum foil. Spray with cooking spray.

2. Mix cheese sauce and cheese in medium bowl. Stir in stir-fry vegetables and potatoes. Arrange one-fourth of the sausage and potato mixture on one side of each foil sheet. Fold foil over sausage and potatoes so edges meet. Seal edges, making tight 1/2-inch fold; fold again. Allow space on sides for circulation and expansion.

3. Cover and grill packets 4 to 6 inches from medium-low heat 20 to 25 minutes, rotating packets 1/2 turn after 10 minutes, until potatoes are tender. Place packets on plates. Cut large X across top of each packet; fold back foil.

1 SERVING Calories 605 (Calories from Fat 395) | Fat 44g (Saturated 19g) | Cholesterol 100mg | Sodium 1510mg | Carbohydrate 29g (Dietary Fiber 3g) | Protein 24g   %DAILY VALUE Vitamin A 14% | Vitamin C 34% | Calcium 22% | Iron 10%   EXCHANGES 2 Starch, 2 1/2 High-Fat Meat, 4 Fat   CARBOHYDRATE CHOICES 2

BETTY'S TIP

Although these packets contain the major portion of your meal, go ahead and add crusty French bread and fresh fruit to complete your picnic.

Southwest Pork Packets

PREP **20 min**   STAND **15 min**   GRILL **20 min**   SERVINGS **4**

1. Heat coals or gas grill for direct heat. Spray half of one side of four 18 × 12-inch sheets of heavy-duty aluminum foil with cooking spray.

2. Mix rice, broth and 1 tablespoon Mexican seasoning in large bowl. Let stand about 15 minutes or until broth is absorbed; drain any remaining broth. Stir corn, bell pepper and onions into rice.

3. Sprinkle each pork chop with 1/2 teaspoon Mexican seasoning; place in center of sprayed foil. Spoon rice mixture over pork. Fold foil over pork and rice so edges meet. Seal edges, making tight 1/2-inch fold; fold again. Allow space on sides for circulation and expansion.

4. Cover and grill packets 4 to 6 inches from medium heat 15 to 20 minutes or until pork is no longer pink in center. Place packets on plates. Cut large X across top of each packet; fold back foil. Serve with salsa.

2 cups uncooked instant rice

1 can (14 ounces) chicken broth

1 tablespoon Mexican seasoning

1 can (15.25 ounces) whole kernel corn, drained

1 small bell pepper, chopped (1/2 cup)

4 medium green onions, sliced (1/4 cup)

4 pork boneless rib or loin chops, 3/4 to 1 inch thick (1 1/4 pounds)

2 teaspoons Mexican seasoning

Salsa, if desired

1 SERVING Calories 560 (Calories from Fat 125) | Fat 14g (Saturated 4g) | Cholesterol 90mg | Sodium 910mg | Carbohydrate 70g (Dietary Fiber 4g) | Protein 42g %DAILY VALUE Vitamin A 12% | Vitamin C 24% | Calcium 6% | Iron 26% EXCHANGES 4 Starch, 2 Vegetable, 4 Lean Meat CARBOHYDRATE CHOICES 4 1/2

BETTY'S TIP

Keep a bunch of grapes in the freezer—they're the ultimate summer treat! Enjoy them for between-meal snacks or to munch on while preparing dinner.

Honey-Cumin Barbecue Pork Packets

1/2 cup barbecue sauce

1/4 cup honey

2 teaspoons ground cumin

4 pork boneless rib or loin chops, 3/4 to 1 inch thick (about 1 1/4 pounds)

2 large ears corn, each cut into 6 pieces

1 cup baby-cut carrots, cut lengthwise in half

2 cups refrigerated cooked new potato wedges (from 1-pound 4-ounce bag)

1 teaspoon salt

PREP 20 min   GRILL 20 min   SERVINGS 4

1. Heat coals or gas grill for direct heat. Cut four 18×12-inch sheets of heavy-duty aluminum foil. Spray with cooking spray.

2. Mix barbecue sauce, honey and cumin in small bowl. Place 1 pork chop on one side of each foil sheet. Top each with one-fourth of the corn, carrots and potatoes; sprinkle with 1/4 teaspoon salt. Spoon 3 tablespoons sauce mixture over each.

3. Fold foil over pork and vegetables so edges meet. Seal edges, making tight 1/2-inch fold; fold again. Allow space on sides for circulation and expansion.

4. Cover and grill packets 4 to 6 inches from medium heat 15 to 20 minutes, turning once, until pork is no longer pink in center. Place packets on plates. Cut large X across top of each packet; fold back foil.

1 SERVING Calories 385 (Calories from Fat 70) | Fat 8g (Saturated 3g) | Cholesterol 55mg | Sodium 960mg | Carbohydrate 59g (Dietary Fiber 4g) | Protein 23g   %DAILY VALUE Vitamin A 100% | Vitamin C 14% | Calcium 4% | Iron 14%   EXCHANGES 3 Starch, 2 Vegetable, 1 1/2 Very Lean Meat CARBOHYDRATE CHOICES 4

BETTY'S TIP

Look for the cooked potato wedges in the refrigerated section of the supermarket. If they are not available, cut 2 medium potatoes into wedges and place in a microwavable bowl. Cover and microwave on High for about 5 minutes or until crisp-tender. Place potatoes in packet and grill as directed.

Grilled Kielbasa and Cabbage

1 ring (1 pound) fully cooked kielbasa sausage

3 cups coleslaw mix (8 ounces)

1/2 medium green bell pepper, cut into 1-inch pieces

1/2 teaspoon celery seed

1/2 teaspoon salt

1/8 teaspoon pepper

1 tablespoon butter or margarine

3 tablespoons water

Bratwurst buns, split, if desired

1. Heat coals or gas grill for direct heat. Place sausage in 8-inch square aluminum foil pan. Mix coleslaw mix, bell pepper, celery seed, salt and pepper. Mound cabbage mixture in center of sausage. Dot with butter; sprinkle with water. Cover with aluminum foil, sealing edges securely.

2. Cover and grill pan 4 to 6 inches from medium heat 15 to 20 minutes or until coleslaw mixture is crisp-tender and sausage is hot.

3. Cut sausage into 4 pieces. Serve sausage and coleslaw mixture on buns.

1 SERVING Calories 390 (Calories from Fat 305) | Fat 34g (Saturated 13g) | Cholesterol 70mg | Sodium 1380mg | Carbohydrate 8g (Dietary Fiber 1g) | Protein 14g   %DAILY VALUE Vitamin A 4% | Vitamin C 24% | Calcium 4% | Iron 8%   EXCHANGES 2 Vegetable, 1 1/2 High-Fat Meat | 4 Fat   CARBOHYDRATE CHOICES 1/2

BETTY'S TIP

What exactly is kielbasa? Well, it's also known as Polish sausage, and it's usually made of pork, sometimes with beef added. It's generally sold smoked and precooked.

Lemon Shrimp with Squash

PREP 10 min   MARINATE 15 min   GRILL 14 min   SERVINGS 4

Lemon-Rosemary Marinade
(below right)

1 pound uncooked large
shrimp in shells, thawed
if frozen

2 medium zucchini, cut into
1-inch slices

2 medium yellow summer
squash, cut into 1-inch slices

1 small bell pepper,
cut into 1-inch wedges

1 small lemon, cut into
wedges

1. Make Lemon-Rosemary Marinade. Add shrimp, zucchini, yellow squash and bell pepper to marinade; stir to coat. Cover dish or seal bag and refrigerate 15 to 30 minutes, stirring occasionally.

2. Heat coals or gas grill for direct heat. Remove shrimp and vegetables from marinade; discard marinade. Place shrimp and vegetables in grill basket (grill "wok").

3. Cover and grill shrimp and vegetables 4 to 5 inches from medium heat 12 to 14 minutes, shaking basket or stirring shrimp mixture occasionally, until shrimp are pink and firm and vegetables are tender. To serve, peel shrimp. Serve with lemon wedges.

Lemon-Rosemary Marinade

2 tablespoons honey

1 teaspoon grated lemon peel

1/4 cup lemon juice

1 teaspoon chopped fresh or 1/2 teaspoon dried rosemary leaves, crumbled

Mix all ingredients in large shallow glass or plastic dish or resealable plastic food-storage bag.

1 SERVING Calories 110 (Calories from Fat 10) | Fat 1g (Saturated 0g) | Cholesterol 105mg | Sodium 130mg | Carbohydrate 14g (Dietary Fiber 3g) | Protein 14g %DAILY VALUE Vitamin A 22% | Vitamin C 34% | Calcium 6% | Iron 14% EXCHANGES 3 Vegetable, 1 1/2 Very Lean Meat CARBOHYDRATE CHOICES 1

BETTY'S TIP

If you use medium shrimp, add the shrimp for the last 5 to 7 minutes of grilling and cook until the shrimp are pink and firm.

Grilled Shrimp Kabobs

PREP **10 min**   MARINATE **30 min**   GRILL **8 min**   SERVINGS **4**

1 pound uncooked peeled deveined large shrimp, thawed if frozen

1 cup fat-free Italian dressing

1 medium red onion, cut into 8 pieces

1 medium bell pepper, cut into 8 pieces

16 medium cherry tomatoes

16 small whole mushrooms

1. Place shrimp and dressing in shallow glass or plastic dish or heavy-duty resealable plastic food-storage bag. Cover dish or seal bag and refrigerate 30 minutes.

2. Heat coals or gas grill for direct heat. Remove shrimp from marinade; reserve marinade. Thread shrimp, onion, bell pepper, tomatoes and mushrooms alternately on each of four 15-inch metal skewers, leaving 1/4-inch space between each piece.

3. Grill kabobs uncovered 4 to 6 inches from medium heat 6 to 8 minutes, turning frequently and brushing several times with marinade, until shrimp are pink and firm. Discard any remaining marinade.

1 SERVING Calories 140 (Calories from Fat 10) | Fat 1 (Saturated 0g) | Cholesterol 160mg | Sodium 730mg | Carbohydrate 13g (Dietary 2g) | Protein 20g   %DAILY VALUE Vitamin A 18% | Vitamin C 36% | Calcium 4% | Iron 20%   EXCHANGES 2 1/2 Vegetable, 2 Very Lean Meat   CARBOHYDRATE CHOICES 1

BETTY'S TIP

A large slice of watermelon makes a fun holder for these colorful kabobs.

Caribbean
Salmon Packets

2 cups uncooked instant rice

1 can (14 ounces) chicken broth

1 small red bell pepper, chopped (1/2 cup)

2 medium green onions, sliced (2 tablespoons)

4 salmon fillets (6 ounces each), skin removed

1 teaspoon salt

1/2 cup chutney

1 cup pineapple chunks

PREP 20 min   STAND 7 min   GRILL 18 min   SERVINGS 4

1. Heat coals or gas grill for direct heat. Cut four 18×12-inch sheets of heavy-duty aluminum foil. Spray with cooking spray.

2. Mix rice and broth in large bowl; let stand about 7 minutes or until broth is almost absorbed. Stir in bell pepper and onions. Place 3/4 cup rice mixture on one side of each foil sheet.

3. Place salmon over rice; sprinkle with salt. Top each with 2 tablespoons chutney and 1/4 cup pineapple chunks. Fold foil over salmon and rice mixture so edges meet. Seal edges, making tight 1/2-inch fold; fold again. Allow space on sides for circulation and expansion.

4. Cover and grill packets 4 to 6 inches from medium heat 12 to 18 minutes or until salmon flakes easily with fork. Place packets on plates. Cut large X across top of each packet; fold back foil.

1 SERVING Calories 525 (Calories from Fat 100) | Fat 11g (Saturated 3g) | Cholesterol 110mg | Sodium 1180mg | Carbohydrate 65g (Dietary Fiber 3g) | Protein 43g %DAILY VALUE Vitamin A 8% | Vitamin C 24% | Calcium 4% | Iron 20% EXCHANGES 3 Starch, 1 Fruit, 1 Vegetable, 4 1/2 Very Lean Meat, 1 Fat CARBOHYDRATE CHOICES 4

BETTY'S TIP

You can use either fresh or canned pineapple chunks in these easy fish packets.

Lemon and Herb Salmon Packets

PREP **15 min**   STAND **5 min**   GRILL **14 min**   SERVINGS **4**

2 cups uncooked instant rice

1 can (14 ounces) chicken broth

1 cup matchstick-cut carrots (from 10-ounce bag)

4 salmon fillets (4 to 6 ounces each)

1 teaspoon lemon pepper seasoning salt

1/2 teaspoon salt

1/3 cup chopped fresh chives

1 medium lemon, cut lengthwise in half, then cut crosswise into 1/4-inch slices

1. Heat coals or gas grill for direct heat. Cut four 18 × 12-inch sheets of heavy-duty aluminum foil. Spray with cooking spray. Mix rice and broth in medium bowl. Let stand about 5 minutes or until most of broth is absorbed. Stir in carrots.

2. Place salmon fillet on one side of each foil sheet. Sprinkle with lemon pepper seasoning salt and salt; top with chives. Arrange lemon slices over salmon. Spoon one-fourth of the rice mixture around each fillet.

3. Fold foil over salmon and rice so edges meet. Seal edges, making tight 1/2-inch fold; fold again. Allow space on sides for circulation and expansion.

4. Cover and grill packets 4 to 6 inches from low heat 11 to 14 minutes or until salmon flakes easily with fork. Place packets on plates. Cut large X across top of each packet; fold back foil.

1 SERVING Calories 400 (Calories from Fat 70) | Fat 8g (Saturated 2g) | Cholesterol 75mg | Sodium 1160mg | Carbohydrate 51g (Dietary Fiber 2g) | Protein 31g   %DAILY VALUE Vitamin A 100% | Vitamin C 4% | Calcium 4% | Iron 18%   EXCHANGES 3 1/2 Starch, 3 Very Lean Meat   CARBOHYDRATE CHOICES 3 1/2

BETTY'S TIP

Use whatever fresh herbs you have on hand. Basil, parsley or thyme would all taste delicious with the salmon.

Fisherman's Grilled Packet

1 can (14 1/2 ounces) stewed tomatoes, undrained

1 can (2 1/4 ounces) sliced ripe olives

1/4 cup basil pesto

1 whitefish fillet (about 2 pounds)

1/2 teaspoon salt

1/4 teaspoon pepper

2 tablespoons chopped fresh parsley

PREP 5 min   **GRILL** 30 min   **SERVINGS** 6

1. Heat coals or gas grill for direct heat. Cut 24 × 12-inch sheet of heavy-duty aluminum foil. Mix tomatoes, olives and pesto in nonmetal bowl.

2. Place fish on foil. Sprinkle with salt and pepper. Top with tomato mixture. Fold foil over fish and tomato mixture so edges meet. Seal edges, making tight 1/2-inch fold; fold again. Allow space on sides for circulation and expansion.

3. Cover and grill packet 4 to 6 inches from medium heat 20 to 30 minutes or until fish flakes easily with fork. Top with parsley.

1 SERVING Calories 275 (Calories from Fat 135) | Fat 15g (Saturated 3g) | Cholesterol 75mg | Sodium 630mg | Carbohydrate 6g (Dietary Fiber 1g) | Protein 29g   %DAILY VALUE Vitamin A 10% | Vitamin C 8% | Calcium 8% | Iron 10%   EXCHANGES 1 Vegetable, 4 Very Lean Meat, 1/2 Fat   CARBOHYDRATE CHOICES 1/2

BETTY'S TIP

Other fish choices for this recipe include cod, haddock, halibut, perch, pollock and red snapper.

Mexican Fish in Foil

PREP 15 min   GRILL 15 min   SERVINGS 6

1. Heat coals or gas grill for direct heat. If fish fillets are large, cut into 6 serving pieces. Place fish in heavy-duty aluminum foil bag. Mix olives, capers, tomato, green onions and garlic; spoon over fish. Drizzle with lemon juice. Sprinkle with salt and pepper. Double-fold open end of bag.

2. Cover and grill bag 5 to 6 inches from medium heat about 15 minutes or until fish flakes easily with fork. Place bag on serving plate. Cut large X across top of bag; fold back foil. Serve fish with lemon wedges.

1 SERVING Calories 115 (Calories from Fat 20) | Fat 2g (Saturated 0g) | Cholesterol 50mg | Sodium 380mg | Carbohydrate 2g (Dietary Fiber 1g) | Protein 22g %DAILY VALUE Vitamin A 4% | Vitamin C 4% | Calcium 2% | Iron 2% EXCHANGES 3 Very Lean Meat CARBOHYDRATE CHOICES 0

1 1/2 pounds halibut fillets, 1/2 to 3/4 inch thick

1/4 cup sliced pimiento-stuffed olives

2 teaspoons capers

1 medium tomato, seeded and coarsely chopped (3/4 cup)

3 medium green onions, thinly sliced (3 tablespoons)

1 clove garlic, finely chopped

2 tablespoons lemon juice

1/4 teaspoon salt

1/8 teaspoon pepper

Lemon wedges

BETTY'S TIP

You can make your own foil packet by centering food on half of an 18 × 12-inch sheet of heavy-duty aluminum foil. Fold other half of foil so edges meet. Seal edges, making a tight 1/2-inch fold; fold again. Allow space on sides for heat circulation and expansion.

Pineapple-Lime Shrimp Kabobs

Pineapple-Lime Marinade
(below right)

3/4 pound uncooked peeled deveined large shrimp, thawed if frozen and tails peeled

1 can (8 ounces) pineapple chunks in juice, drained and 2 tablespoons juice reserved

1 orange bell pepper, cut into 12 pieces

4 medium green onions, cut into 1 1/2-inch pieces

PREP 10 min   **MARINATE** 15 min   **GRILL** 7 min   **SERVINGS** 4

1. Make Pineapple-Lime Marinade. Add shrimp, pineapple, bell pepper and onions to marinade; stir to coat. Cover dish or seal bag and refrigerate 15 to 30 minutes, turning once or twice.

2. Brush vegetable oil on grill rack. Heat coals or gas grill for direct heat. Thread shrimp, pineapple, bell pepper and onions alternately on each of four 12- to 14-inch metal skewers; reserve marinade.

3. Cover and grill kabobs 4 to 5 inches from medium heat 5 to 7 minutes, turning and brushing with marinade once, until shrimp are pink and firm and vegetables are tender. Discard any remaining marinade.

Pineapple-Lime Marinade

2 tablespoons olive or vegetable oil

1 teaspoon grated lime peel

2 tablespoons lime juice

2 tablespoons reserved pineapple juice

1/4 teaspoon salt

1/4 teaspoon red pepper sauce

2 cloves garlic, finely chopped

Mix all ingredients in large shallow glass or plastic dish or resealable plastic food-storage bag.

1 SERVING Calories 220 (Calories from Fat 70) | Fat 8g (Saturated 1g) | Cholesterol 185mg | Sodium 350mg | Carbohydrate 6g (Dietary Fiber 1g) | Protein 31g   **%DAILY VALUE** Vitamin A 100% | Vitamin C 6% | Calcium 12% | Iron 26%   **EXCHANGES** 1 Vegetable, 4 Lean Meat, 1 Fat   **CARBOHYDRATE CHOICES** 1/2

BETTY'S TIP

Marinating for a little longer will intensify the flavor slightly, but don't leave it for more than 2 hours. The marinade will start to break down the tissues in the shrimp, and the bell peppers will not be as pretty.

Pesto-Artichoke Pizza

PREP 10 min   GRILL 10 min   SERVINGS 8

1. Heat coals or gas grill for direct heat. Grill pizza crusts, top sides down, 4 to 6 inches from medium heat 3 to 5 minutes or until light brown. Remove from grill.

2. Spread pesto over grilled side of crusts. Top with artichokes and tomatoes. Sprinkle with cheese.

3. Cover and grill about 5 minutes or until cheese is melted. Cut each pizza in half.

1 SERVING Calories 520 (Calories from Fat 280) | Fat 31g (Saturated 10g) | Cholesterol 30mg | Sodium 890mg | Carbohydrate 43g (Dietary Fiber 5g) | Protein 17g %DAILY VALUE Vitamin A 18% | Vitamin C 12% | Calcium 36% | Iron 22% EXCHANGES 2 1/2 Starch, 1 Vegetable, 1 High-Fat Meat, 4 1/2 Fat CARBOHYDRATE CHOICES 3

2 packages (10 ounces each) ready-to-serve Italian pizza crusts (6 inches in diameter)

1 cup basil pesto

2 jars (6 to 7 ounces each) marinated artichoke hearts, drained and chopped

6 large roma (plum) tomatoes, sliced (2 cups)

2 cups shredded Monterey Jack cheese (8 ounces)

BETTY'S TIP

You can serve this easy grilled pizza as an appetizer, too. Simply cut each pizza into 8 wedges and serve.

Grilled Italian Pesto Pizza

1 package (14 ounces)
ready-to-serve original
Italian pizza crust or other
12-inch ready-to-serve
pizza crust

1/2 cup basil pesto

2 cups shredded
mozzarella cheese
(8 ounces)

3 large roma (plum)
tomatoes, cut into
1/4-inch slices

1/2 cup whole basil leaves

1/4 cup shredded
Parmesan cheese

PREP **15 min**   GRILL **8 min**   SERVINGS **4**

1. Heat coals or gas grill for direct heat. Brush pizza crust with pesto. Sprinkle 1 cup of the mozzarella cheese over pesto. Arrange tomato slices and basil leaves on cheese. Sprinkle with remaining 1 cup mozzarella cheese and the Parmesan cheese.

2. Cover and grill pizza 4 to 6 inches from medium heat 6 to 8 minutes or until crust is crisp and cheese is melted. (If crust browns too quickly, place a piece of aluminum foil between crust and grill.)

1 SERVING Calories 665 (Calories from Fat 295) | Fat 33g (Saturated 11g) | Cholesterol 40mg | Sodium 1220mg | Carbohydrate 66g (Dietary Fiber 4g) | Protein 30g   %DAILY VALUE Vitamin A 28% | Vitamin C 8% | Calcium 64% | Iron 26%   EXCHANGES 4 Starch, 1 Vegetable, 2 High-Fat Meat, 2 1/2 Fat CARBOHYDRATE CHOICES 4 1/2

BETTY'S TIP

If you have lots of fresh basil on hand, try making your own pesto. Place 2 cups firmly packed basil leaves, 3/4 cup grated Parmesan cheese, 1/4 cup pine nuts, 1/2 cup olive oil and 3 cloves garlic in a blender or food processor. Cover and blend on medium speed about 3 minutes or until smooth.

BettyCrocker.com

Grilled Antipasto Pizza

1/4 pound small whole
mushrooms (1 1/2 cups)

1 medium yellow bell
pepper, cut into 8 pieces

1/4 cup Italian dressing

1 package (14 ounces)
ready-to-serve original
Italian pizza crust or other
12-inch ready-to-serve
pizza crust

1 cup shredded mozzarella
cheese (4 ounces)

2 roma (plum) tomatoes,
thinly sliced

4 medium green onions,
sliced (1/4 cup)

1/4 cup sliced ripe olives

1. Heat coals or gas grill for direct heat. Toss mushrooms, bell pepper and 2 tablespoons of the dressing in medium bowl. Place vegetables in grill basket (grill "wok"). Cover and grill vegetables 4 to 5 inches from medium heat 4 to 6 minutes, shaking basket or stirring vegetables occasionally, until bell pepper is crisp-tender. Coarsely chop vegetables.

2. Brush pizza crust with remaining 2 tablespoons dressing. Sprinkle with 1/2 cup of the cheese. Arrange tomatoes on cheese. Top with grilled vegetables, onions, olives and remaining 1/2 cup cheese.

3. Place pizza directly on grill. Cover and grill 4 to 5 inches from medium heat 8 to 10 minutes or until crust is crisp and cheese is melted.

1 SERVING Calories 240 (Calories from Fat 90) | Fat 10g (Saturated 3g) | Cholesterol 10mg | Sodium 440mg | Carbohydrate 32g (Dietary Fiber 2g) | Protein 8g %DAILY VALUE Vitamin A 6% | Vitamin C 26% | Calcium 12% | Iron 12% EXCHANGES 2 Starch, 2 Fat CARBOHYDRATE CHOICES 2

BETTY'S TIP

If you don't have a grill basket, a sheet of heavy-duty aluminum foil with a few holes poked in it will work just fine.

Helpful Nutrition and Cooking Information

Nutrition Guidelines

We provide nutrition information for each recipe that includes calories, fat, cholesterol, sodium, carbohydrate, fiber and protein. Individual food choices can be based on this information.

Recommended intake for a daily diet of 2,000 calories as set by the Food and Drug Administration

Total Fat	Less than 65g
Saturated Fat	Less than 20g
Cholesterol	Less than 300mg
Sodium	Less than 2,400mg
Total Carbohydrate	300g
Dietary Fiber	25g

Criteria Used for Calculating Nutrition Information

- The first ingredient was used wherever a choice is given (such as 1/3 cup sour cream or plain yogurt).
- The first ingredient amount was used wherever a range is given (such as 3- to 3 1/2-pound cut-up broiler-fryer chicken).
- The first serving number was used wherever a range is given (such as 4 to 6 servings).
- "If desired" ingredients and recipe variations were not included (such as sprinkle with brown sugar, if desired).
- Only the amount of a marinade or frying oil that is estimated to be absorbed by the food during preparation or cooking was calculated.

Ingredients Used in Recipe Testing and Nutrition Calculations

- Ingredients used for testing represent those that the majority of consumers use in their homes: large eggs, 2% milk, 80%-lean ground beef, canned ready-to-use chicken broth and vegetable oil spread containing not less than 65% fat.
- Fat-free, low-fat or low-sodium products were not used, unless otherwise indicated.
- Solid vegetable shortening (not butter, margarine, nonstick cooking sprays or vegetable oil spread as they can cause sticking problems) was used to grease pans, unless otherwise indicated.

Equipment Used in Recipe Testing

We use equipment for testing that the majority of consumers use in their homes. If a specific piece of equipment (such as a wire whisk) is necessary for recipe success, it is listed in the recipe.

- Cookware and bakeware without nonstick coatings were used, unless otherwise indicated.
- No dark-colored, black or insulated bakeware was used.
- When a pan is specified in a recipe, a metal pan was used; a baking dish or pie plate means ovenproof glass was used.
- An electric hand mixer was used for mixing only when mixer speeds are specified in the recipe directions. When a mixer speed is not given, a spoon or fork was used.

Cooking Terms Glossary

Beat: Mix ingredients vigorously with spoon, fork, wire whisk, hand beater or electric mixer until smooth and uniform.

Boil: Heat liquid until bubbles rise continuously and break on the surface and steam is given off. For rolling boil, the bubbles form rapidly.

Chop: Cut into coarse or fine irregular pieces with a knife, food chopper, blender or food processor.

Cube: Cut into squares 1/2 inch or larger.

Dice: Cut into squares smaller than 1/2 inch.

Grate: Cut into tiny particles using small rough holes of grater (citrus peel or chocolate).

Grease: Rub the inside surface of a pan with shortening, using pastry brush, piece of waxed paper or paper towel, to prevent food from sticking during baking (as for some casseroles).

Julienne: Cut into thin, matchlike strips, using knife or food processor (vegetables, fruits, meats).

Mix: Combine ingredients in any way that distributes them evenly.

Sauté: Cook foods in hot oil or margarine over medium-high heat with frequent tossing and turning motion.

Shred: Cut into long thin pieces by rubbing food across the holes of a shredder, as for cheese, or by using a knife to slice very thinly, as for cabbage.

Simmer: Cook in liquid just below the boiling point on top of the stove; usually after reducing heat from a boil. Bubbles will rise slowly and break just below the surface.

Stir: Mix ingredients until uniform consistency. Stir once in a while for stirring occasionally, often for stirring frequently and continuously for stirring constantly.

Toss: Tumble ingredients (such as green salad) lightly with a lifting motion, usually to coat evenly or mix with another food.

Metric Conversion Guide

Volume

U.S. UNITS	CANADIAN METRIC	AUSTRALIAN METRIC
1/4 teaspoon	1 mL	1 ml
1/2 teaspoon	2 mL	2 ml
1 teaspoon	5 mL	5 ml
1 tablespoon	15 mL	20 ml
1/4 cup	50 mL	60 ml
1/3 cup	75 mL	80 ml
1/2 cup	125 mL	125 ml
2/3 cup	150 mL	170 ml
3/4 cup	175 mL	190 ml
1 cup	250 mL	250 ml
1 quart	1 liter	1 liter
1 1/2 quarts	1.5 liters	1.5 liters
2 quarts	2 liters	2 liters
2 1/2 quarts	2.5 liters	2.5 liters
3 quarts	3 liters	3 liters
4 quarts	4 liters	4 liters

Weight

U.S. UNITS	CANADIAN METRIC	AUSTRALIAN METRIC
1 ounce	30 grams	30 grams
2 ounces	55 grams	60 grams
3 ounces	85 grams	90 grams
4 ounces (1/4 pound)	115 grams	125 grams
8 ounces (1/2 pound)	225 grams	225 grams
16 ounces (1 pound)	455 grams	500 grams
1 pound	455 grams	1/2 kilogram

Measurements

INCHES	CENTIMETERS
1	2.5
2	5.0
3	7.5
4	10.0
5	12.5
6	15.0
7	17.5
8	20.5
9	23.0
10	25.5
11	28.0
12	30.5
13	33.0

Temperatures

FAHRENHEIT	CELSIUS
32°	0°
212°	100°
250°	120°
275°	140°
300°	150°
325°	160°
350°	180°
375°	190°
400°	200°
425°	220°
450°	230°
475°	240°
500°	260°

NOTE: The recipes in this cookbook have not been developed or tested using metric measures. When converting recipes to metric, some variations in quality may be noted.

Index

Complete your cookbook library with these
Betty Crocker titles